Widowhoo
and Early M

WOMEN AND MEN IN HISTORY

This series, published for students, scholars and interested general readers, will tackle themes in gender history from the early medieval period through to the present day. Gender issues are now an integral part of all history courses and yet many traditional texts do not reflect this change. Much exciting work is now being done to redress the gender imbalances of the past, and we hope that these books will make their own substantial contribution to that process. This is an open-ended series, which means that many new titles can be included. We hope that these will both synthesise and shape future developments in gender studies.

The General Editors of the series are *Patricia Skinner* (University of Southampton) for the medieval period; *Pamela Sharpe* (University of Bristol) for the early modern period; and *Penny Summerfield* (University of Lancaster) for the modern period. *Margaret Walsh* (University of Nottingham) was the Founding Editor of the series.

Published books:

Masculinity in Medieval Europe
D.M. Hadley (ed.)

Gender and Society in Renaissance Italy
Judith C. Brown and Robert C. Davis (eds)

Gender, Church and State in Early Modern Germany: Essays by Merry E. Wiesner
Merry E. Wiesner

Manhood in Early Modern England: Honour, Sex and Marriage
Elizabeth W. Foyster

Disorderly Women in Eighteenth-Century London: Prostitution in the Metropolis 1730–1830
Tony Henderson

Gender, Power and the Unitarians in England, 1760–1860
Ruth Watts

Women and Work in Russia, 1880–1930: A Study in Continuity through Change
Jane McDermid and Anna Hillyar

The Family Story: Blood, Contract and Intimacy, 1830–1960
Leonore Davidoff, Megan Doolittle, Janet Fink and Katherine Holden

More than Munitions: Women, Work and the Engineering Industries 1900–1950
Clare Wightman

Widowhood in Medieval and Early Modern Europe

Edited by

SANDRA CAVALLO

AND

LYNDAN WARNER

Longman

Pearson Education Limited
Edinburgh Gate
Harlow
Essex CM20 2JE
United Kingdom
and Associated Companies throughout the world

Published in the United States of America
by Pearson Education Inc., New York

First published 1999 by Pearson Education

ISBN 0 582 317479 CSD
ISBN 0 582 317487 PPR

Visit our world wide web site at
hhtp://www.awl-he.com

British Library Cataloguing in Publication Data

A catalogue record for this book is available from the British Library

Library of Congress Cataloging-in-Publication Data

Widowhood in medieval and early modern Europe / edited by Sandra Cavallo and Lyndan Warner.
p. cm. — (Women and men in history)
Includes bibliographical references.
ISBN 0-582-31748-7 (ppr). — ISBN 0-582-31747-9 (csd)
1. Widowhood—Europe—History. 2. Widows—Europe—History. 3. Widowers—Europe—History. I. Cavallo, Sandra. II. Warner, Lyndan. III Series.
HQ1058.5.E97W53 1999
305.48′9654′094—dc21 98-52954
CIP

Set by 35 in 10/12pt Baskerville
Produced by Addison Wesley Longman Singapore (Pte) Ltd.,
Printed in Singapore

Contents

Acknowledgements

We would like to thank former colleagues at the University of Exeter, Julia Crick and Tim Rees, for their help in the initial stages of this project – back in the days when it was an idea for a symposium. We would also like to thank David Vassberg, a speaker at the *Widowhood: Conditions and Constructions* Symposium, for generously allowing the citation of his unpublished work in the Introduction.

Lyndan is grateful to members of the History Department at the University of Warwick, especially Colin Jones, for making it such a stimulating and wonderful place to work, and to the Department of History at the University of Waikato, New Zealand for giving her the time to do some of the writing and editing. We would also like to thank Tim Stretton for helping us to 'english' (as they used to say in the early modern period) some of the chapters.

Notes on Contributors

JODI BILINKOFF earned her PhD from Princeton University in 1983. She is the author of *The Avila of Saint Teresa: Religious Reform in a Sixteenth-Century City* (Ithaca, NY, 1989; paperback 1992) and a number of essays and articles exploring religion, gender and authority in early modern Spain. She is Associate Professor of History at the University of North Carolina at Greensboro, USA.

GIULIA CALVI teaches History at the University of Siena. She is the author of *Il Contratto Morale, Madri e Figli nella Toscana Moderna* (Rome, 1994). Her book *Storie di un Anno di Peste* (Milan, 1984) was translated as *Histories of a Plague Year: The Social and the Imaginary in Baroque Florence* (Berkeley, Calif., 1989). She is the editor of *Barocco al Femminile* (Rome, 1992) and co-editor with Isabelle Chabot of *Le Richezze Delle Donne. Diritti Patrimoniali e Poteri Familiari (XIII–XIX sec.)* (Turin, 1998).

SANDRA CAVALLO is Lecturer in Early Modern European History at Royal Holloway, University of London. She is the author of *Charity and Power in Early Modern Italy: Benefactors and their Motives in Turin 1541–1789* (Cambridge, 1995) and of numerous articles on poor relief and health care, family and gender relations in seventeenth- and eighteenth-century Italy.

ISABELLE CHABOT is Research Fellow at the University of Florence. She has published many articles on women and widowhood in edited collections and journals such as *Quaderni Storici* and *Continuity and Change*. She is currently preparing her book *La Dette des Familles: Femmes, Lignages et Patrimoine à Florence aux XIVe et XVe siècles* and is co-editor with Giulia Calvi of *Le Richezze Delle Donne. Diritti Patrimoniali e Poteri Familiari (XIII–XIX sec.)* (Turin, 1998).

JULIA CRICK is Lecturer in History at the University of Exeter. She has published articles on female religious communities and on women's and family property in pre-Conquest England. She has authored two volumes on Geoffrey of Monmouth's *Historia Regum Britanniae* (Cambridge, 1989 and 1991). Her article 'Women, post-humous benefaction, and family strategy in pre-Conquest England' is forthcoming in *Journal of British Studies.*

AMY LOUISE ERICKSON is Research Fellow at the University of Sussex and the author of *Women and Property in Early Modern England* (London, 1993; paperback 1995). She has published several articles and essays, including an Introduction to Alice Clark's *Working Life of Women in the Seventeenth Century* (London, 1992) and the chapter on 'Family, Household and Community' for *The Oxford Illustrated History of Tudor and Stuart England,* ed. John Morrill (Oxford, 1996).

ELIZABETH FOYSTER is Lecturer at the University of Dundee. She has worked as a Lecturer at the University of Wales, Bangor and held a British Academy Postdoctoral Research Fellowship at Clare College, Cambridge. Among her published articles on marriage in seventeenth-century England is 'Male honour, social control and wife beating in late Stuart England', *Transactions of the Royal Historical Society* (1996). Her book *Manhood in Early Modern England* will be published by Longman in 1999.

DAGMAR FREIST is Assistant Lecturer at the Department of History, University of Osnabrück and a member of the Interdisciplinary Institute for Early Modern Cultural History, University of Osnabrück. Formerly a Research Fellow at the German Historical Institute, London, her book *Governed by Opinion, Politics, Religion and the Dynamics of Communication in Stuart London 1637–1645* was published in 1997. In her published work and in her teaching she specializes in the study of political culture, and the social and gender history of Germany and England.

MARGARET PELLING is University Research Lecturer in the Modern History Faculty, University of Oxford. Her research interests focus on health, medicine and social conditions at and below the level of the 'middling sort' in early modern English towns. Her recent publications include (with Hilary Marland), *The Task of Healing: Medicine, Religion and Gender in England and the Netherlands 1450–1800* (Rotterdam, 1996), and a volume of her essays, *The Common Lot: Sickness, Medical Occupations and the Urban Poor in Early Modern England* (London, 1998). She is completing a monograph on the

College of unlicensed practitioners, 1550–1640, to be published by Macmillan.

Pamela Sharpe is Lecturer in Social and Economic History at the University of Bristol. She has written a number of articles on women's work, poverty and demographic change in England from the seventeenth to the nineteenth century, and a monograph *Adapting to Capitalism: Working Women in the English Economy 1700–1850* (London, 1996). She has recently edited *Women's Work: The English Experience 1650–1914* (London, 1998) and with Tim Hitchcock and Peter King, *Chronicling Poverty: The Voices and Strategies of the English Poor 1640–1840* (London, 1997).

Patricia Skinner is Lecturer in Medieval History at the University of Southampton. Her PhD thesis was published as *Family Power in Southern Italy: The Duchy of Gaeta and its Neighbours 850–1139* by Cambridge University Press in 1995. She has since published *Health and Medicine in Early Medieval Southern Italy* (Leiden, 1997) and is the author of numerous articles on women and family life in medieval Italy.

Tim Stretton is the author of *Women Waging Law in Elizabethan England* (Cambridge, 1998) and a number of articles on women, litigation and court records. After gaining law and history degrees from the University of Adelaide, and a PhD in history from the University of Cambridge, he worked as a lecturer at the University of Durham, and then as a Research Fellow at Clare Hall, Cambridge. He is currently a Teaching and Research Fellow at the University of Waikato in New Zealand, where he is working on a history of married women and English law over four centuries.

Barbara Todd is Associate Professor of History at the University of Toronto, Canada. She has published pioneering articles on widowhood such as 'The remarrying widow: a stereotype reconsidered' in Mary Prior's *Women in English Society 1500–1800* (London, 1985) and 'Demographic determinism and female agency: the remarrying widow reconsidered . . . again' in *Continuity and Change* (1994). She is currently preparing a book on women and investment in early modern England.

Lyndan Warner is Assistant Professor of History at Saint Mary's University, Halifax, Canada. She has worked as a Research Fellow at the University of Exeter, as a Lecturer in Early Modern European History at the University of Warwick and as a Teaching and Research Fellow at the University of Waikato in New Zealand. She has published articles on book history and women writers and is currently preparing the book of her Cambridge doctoral thesis as *Renaissance Man and Woman: Morals and Government in French Print.*

Foreword

Widowhood in Medieval and Early Modern Europe revisits the territories familiar to the historian of widowhood, pushes out the boundaries, and explores new areas of research. Through case studies of several European countries, and the use of diverse source material, the volume integrates methods and approaches which have often been kept in separate historical compartments. For example, we focus attention on the early modern period, although we also include two medieval papers in order to trace the emergence of the conventional association of widowhood with women. The volume studies widowhood, often analysed as a predominantly female experience, from both the male and the female perspectives. Scholars have tended to examine widowhood either as a condition determined primarily by demographic and economic constraints, or as a mere reflection of the models and stereotypes through which the widow was represented in prescriptive literature and normative sources. In this volume, by contrast, the investigation concentrates on the ways in which ideological assumptions crystallized into patterns of demographic behaviour, legal codes, inheritance practices, terminologies and social perceptions, making the experience of widowhood so different for men and for women. A third feature, which lies at the heart of this project, is the attention paid to human agency, to the self-construction of widowhood and the ways in which the widowed negotiated the ideals and social practices associated with their condition. In so doing our volume will demonstrate, we hope, how persistent stereotypes, such as those of the powerful widow and the poor dependent widow, may be oversimplified.

Our main concern in putting together this volume has been to provide examples of new approaches to the study of the widowed. Although we also endeavoured to achieve a thematic and geographical coverage, we inevitably gathered the material for these new perspectives from European countries where research on widowhood has attracted special attention. Much research is in progress, however, for areas which are under-represented in this volume. We hope that this collection will be helpful in furthering cross-cultural comparisons.

Illustrations and Tables

Illustrations

Tables

PART ONE

Defining Widowhood

CHAPTER ONE

Introduction

SANDRA CAVALLO AND LYNDAN WARNER

Widowhood, 'widowerhood': problems of visibility and definition

In recent decades historical research has seen a shift from a focus on women's experience to an emphasis on studies of gender which compare and contrast the lives of men and women. In studies of the pre-industrial period, however, widowhood has often been presented solely as a female experience, making the topic of widowhood a virtual province of women's history. In reality, the death of a wife, especially in her childbearing years, meant that men, too, frequently experienced widowhood, although widowers tended to remarry more often, and after shorter intervals, than widows. Ironically, despite the usual invisibility of women in the historical record, in the case of widowhood, it is more often the widower who is 'invisible'. One of the aims of the collection is to seek out the 'invisible widower' and set up a series of comparisons with widows.

In some ways the death of a spouse affected women more than men. Upon widowhood a wife's legal and patrimonial condition changed. She was no longer a 'feme covert': a woman whose legal entity was 'covered' by her husband. And the widow often becomes visible to the historian because she left traces of her new 'uncovered' legal status. Scholars have sought to examine the widow's actions and options at a time when she could be said to be operating at her most independent, although subject to family and financial constraints. Many of the chapters in this volume examine how widows negotiated these constraints, how widows were both vulnerable and resourceful, and in some cases exploited their vulnerability to advantage. By contrast, the widower's legal status did not change at the death of his wife.

Several of the chapters consider the experience of widowhood from 'the male perspective' and embark on a new research enterprise, which has been tentatively termed 'widowerhood' by some of the contributors. 'Widowerhood' is not a particularly defined state. In Chapter 2, for example, Julia Crick reminds us that in the medieval period, charters and legal records define men by rank not marital status. Margaret Pelling encounters the same difficulties tracing widowers in early modern England in Chapter 3. When officials in Norwich took a census of the poor in the 1570s, the word 'widower' was rarely used and the closest designation was 'single men'.[1]

The terminology of widowhood is fascinating because it is one of the rare cases where the male term, widower, derives from the female term. The terms widow in English, *widewe* in Old English, *weduwe* in Middle Dutch and Dutch, *Witwe* in German, *vidua* in Latin, *viuda* in Spanish, *vedova* in Italian, *veuve* in French, all derive from an Indo-European base word meaning 'to separate' or 'to divide'. The Latin *vidua* meant 'to be deprived of' as well as 'widow' and the masculine and neutral forms *viduus* and *viduum* derived from the feminine.[2] Hence the terms for widower become *weduwnaar* in Dutch, *Witwer* in German, *viudo* in Spanish, *vedovo* in Italian, *veuf* in French. So it is perhaps not surprising that historians have explored the conditions of widows more thoroughly than widowers, given the long association of the state of widowhood with women.

However, the problems of tracing widows and widowers go beyond this gender question of whether the terms of widowhood applied to both men and women. Widowhood seems a fairly straightforward term. A stage of life which begins with the death of a spouse, it is defined as the 'state or condition of a widow or widower, or (contextually) the time during which one is a widow or widower'.[3] As many of our contributors demonstrate, however, the 'condition of a widow or widower' was never as straightforward as the definition might suggest. In medieval Europe, for example, monogamous Christian marriage was far from the norm. The practice of concubinage was common.[4] In Anglo-Saxon England, as

1. See also Barbara Todd, 'Demographic determinism and female agency: the remarrying widow reconsidered . . . again', *Continuity and Change* 9 (1994), p. 437 n. 66.

2. Ernst Klein, *A Comprehensive Etymological Dictionary of the English Language* (Amsterdam, 1967); *Dictionnaire Étymologique de la Langue Latine: Histoire des Mots*, 4th edn (Paris, 1985).

3. *The Shorter Oxford English Dictionary*.

4. James Brundage, *Law, Sex and Christian Society in Medieval Europe* (Chicago, 1987), pp. 98–103 and 297–300.

Crick argues, the widespread existence of sexual partners, or concubines, meant that in the event of a death a whole range of terms might be used to describe the surviving partner. The survivor might be known as a bedfellow, a wife (rather than widow), or a *laf* (meaning the one left behind). Therefore, the death of a husband or sexual partner and the change of status wrought by widowhood is not certain; it must be inferred. 'Widows have to be prised out of the documentary record; the process is as labour-intensive as identifying widowers in other periods' (p. 32).

Furthermore, it would be misleading to suggest that sexual liaisons outside Christian marriage are symptomatic of the medieval period alone. Among the Dutch gentry in the sixteenth and seventeenth centuries, widowers took mistresses and fathered illegitimate children. When these widowers died they left provisions for their widowed companions and orphaned children and, in doing so, exhibited attitudes 'similar in many respects to a legitimate marital relationship'.[5] Little is known about the status of the widowed concubine. It is sometimes assumed that this condition was frowned upon or reserved to women of low station – however, in Chapter 11 Jodi Bilinkoff provides an excellent example of a widowed clerical concubine in fifteenth-century Spain. Although not formally a wife, Elvira González de Medina was the companion of a prominent noble member of the clergy and after his death she founded a religious community of women. Doña Elvira's religious foundation eventually became a Carmelite convent – one of the most important convents in Spain – headed by her illegitimate children and their heirs.

Taking a companion was not a socially acceptable possibility for a bereaved and lonely wife. Withdrawal from the world – whether as a vowess, vowed to chastity, a lay *Deo devota* in mourning clothes, or through retreat behind the convent wall – was a more suitable option for the medieval widow or the early modern Catholic widow.[6] Entry into a religious order was a path which could itself produce the condition of widowhood. As Patricia Skinner notes in Chapter 4, a husband might enter a monastery while his wife was alive, but this left her effectively a widow.

5. Sherrin Marshall, *The Dutch Gentry, 1500–1650: Family, Faith and Fortune* (New York, 1987), pp. 66–7.

6. Bernhard Jussen, 'On church organization and the definition of an estate: the idea of widowhood in late antique and early medieval Christianity', *Tel Aviver Jahrbuch für deutsche Geschichte* 22 (1993), pp. 31, 33–5; St Francis de Sales, 'Advice to widows', in *Introduction to the Devout Life* (London and New York, 1961), p. 195.

Similarly, husbands also left their wives without giving any indication of their whereabouts. The numbers of abandoned wives should not be underestimated and some legal systems made provisions for marital desertion. Under Lombard laws in medieval southern Italy, as Skinner comments, for example, the absence of a husband for more than three years allowed his wife to assume his death. For early modern England, Pelling draws attention to the high numbers of deserted wives in the Norwich Census of the Poor. David Vassberg's research on migration in sixteenth- and seventeenth-century Spain supports the claims of Skinner and Pelling on desertion. Vassberg has identified a category of 'virtual widows' in the censuses of Castilian villages – abandoned wives whose husbands deserted them, usually to avoid debt imprisonment.[7]

From the early church to the early modern parish and the emerging state, attempts to reform or eliminate irregular practices shaped the widow's and widower's experience. These institutional changes reveal what medieval and early modern societies expected of a widow or widower; in particular how the survivor should behave at the death of a spouse. The stereotypes associated with female widowhood – the ideal models encouraged by legal codes and biblical stories as well as the worrisome examples of vice and profligacy feared by legislators and magistrates – have been well-studied. The typical or model widower is much less obvious largely because, as Pelling, Skinner, Sharpe, Foyster and Warner point out, there was no clear ideal model to which the widower was meant to aspire. This volume, therefore, seeks to sketch the figure of the widower and compare him with his female counterpart as well as to highlight the extent to which women and others manipulated positive and negative stereotypes for the widow. And, as we shall see, widows regularly gave the appearance of conforming to idealized models whenever they found themselves face-to-face with authority in negotiations for poor relief, in the law courts, or in the defence of their interests.

Models and stereotypes

Perhaps the most well-known stereotypes are the good or ideal widow, the merry widow, and the poor widow. For the Spanish

7. David E. Vassberg, 'Widows and their children in early modern rural Castile', paper presented at Symposium 'Widowhood: Conditions and Constructions', University of Exeter, 16–17 May 1996, p. 2; Vassberg, *The Village and the Outside World in Golden Age Castile: Mobility and Migration in Everyday Life* (Cambridge, 1996), pp. 114–15.

humanist Juan Luis Vives, the ideal widow maintained the memory of her late husband and lived as a 'perpetual wife'. Vives' *Instruction of a Christian Woman*, discussed in Chapters 5 and 12, was translated in the first half of the sixteenth century from Latin into English, French, German, Spanish and Italian. His emphasis on chastity and continued obedience, however, inhibited any public transactions which might expose the widow to dishonour and in some ways encouraged inaction or passivity at a time when a widow faced financial and legal responsibilities for herself and her children. In Chapter 5 Barbara Todd contrasts Vives' ideal widow with advice which sought to teach the widow self-control. The Protestant author of the seventeenth-century English manuscript 'The Widdowe Indeed' stressed the requisite chastity, solitariness, charity to others, and the obvious desolation of widowhood, but he also recognized how of all women the widow came closest to experiencing the 'preeminence and prerogative of a man'. This ideal Protestant widow may have had the opportunities to exercise her independence; nevertheless, her bereavement meant that she channelled her energies into spiritual matters, salvation and the attainment of Christian virtues.

The merry widow was usually portrayed as rich, worldly, ready to enjoy her independence and satisfy her sensual appetite; a stereotype which contrasts sharply with the glimpses into the lives of bereaved widows provided by Todd's chapter. The caricatures of the worldly widow and the faithful, chaste widow can be found in drama, ballads, prescriptive literature and memoirs and, as we see in the chapters by Foyster, Stretton and Warner, these characterizations played a noticeable role in the way widows, or at least their lawyers and witnesses, represented their lives to authorities.

While the stereotypical merry widow did not have a direct male counterpart, the 'lusty old man' stereotype examined in Chapters 3 and 6 mocked men in a similar fashion. European satires often targeted the foolish old man lusting after a young maiden as either an ageing bachelor seeking to marry for the first time or a widower marrying a wife too young for him. Alciati mocked this 'old man in love' in his sixteenth-century Latin moral emblems translated into French, German, Italian and Spanish.[8] Molière mocked the ageing widower's love for a young maiden in his 1668 play *The Miser*. As a potential husband, the widower may have been deluged with advice on whether to remarry and on the type of bride he might choose,

8. Andreas Alciatus, *Index Emblematicus*, P. Daly, ed., 2 vols (Toronto, 1985), I, Emblem 117, 'Senex puellam amans', and II, Emblem 117.

but he was not inundated with advice on his conduct, the remembrance of his first wife, or the administration of the estate.

A recently bereaved, and suddenly 'independent' widow, it seems, needed more guidance on how to make the adjustment from 'obedient' wife to autonomous head of household, judging by the quantity of advice available to her. In the sixteenth century, as Stretton indicates in Chapter 12, the humanist Vives argued that the widow should either allow others to defend her interests or should not push hard to protect her interests because the need to preserve her modesty outweighed the need to protect her rights. The continuity of this advice is perhaps more striking than any change. The Counter-Reformation figure Saint Francis de Sales echoes this admonition to the widow to 'take no part in lawsuits, but rather conduct her affairs in the most peaceful (even though perhaps not the most profitable) way'. He reasons that lawsuits lay the widow's heart open to the 'enemies of chastity, encouraging behaviour neither devout nor pleasing to God'.[9] Many widows ignored prescription and did go to law to protect their interests. In most English civil courts, as Stretton observes, widows were proportionally 'the most prominent group of female litigants'. We cannot, however, entirely ignore the possibility that some widows internalized society's expectations and faced the legal difficulties accompanying widowhood in the manner of an eleventh-century noble French widow who refused to face her adversaries in court, choosing instead to retreat to a chapel and put all her faith in the Lord, 'the advocate under whose protection I will plead'.[10] The salutary example of this medieval noblewoman could have been drawn from the pages of Vives or the seventeenth-century handbook *The English Gentlewoman* discussed in Chapter 12. The tone of advice to and expectations of the widow are remarkably stable through the centuries and across borders – perhaps as stable as their persistent presence in the courts.

Beyond the positive and negative portrayals of the widow lay the third option and probably the stereotype closest to reality for women – the poor widow. As Stretton explains, even when widows did protect their interests in the law courts of Tudor and Stuart England

9. St Francis de Sales, 'Advice to widows', p. 197; see the similar advice offered by the medieval widow Christine de Pisan, although she was also careful to counsel the potential widow litigant to 'avoid being injured or dominated by other people', *The Treasure of the City of Ladies or the Book of the Three Virtues* (Harmondsworth, 1985), pp. 157–9.

10. John Benton, ed., *Self and Society in Medieval France: The Memoirs of Abbot Guibert of Nogent* (1064–*c.* 1125), 2nd edn (Toronto, 1984), pp. 70–1.

they often played on their weakness and vulnerability and emphasized their 'poverty in its widest sense', that is, not just in financial terms but also through 'declarations of impotence' that emphasized their lack of support. These tactics had parallels throughout Europe, where, for example, Merry Wiesner has observed how widows in early modern Germany tended to emphasize the individual and specific nature of their hardship when faced with increasing restrictions on their rights to work.[11]

In paupers' letters to poor relief overseers in early industrial England, analysed by Sharpe in Chapter 14, widows articulated their distress, reminded authorities of their age and infirmities, emphasized the seasonal nature of their work and their attempts at self-sufficiency, and sometimes threatened to return to their home parishes if they were not granted relief. Widows also adopted certain formulae and timed their appeals in order to gain as much support as possible. Across Europe from late medieval Italy to sixteenth-century Spain, the poor widow was a familiar figure as the 'deserving' object of charity.[12] Sharpe, however, suggests that 'during industrialization it did become necessary for widows to strengthen their historic claim to relief' – a claim which became harder to stake in urban centres than in village communities. Chapters 3 and 14 reflect on why the widower had never been able to stake an historic claim to relief.

The choice to remarry

Did widowhood only exist, as the definition suggests, for 'the time during which one is a widow or widower' or could it be said to carry over into remarriage? A widow's previous marriage could be a source of empowerment and provide her with greater financial awareness and expectations, as Foyster and Erickson acknowledge in Chapters 7 and 9. Knowledge of financial or legal apparatus meant that widowhood marked a woman for life, and it did not disappear upon remarriage when a widow's independent legal status reverted

11. Merry Wiesner, 'Spinning out capital: women's work in the early modern economy', p. 144; Wiesner, 'Women's defence of their public role', pp. 12, 15; Wiesner, 'Guilds, male bonding, and women's work in early modern Germany', p. 175; all three essays in Merry Wiesner, *Gender, Church and State in Early Modern Germany* (London, 1998).

12. Isabelle Chabot, 'Widowhood and poverty in late medieval Florence', *Continuity and Change* 3 (1988), pp. 291–311; David Vassberg, 'The status of widows in sixteenth-century rural Castile', in John Henderson and Richard Wall, eds, *Poor Women and Children in the European Past* (London, 1994), pp. 182 and 185.

to its diminished capacity as a 'feme covert', a 'covered woman'. This was a problem contemporaries recognized, particularly in satires and advice books warning grooms away from the widow bride.[13] Moreover, as Foyster points out, the widow brought with her into a second or later marriage not only experience of financial and legal transactions, but her previous marital and sexual experience as well. This chapter on marital litigation in the Court of Arches reveals how important it was for both defendants and plaintiffs in separation cases to remind the courtroom of a remarried widow's 'previous status as somebody else's wife'. When the second marriage broke down, it was not simply a widow's period of legal, financial and sexual independence which could be cited in blame, rather, as Foyster makes clear, 'it is this reputation as a former wife, rather than as a widow, which is recalled'.

Barbara Todd has dispelled the myth that widows were desperate to remarry and did so at a great rate.[14] In fact, widowers were the most likely candidates for a remarriage. As Pelling points out in her chapter, the most striking aspect about the widower is precisely that the 'widower seems not so much submerged as shortlived'. The rapid rate of remarriage by widowers seems to be a constant throughout the medieval and early modern period – they married sooner after the death of their wives and they continued to marry at an older age than widows.[15] The widower, too, took the experience of his first marriage into the next, precisely because he knew how important a role the wife played in the running of the household. At the death of his wife, the widower lost her expertise and manifold capabilities. The nineteenth-century widower, described in Chapter 14, relied on his eldest daughter to fill the maternal role in the household until he eventually remarried.

This tendency for widowers to remarry can perhaps be explained by the fact that across Europe and across time, the widower faced fewer restrictions to remarriage. The medieval widower knew that if he remarried he could never enter the church, but the impact of such a restriction was negligible, and undeniably lessened after the

13. Todd, 'Demographic determinism', p. 425.

14. Barbara Todd, 'The remarrying widow: a stereotype reconsidered', in Mary Prior, ed., *Women in English Society 1500–1800* (London, 1985), pp. 54–92.

15. Todd has recently added some nuances to the evidence on widower remarriage. She suggests that by the late seventeenth century 'while widowers were continuing to remarry in the same proportions, the time that elapsed before they did so increased, if only slightly'. Among another group of widowers in Todd's study, those with wives who died between 1680 and 1719, the remarriage interval was even longer: see Todd, 'Demographic determinism', p. 440.

Protestant Reformation.[16] While widows generally faced some kind of 'year of mourning' prohibition to prevent any confusion over the paternity of a child, the widower was usually a free agent from the time of his wife's death.[17] With few barriers to remarriage, it remains to be seen whether any factors beyond 'replacement' actually encouraged widowers to seek a new wife. Lyndal Roper has noted that the 'connection between political capacity and marriage' was so strong that a council decree in fifteenth-century Augsburg 'stipulated that only those currently married could hold urban office – a provision that would have disqualified all widowers'.[18] In England in the 1690s the government, ostensibly to raise money for the war against France, instructed its 'surveyors' on how to 'ascertain' the duties or taxes upon houses, bachelors and childless widowers.[19] Did council decrees or the imposition of taxes encourage remarriage by widowers or did they simply add another factor to the need to replace a wife? Little is known about 'widowerhood' and widower remarriage beyond demographics, but this volume attempts to ask some of the questions.

A widow's remarriage, however, was subject to a series of restrictions. In the 1530s the English Parliament went so far as to introduce a bill to prevent young men marrying widows. It did not proceed to a second reading.[20] In France the 1560 Edict of Second Marriages placed restrictions on remarrying widows and, as discussed in Chapter 6, it was nearly two decades before a court case challenged the interpretation of the edict and led the highest court of appeal in France to issue a verdict extending the law to widowers. In the Dutch province of Friesland a widow under the age of 25 could not remarry without her father's consent, although widows and widowers seem to have been on a more equal footing under Dutch customary law, which allowed the 'longest-lived of Husband

16. Brundage, *Law, Sex*, pp. 58, 98.

17. Although the Dutch province of Friesland introduced a mandatory six-month period of mourning in 1723 preventing widower remarriage. See Dierneke Hempernias-van Dijk, 'Widows and the law: the legal position of widows in the Dutch Republic during the seventeenth and eighteenth centuries', in J. Bremmer and L. van den Bosch, eds, *Between Poverty and the Pyre: Moments in the History of Widowhood* (London, 1995), p. 97.

18. Lyndal Roper, *The Holy Household: Women and Morals in Reformation Augsburg* (Oxford, 1989), p. 31.

19. *Instructions to be Held & Observed by the Several Surveyors Appointed Ascertaining the Duties upon Houses, and upon Marriages, Births, Burials, and upon Batchelors and Widowers, pursuant to the Act of Parliament in that behalf* (London, 1697).

20. Charles Carlton, 'The widow's tale: male myths and female reality in 16th and 17th century England', *Albion* 10 (1978), p. 121.

or Wife' to 'govern and administer the Goods, feudal and personal, gained and lost in common, until the death of that survivor'.[21] In seventeenth-century England, a widow knew that by remarriage she would relinquish her legal personality and would not be able to protect her interests or the interests of her children. As the London widow Katherine Austen wrote in her diary, 'For my part I doe noe Injury to none by not Loveing. But if I doe I may doe real Injuries where I am already engadged. To my Deceased friends [husband's] posterity.'[22]

Inheritance and property

Property was another area which set apart women's and men's experiences of widowhood. When a woman became a widow, both her inheritance from her husband and the recovery of her own property had to be settled. For men, by contrast, widowhood did not involve any transfer of property because, in most instances, especially when there were children from the marriage, the husband simply maintained the same control over his spouse's goods that he had enjoyed during her lifetime. This seems to have been the case both in Mediterranean and Northern Europe, despite the different regional systems of marriage settlement. In the Mediterranean basin from the twelfth century onward a wife's property was largely constituted by the dowry set by the father of the bride at her marriage. The dowry, an institution of Roman origin, had replaced the *morgengab* or morning gift provided by the husband, a practice of Lombard origin.[23] In England and parts of Northern Europe, by contrast, the economic security of the widow was represented by the dower, that is, her entitlement to a third of her husband's property if she outlived him.[24] Although prescribed by law, both the recovery of dowry and the transfer of dower often led to conflict. In the early Middle Ages, these problems could partly be attributed to

21. Hempernias-van Dijk, 'Widows and the law', p. 97; Marshall, *Dutch Gentry*, pp. 57–8.

22. Todd, 'The remarrying widow', p. 77.

23. D.O. Hughes, 'From brideprice to dowry in Mediterranean Europe', *Journal of Family History* 3 (1978), pp. 262–96 and, more recently, B.M. Kreutz, 'The twilight of the *Morgengabe*', in S.K. Cohn and S.A. Epstein, eds, *Portraits of Medieval and Renaissance Living: Essays in Honor of David Herlihy* (Ann Arbor, Mich., 1996), pp. 131–47.

24. L.J. Senderowitz, '"Of the gift of her husband": English dower and its consequences in the year 1200', in J. Kirshner and S. Wemple, eds, *Women of the Medieval World* (Oxford, 1985), pp. 215–55.

the nature of the assets, which were 'resistant to division', as Crick puts it, being largely made up of immovable goods or real property. When dowries started to take a monetary form in the late Middle Ages it became technically easier to return them, although interested parties employed several devices to delay the process or prevent it all together.[25]

In Chapter 8 Isabelle Chabot points out that the heart of the issue was a crucial conflict of interests between the property rights of the widow and those of her children. In fifteenth-century Florence a widow's entitlement to her dowry was played against her position as a mother and her rights to the custody or guardianship of her children. A widow who wanted to stay with her children was expected to give up her dowry in favour of her offspring, as well as any idea of remarriage (which would deprive children of a first marriage of any right to their mother's property). It must be underlined that if the widow stayed in her late husband's house with her children this amounted to giving up her rights to control and dispose of her goods as she wished. The practice meant that, in these cases, a widowed mother's goods remained incorporated in her husband's property and thus were passed down to the heirs designated by him.[26]

This denial of a woman's right to separate property – to control it or to transmit it – becomes more and more the rule as we move into the early modern period. In the eighteenth century, in particular, this was justified by the ideal of the conjugal family. In Chapter 9 Amy Louise Erickson shows how marriage settlements in England had sharply declined in numbers by the early eighteenth century, a process which paralleled the new popularity of romantic ideals of marriage. These findings clearly undermine or complicate the idea that a more 'egalitarian' family emerged in this period, as a result of a romantic revolution.[27] Although we should consider the compensations of an enhanced maternal role, women undoubtedly lost ground in terms of their economic power and independence.[28]

25. Hughes, 'From brideprice', pp. 281–2.

26. Sandra Cavallo, 'Proprietà o possesso? Composizione e controllo dei beni delle donne a Torino, 1650–1710', in Giulia Calvi and Isabelle Chabot, eds, *Le Ricchezze delle Donne* (Turin, 1998), pp. 183, 191.

27. Lawrence Stone, *The Family, Sex and Marriage in England 1500–1800* (London, 1977); Randolph Trumbach, *The Rise of the Egalitarian Family: Aristocratic Kinship and Domestic Relations in Eighteenth-Century England* (New York, 1978), pp. 84–93.

28. On the growing idealization of motherhood in the eighteenth century see the recent discussion in Amanda Vickery, *The Gentleman's Daughter: Women's Lives in Georgian England* (New Haven, Conn., 1998), pp. 91–4.

While widows in some parts of Europe may have lost their entitlement to direct control over their dowries or dower portions, it is often assumed that they retained their roles as managers of the family property – a role that gave women responsibility, authority and a presence in the public sphere. Widowed mothers were normally made responsible (in their husbands' wills) for the management of the family estate while the children were under age, as long as they renounced any claim to dispose of their own property and promised not to enter a new marital union. The contributors in this volume, however, are sceptical that widowhood was necessarily a liberating phase in women's lives when women acquired the legal right to administer, buy and sell goods. This optimistic interpretation tends to rely on sources such as widows' wills because in many testaments women do appear to be exercising their ownership rights and decision-making powers regarding property.[29] Yet, as the Anglo-Saxon cases studied by Crick illustrate, widows' wills often simply reconfirmed (at the end of the woman's period of control of the family property) the choices previously made by their husbands. Moreover, as Erickson demonstrates, the widow's responsibility for the family property seems to have been curtailed over time: in England, as we move from the seventeenth into the eighteenth century, widows were less and less likely to be assigned the important role as executors of their husbands' wills.

What property actually came under the widow's control and how free was she in her ability to administer it? Chabot draws attention to the fact that in Renaissance Florence the expression 'usufruct of all goods' might mean the mere right to clothing and food rather than the right to manage the estate. Skinner further notes that most of the transactions undertaken by widows in medieval southern Italy were land sales. A similar pattern of widows as sellers of land, rather than purchasers, appears in early modern France.[30] As Skinner notes, when the reasons for these sales are investigated cultural and legal constraints appear, which may have prevented widows from managing property dynamically. According to Lombard law any alienation of property, if it affected children's interests and was not sold or donated to the church, could be justified only on the grounds of poverty – a reason often cited by widows. In the early modern

29. For example Barbara Diefendorf, 'Women and property in *ancien régime* France: theory and practice in Dauphiné and Paris', in J. Brewer and S. Staves, eds, *Early Modern Conceptions of Property* (New York, 1995), pp. 170–93.

30. James B. Collins, 'The economic role of women in seventeenth-century France', *French Historical Studies* 16 (1989), pp. 457–8.

period, the forms of investment available to widows also decreased, as membership of guilds became increasingly restricted and other common purchases such as civic or state officeholding positions were obviously off limits to female investors.[31] Local forms of landholding also played an important part in determining a widowed mother's role as custodian of the children's patrimony. Hence, widows operating under systems of life interest in a property (such as 'freebench') were expected to maintain the property prudently for their children – not to take risks and expand it.[32] A general lack of confidence in widows' abilities as administrators finds a reflection in the fact that authorities in parts of Germany from the mid-sixteenth century onwards imposed male guardians on widows and often a son, brother, or another male appointed by the local city council had to represent widows in any legal or financial dealings.[33] Moreover, in areas where they did have access to the administration of property widows, unlike widowers, were regularly subject to checks by authorities, such as the Tuscan magistrates or Officials of the Wards discussed in Giulia Calvi's chapter, and made to account for their administration of the estate destined for their offspring. Kin also contributed to this 'close supervision' of the widow's actions, which extended, as Calvi argues, to her decisions concerning the 'lifestyle, consumption, and education' of her children.[34] It is likely that many widows internalized these anxieties and felt that the scope of their initiative as guardians and managers of property was in practice much more limited than the legal autonomy theoretically assigned to them.

Children

Parental authority over children (the Roman concept of *patria potestas*) formed another sphere in which the inequality between

31. Ibid.; Wiesner, 'Spinning out capital', p. 144; Wiesner, 'Women's defence', pp. 12, 15; Wiesner, 'Guilds', pp. 174–6.

32. Barbara Todd, 'Freebench and free enterprise: widows and their property in two Berkshire villages', in John Chartres and David Hey, eds, *English Rural Society, 1500–1800: Essays in Honour of Joan Thirsk* (Cambridge, 1990), pp. 175–200.

33. Wiesner, 'Spinning out capital', p. 140; Wiesner, 'Frail, weak and helpless: women's legal position in theory and reality', in Wiesner, *Gender*, pp. 86, 88, 91.

34. Julia Hardwick also offers evidence of these continuous interferences by members of the family: see Hardwick, 'Widowhood and patriarchy in seventeenth century France', *Journal of Social History* 26 (1992), pp. 133–48.

widowed mothers and fathers emerged. Although little research has been carried out on this important issue, it is usually assumed that the father, rather than the mother, retained full rights to decide the fate of the children in matters such as education, trade or profession, religious affiliation or place of residence and that a widow was obliged to comply with her late husband's prescriptions.[35] In Chapter 10 on early modern Germany, however, Dagmar Freist demonstrates that in marriages of mixed religious faith, the death of a spouse could trigger a struggle about the religion in which the children should be raised, and pose a challenge to the idea of *patria potestas*. As we proceed into the eighteenth century, the right of mothers to have a say in their children's religious faith was increasingly recognized. Further research should determine to what extent this shift in authority from the father to the mother – or rather a shift towards a more balanced distribution of parental authority – extended to other areas of decision-making. It is worth noting that the transmission of religious faith from parents to children in Germany seems to some extent to have followed gender lines (following a pattern similar to the one which, as we shall see, sometimes characterizes the distribution of property). As Freist comments, mothers were more likely to achieve recognition of their right to transmit their religious faith to their daughters, whereas sons were expected to adopt the religion of the father.

On the Continent the practice of appointing widows as guardians, and often as sole guardians, of their children became more common in the early modern period. Freist suggests that this was the usual practice in Germany in the seventeenth and eighteenth centuries. According to Giulia Calvi in Chapter 13, the legal principle which prevented mothers from inheriting from their children was responsible for the recognition of mothers' rights to guardianship. Mothers came to be seen as the most disinterested protectors of children's property rights and were preferred to paternal kin such as uncles and grandfathers who stood to benefit from a child's death. In areas of Europe, this restriction on inheritance was already in place in the late Middle Ages as an obvious corollary of patrilineal systems of succession. In London, for example, as well as in the early modern Tuscan case examined by Calvi, custody laws favoured the mother and her kin because 'no one who would profit from

35. The idea of joint parental authority over children had gained popularity in the Middle Ages, at least in Germany, but it died out in the sixteenth century: see Wiesner, 'Frail, weak and helpless', pp. 86, 88.

the death of the child could serve as guardian'.[36] This exclusion of mothers from the succession of their children gained popularity with the reintroduction of Roman law across parts of Europe in the sixteenth century, such as the French crown's 1567 *Edict des Mères*. The versions of Roman law adopted in early modern Europe add a further dimension to this issue of the mother's abilities as guardian, because these adaptations tended to reinforce the authority of the head of the household at the same time as they accentuated the fragility or *imbecilitas* of women.[37] Hence, early modern versions of Roman law often reflect an ambivalence to the widow as head of household and guardian of her children's interests.[38]

In early modern continental Europe, the property rights of children appear to have become increasingly protected from the possible foolishness of both mothers and fathers. The state extended its authority over family matters and, in particular, limited parents' freedom in actions affecting their children. The potential for conflict between a surviving parent's actions and the implications for the material wealth of his or her children conferred a new rigidity on widowed parents' use of property, and constrained their freedom to remarry. As the amount of legislation issued on this matter in sixteenth-century France indicates, relationships between step-parents and step-children, half-brothers and half-sisters clearly provoked growing concern, and remarriage was increasingly seen as a source of disputes over inheritance rights. Although no chapter in this volume studies the important issue of the relative status of children from the first and second marriage bed (were children from the first marriage disadvantaged?), some of the examples do suggest that there may have been a move towards more equitable treatment in the early modern period. The principles adopted by the French state to protect the family name and inheritance of children from both the first and second marriage beds, discussed in Chapter 6, contrast sharply with the harsh treatment that Florentine statutory law reserved, a century earlier, for the children of a first marriage. As noted in Chapter 8, these children were excluded

36. Barbara Hanawalt, 'Patriarchal provisions for widows and children in medieval London', in M.J. Maynes *et al.*, eds, *Gender, Kinship, Power: A Comparative and Interdisciplinary History* (New York, 1996), p. 203.

37. The impact of Roman law on women's condition in early modern Germany has been analysed by Wiesner, 'Frail, weak and helpless', pp. 84–93.

38. An ambivalence only exacerbated by the fact that in ancient Rome, in contrast to early modern Europe, a mother could never act as the guardian of her children. On early modern versions of Roman law, see Chapter 6.

from any right to inherit from the mother's property, if she had children from a second husband.

The extent to which the presence or absence of children modified the experience of widowhood merits further attention. It may well be that the death of a spouse had very different implications for men and women with and without issue. In Renaissance Florence, the childless widow enjoyed unusually generous inheritance rights. Her husband's will often nominated her as beneficiary, during her lifetime, of all his goods. Moreover, she could freely dispose of her dowry, which could in no case be claimed by her husband's heirs. In early modern England too, as Erickson notes, the widow with no surviving offspring was entitled, under ecclesiastical law, to the whole of her husband's patrimony when he died intestate (that is, about 70 per cent of the time). The widowed mother had the right to one-third of her husband's personal property, although in practice the ecclesiastical courts were often more benevolent and accorded her more than her legal share. From 1670 an Act introduced by Parliament significantly reduced the property rights of widows, especially of those with no children (their share was curtailed to one-half of the husband's estate), but maintained nevertheless the imbalance between the latter and widowed mothers (whose share was thereafter strictly limited to one-third of the husband's property). The situation of the childless widow raises the question, addressed in this volume by Chabot, of the relationship between maternity roles and property rights. To what extent was motherhood (as opposed to womanhood) seen as incompatible with property ownership? A lack of children, by contrast, may have implied for the widower the imposition of sanctions or taxes, not on his portion of his wife's property but, as Pelling notes with respect to England in the 1690s, as a result of the nation's concern for fertility and its need to raise revenue.

Several of the contributors further point out how widows and widowers behaved differently, and faced different types of pressures and concerns, depending on whether they had male children only, female children only or a mixture of both. As Chabot suggests in her study of Renaissance Florence, at the death of a father who only had daughters, the pressure on his family to keep his patrimony intact and to prevent the widow's recovery of her dowry diminished. These husbands were unusually generous with their widows because they seemed to realize that in the absence of male children the property would in any case devolve outside the patrilineage.

It may have been easier, therefore, for a widow with no sons to recover her dowry, claim her dower, or achieve recognition of her property rights. This interpretation is confirmed by evidence from seventeenth-century northern Italy, where husbands with female children frequently split the property equally between their daughters and their wives, treating the spouse exactly as if she was one of the offspring.[39] One could argue that a similar gender bias was at work in an eighteenth-century case studied by Giulia Calvi where the reversion of two daughters' patrimony to their mother – a practice forbidden by law – was allowed to occur after a long battle. The fact that the widow had no sons may have played a part in the magistrates' leniency. The existence of male or female children may have also affected the experience of widowed men. We have already noted that the presence of adolescent daughters capable of looking after younger siblings, and of replacing the mother in some of her tasks, may have made the remarriage of the father less necessary. Daughters, however, may also have been a source of fears and anxiety for the widower, especially when they were sole heirs. According to Crick, widowed fathers of daughters feature more prominently in the historical record of Anglo-Saxon England because they were more likely to leave special provisions to protect vulnerable beneficiaries of their estate.

Church and religion

Chapters in this volume thus reconstruct in detail the constraints which affected the lives of widowed men and women. They analyse the impact of legal prescriptions, ideals of conduct, demographic conditions, and family expectations. In addition, our contributors provide several examples of the various ways widows, widowers and their opponents manipulated norms and stereotypes, and surviving spouses managed to overcome family and social pressures. This manipulation of codes occurred not just in court litigation, in disputes over the guardianship of children and in petitions for poor relief: widows were often able to play competing models of widowhood – proposed by the state, the church and the family – against each other in their efforts to circumvent the prescriptions imposed by customs and laws concerning property. The Catholic

39. Cavallo, 'Proprietà', p. 186.

church, in particular, was often an ally for widowed women wanting to escape conventional patterns of transmission of wealth: this is most clearly illustrated in the examples from Anglo-Saxon England, medieval southern Italy, late medieval Florence and sixteenth-century Spain discussed by Crick, Skinner, Chabot and Bilinkoff in their respective chapters. One of the few ways in which medieval and early modern widows could retain control over their goods in life and exercise their rights of transmission in unorthodox ways – escaping family and social expectations – was to donate part of their property to a religious or charitable establishment or, perhaps more frequently, to commit themselves to a future bequest.[40] Arguably, one of the keys to the church's success in attracting funds, which contributed largely to its consolidation and expansion, lies in the fact that it provided widows with one of the few morally-approved means of escaping the claims of family and kin to their property.[41]

Involvement in religious and charitable initiatives also gave widows the opportunity to play an active role in areas of the public realm usually barred to women. Widows' prominence in the foundation and financing of convents and charities (especially institutions set up for women) in Counter-Reformation Europe has been repeatedly noted in recent studies.[42] Jodi Bilinkoff shows, however, that widows were not simply providers of funds – they extended their activities to all aspects of these institutions. Widows acted as financial administrators and as governors presiding over the organization of internal life. They designed commemorative rituals and determined the aesthetic and functional appearance of the buildings constructed for these religious and charitable establishments. Moreover, analysis of the way in which widows performed these duties reveals the subversive nature of their involvement. Bilinkoff argues that the semi-religious communities for women created by Spanish widows in Avila can be seen as households free from

40. Often the church, convent or charity that was named as beneficiary of the legacy was entitled to claim it only after the death of several usufructuaries nominated by the benefactress: Sandra Cavallo, *Charity and Power in Early Modern Italy: Benefactors and their Motives in Turin 1541–1789* (Cambridge, 1995), pp. 172–3.

41. This complicates Goody's interpretation of the church's expansion through private charity: J. Goody, *The Development of the Family and Marriage in Europe* (Cambridge, 1983).

42. See for example S.K. Cohn, Jr., *Women in the Streets: Essays on Sex and Power in Renaissance Italy* (Baltimore, 1996), ch. 4, as well as the works cited by Bilinkoff in this volume, ch. 11, n. 6.

male authority, where the role of 'the mother' was central. Similarly, in the commemorative provisions prescribed by these women we find a conception of the family which included kin from the woman's family lineage as well as from her marital one – clearly disregarding the conventional hierarchy that placed priority on the patrilineage.[43]

Apart from offering opportunities for the protection of the widow's property and for the expression of subversive and creative roles, as Chabot, Freist and Bilinkoff discuss, religious and charitable establishments presented widows with a respectable route to escape family pressure to remarry and to overcome the ambiguities created by their unbound marital status. Widows (both the wealthy and those of more modest means) were numerous among the women who entered convents or joined other types of religiously inspired female communities. This was true especially in the sixteenth and early seventeenth centuries – a period in which the distinction between cloistered and uncloistered female communities was not yet clear cut. For many widows, embracing a religious or semi-religious communal life was also no doubt a means of ensuring a domestic environment free from conflict. The question of where to live often became a problem after the death of the spouse, especially when the presence of adult children or heirs often forced a redefinition of the living space of the surviving partner. The frequency with which widows are found as members of irregular households, sharing dwelling and resources with other widows, unmarried women or children who were not relatives, is evidence of the crisis that many wives had to face at the death of their husbands. Clearly, there are parallels between these unconventional living arrangements, described for many parts of early modern Europe, from fifteenth-century Florence to sixteenth-century Norwich or seventeenth-century Rome, and the female religious communities just discussed. Both types of arrangements can be seen as responses to the frequent isolation of the widow.[44]

43. For similar remarks concerning masses for the dead ordered by women see Sharon Strocchia, 'Women, kin and commemorative masses in Renaissance Florence', *Renaissance Quarterly* 42 (1989), pp. 635–54.

44. Isabelle Chabot, 'Widowhood and poverty in late medieval Florence', *Continuity and Change* 3 (1988), pp. 291–311; Margaret Pelling, 'Old age, poverty and disability in early modern Norwich: work, remarriage and other expedients', in Pelling and Richard Smith, eds, *Life, Death and the Elderly: Historical Perspectives* (London, 1991), pp. 74–101; Marina D'Amelia, 'Scatole cinesi: vedove e donne sole in una società d'antico regime', *Memoria* 3 (1986), pp. 58–79.

Facing loneliness and poverty

This issue of residence and widowhood deserves further consideration because tensions often arose with heirs not just over property and authority in the house but also over the continuity of the household itself. What kind of negotiation took place between the surviving parent and the children? Who stayed? Who left? Were children's attitudes different towards widowed mothers and widowed fathers? Sharpe argues in Chapter 14 that women gained more control over the family purse after the death of a husband. How enduring was the widow's autonomy? Did her new authority start to be questioned when children approached the age of majority? Even in the absence of remarriage, widowhood has a life cycle which we need to take into account and this cycle may differ notably for widows and widowers.

Evidence about attitudes to widowed parents and on the possible differences in attitudes to fathers and mothers is still sparse. Across Europe widows are found living on their own in much greater numbers than widowers; and the proportion of widows sharing with their married children (usually with their daughters) is very small. For widowed men we face an apparent paradox. Despite the fact that, at least in early modern England, it was highly unusual for widowers to reside with their grown-up children, households composed of single men were extremely rare. Pelling argues that this situation reflects a general anxiety about the existence of lonely males. The invisibility of the widowed man could, therefore, be a result of the various provisions made to avoid male loneliness. Concern about solitary men influenced attitudes to male remarriage, making it fairly acceptable, socially, for elderly widowers to take much younger women as second wives. It is also likely, although this is an area which is difficult to document, that concern for male loneliness shaped the attitudes of children and kin, for example, in terms of their willingness to provide support and care. Finally, as Pelling remarks, it certainly informs institutional care, at least in England, where men rather than women are given preference.

Pelling's thesis has important implications for the way in which welfare systems in European pre-industrial societies have been understood. It is a commonplace that in these systems women – especially unmarried women or widows – were the objects of charity *par excellence.* The benevolent attitude to widows, in particular, is a characteristic of Judaeo-Christian doctrines, as Sharpe demonstrates, whereas nothing similar is found in Africa and Asia. The widow's visibility in the rhetoric and practice of welfare is usually seen as a sign of vulnerability and dependency. Yet it may also indicate that less visible forms of aid and support directed to widowers prevented their pauperization and spared them the experience of public charity.

The prominence of widows as recipients of poor relief made a crucial contribution to the construction of the enduring stereotype of the frail woman. As Sharpe warns in Chapter 14, poor relief is a form of control, not just of protection: it plays an important ideological role. The widow's unquestioned entitlement to poor relief greatly contributes to reinforcing images of female vulnerability – images at odds with the reality of the resourceful widow who often spent long years of her life on her own, or in unconventional living arrangements, and who had to work and support herself for much longer than her male counterpart.

The example of poor relief, and of formal and informal provisions for the widowed more generally, demonstrates with clarity the tension between conventional images of widowhood and the actual conditions in which widows and widowers lived. Dominant representations of the widowed were neither a mere result nor a determinant of social practice, though representations often concealed an unsettling reality and reconfirmed gender divisions and hierarchies. The ways in which medieval and early modern widows and widowers negotiated the stereotypes, laws and expectations associated with widowhood, as well as how their contemporaries perceived their actions, are the subjects of this volume.

CHAPTER TWO

Men, women and widows: widowhood in pre-Conquest England[1]

JULIA CRICK

Widowhood can be said to comprise two component parts: the event – the loss of a partner – and the construct – the deployment of the rhetoric of widowhood. This chapter concerns a situation in which the hiatus between these elements is more than usually evident. Although the loss of a partner must have been a relatively frequent occurrence in England before the Norman Conquest, the terminology of widowhood occupies a very marginal place in the documentary record. No special designation marks most of the widowed population – a situation familiar in many periods in which male widowed do not carry any special style – but neither do the written sources give much suggestion of a stable and developed terminology of widowhood:[2] no one term for widow, no verb to be widowed, no widely used description of the state of widowhood.[3]

Without a clear signal in the written record, few historians investigating Anglo-Saxon society have given much attention to the widowed.[4] It is necessary at the outset, therefore, to demonstrate the importance of the event of widowhood in pre-Conquest England,

1. I am indebted to Julia Smith for acute comments on a draft of this paper.

2. For a contrary view, see R.H. Bremmer, 'Widows in Anglo-Saxon England', in Jan Bremmer and Lourens van den Bosch, eds, *Between Poverty and the Pyre: Moments in the History of Widowhood* (London, 1995), p. 59.

3. *Wuduwanhad* (meaning 'husbandless state' or 'widowhood') is attested but very rare: J.R. Clark-Hall, *A Concise Anglo-Saxon Dictionary*, 4th edn (Cambridge, 1960), p. 424. See also P.H. Sawyer, *Anglo-Saxon Charters: An Annotated List and Bibliography* (London, 1968), no. 1517.

4. Although see Bremmer, 'Widows'; Carole A. Hough, 'The early Kentish "divorce laws": a reconsideration of Æthelberht, chs. 79 and 80', *Anglo-Saxon England* 23 (1994), pp. 19–34; Pauline Stafford, *Unification and Conquest: A Political and Social History of England in the Tenth and Eleventh Centuries* (London, 1989), pp. 174–6; Stafford, 'Women in Domesday', *Reading Medieval Studies* 15 (1989), pp. 77–82, 84–9. See also Theodore John Rivers, 'Widows' rights in Anglo-Saxon law', *American Journal of Legal History* 19 (1975), pp. 208–15.

by which I mean the consequences of the termination by death of the reproductive unit. In all documented cases this unit held property and would probably have been recognized by the church. The second half of the discussion will be concerned with the meagre lexicography of widowhood. The frequent failure of our sources, all ultimately ecclesiastical, to identify widows and to employ the vocabulary of *viduitas* poses wider and more difficult questions about the construction and representation of widowhood.

Widowhood in pre-Conquest England

Both by analogy with other early medieval societies and by observation of individual cases, we can predict that in pre-Conquest England widowhood is likely to have been a significant occurrence both statistically and economically. This was a violent society, prone to disease, with no useful medical or obstetric intervention to speak of: it is highly probable that by the age of 30 many men and women would have lost one or more marital partners.[5] Besides the many young widows found among the documented classes (the ruling elite), so many cases of multiple male and female remarriage occur that it is often difficult to be sure that the marriages were indeed serial and not concurrent.[6] When at the age of nineteen Judith, a Frankish princess, was married to a count of Flanders, she had already been widowed twice, having married successive kings of Wessex at the age of fourteen and seventeen.[7]

Presumed high mortality coincided with a lack of economic liquidity.[8] In ninth-, tenth- and eleventh-century England, as in other

5. Don Brothwell, 'Palaeodemography and earlier British populations', *World Archaeology* 4 (1972), pp. 82–5; David Herlihy, 'Life expectancies for women in medieval society', in Rosmarie Thee Morewedge, ed., *The Role of Woman in the Middle Ages* (Albany, NY, 1975), pp. 1–22; and Suzanne Fonay Wemple, *Women in Frankish Society: Marriage and the Cloister 500 to 900* (Philadelphia, 1985), pp. 101–2.

6. On the wives of King Edward the Elder (AD 899–924) see Barbara Yorke, 'Æthelwold and the politics of the tenth century', in Barbara Yorke, ed., *Bishop Æthelwold: His Career and Influence* (Woodbridge, 1988), pp. 74–7, 80. See also James A. Brundage, *Law, Sex and Christian Society in Medieval Europe* (London, 1987), pp. 128, 135–7, 145.

7. Discussed by Bremmer, 'Widows', p. 64. I disagree with his interpretation of this case. See also Pauline Stafford, 'Charles the Bald, Judith and England', in Margaret Gibson and Janet Nelson, eds, *Charles the Bald: Court and Kingdom* (Oxford, 1981), pp. 144–5.

8. Although the case should not be overstated. See James Campbell, 'Was it infancy in England? Some questions of comparison', in Michael Jones and Malcolm Vale, eds, *England and her Neighbours, 1066–1453: Essays in Honour of Pierre Chaplais*

medieval societies, wealth was overwhelmingly immovable and therefore resistant to division; the death of a male head of household consequently presented the families of the elite with a difficult and important problem: how to deal with high-status females without damaging either the claims of subsequent generations or the social prestige of the family. Given the impossibility of splitting up working estates, the equitable division of the assets of the conjugal household could prove impossible (much like the early modern businesses in which widows played a prominent role);[9] on the other hand, maintaining the family property intact meant either removing the widow from any claim or giving her custody of the property, perhaps for her lifetime.[10] An eminently practical solution presented itself, particularly if the widow lacked children: the widow could marry a near relative of her husband and so ensure smooth succession to the property.[11] Two kings famously married their stepmothers and so secured title as well: Eadbald of Kent in 616 and Æthelbald of Wessex in 858 (Judith's second husband). The church had long striven against serial remarriage – twice was enough[12] – but marriage to a stepmother involved transgressing a much more serious taboo: exposing the nakedness of one's father.[13] Clerics fulminated at Eadbald's and Æthelbald's marriages, with more success in the first case, in the seventh century, than two centuries later.[14] Royal legislation issued under Cnut 150 years later still included measures

(London, 1989), pp. 1–17, and his 'Observations on English government from the tenth to the twelfth century', *Transactions of the Royal Historical Society* 25 (1975), pp. 39–54.

9. See Olwen Hufton, 'Women without men: widows and spinsters in Britain and France in the eighteenth century', in Bremmer and van den Bosch, eds, *Between Poverty and the Pyre*, pp. 133–4.

10. As much property passed to heirs without testament, although the exact nature of the devolution of the land remains unclear. By the century before the Norman Conquest, a woman at the time of betrothal could be promised named estates in the event of her husband's predeceasing her. Compare F. Pollock and F.W. Maitland, *The History of English Law*, 2 vols, 2nd edn (Cambridge, 1898; repr. 1968), II, pp. 240–55. Marc A. Meyer, 'Land charters and the legal position of Anglo-Saxon women', in Barbara Kanner, ed., *The Women of England from Anglo-Saxon Times to the Present* (London, 1980), pp. 62–5.

11. Bremmer, 'Widows', p. 62.

12. Brundage, *Law*, pp. 61, 68, 97–8, 142.

13. Genesis 9:25, when Ham is cursed for looking on Noah's nakedness. Compare Pope Gregory I's advice to Augustine in AD 601: Bede, *Historia Ecclesiastica*, bk I, ch. 27, no. 5, in Bertram Colgrave and R.A.B. Mynors, eds, *Bede's Ecclesiastical History of the English People* (Oxford, 1969; rev. 1991), pp. 84–7.

14. Bede, *Historia Ecclesiastica*, bk II, chs 5–6, pp. 150–5; Asser, *De gestis Alfredi regis*, ch. 17, in William Henry Stevenson, ed., *Asser's Life of King Alfred* (Oxford, 1904; rev. 1959), p. 16. Discussed by Stafford, 'Charles', pp. 144–5.

to prevent marriage to the widows of near kindred.[15] Controlling marriage law was a remarkably slow and obstacle-strewn process.[16]

Wherever and whenever ecclesiastical law had a foothold, less satisfactory alternatives had to be found for dealing with widows.[17] Two main options are attested. First, the widow could be detached from the conjugal property and consequently would become an economic burden elsewhere, perhaps to her natal family or an institution: eleventh-century kings, like their earlier Continental counterparts, passed laws to prevent such women being forcibly remarried or consigned to monasteries within a year of their husband's death – presumably by relatives eager to be freed from this particular obligation.[18] Alternatively, the widow could acquire usufruct (life interest), or even a certain amount of freedom of disposition, over a substantial part of her husband's property, defined at the time of her marriage or specified in a will (or both).[19] Such legacies frequently fell prey to the husband's relatives, to judge from a number of surviving lawsuits.[20] So this solution, too, presented problems for both the widow and the family.

15. AD 1027–34. I Cnut 7, in F. Liebermann, ed., *Die Gesetze der Angelsachsen*, 3 vols (Halle, 1903–16), I, pp. 290–1. See also Pauline Stafford, 'Women and the Norman Conquest', *Transactions of the Royal Historical Society* 4 (1994), p. 231.

16. T.J. Rivers, 'Adultery in early Anglo-Saxon society: Æthelberht 31 in comparison with Continental Germanic law', *Anglo-Saxon England* 20 (1991), pp. 20–1; Brundage, *Law*, pp. 137, 143–5, 183–4; Mayke de Jong, 'To the limits of kinship: anti-incest legislation in the early medieval west (500–900)', in Jan Bremmer, ed., *From Sappho to de Sade: Moments in the History of Sexuality* (London, 1989), pp. 38–45.

17. See Pope Zacharias's letter to the English missionary Boniface, AD 743, advising him on dealing with problems of remarriage among the Continental Saxons, in Michael Tangl, ed., *Die Briefe des Heiligen Bonifatius und Lullus* (Berlin, 1955), no. 51, pp. 86–92; *The Anglo-Saxon Missionaries in Germany*, trans. C.H. Talbot (London, 1954), no. 28, pp. 102–6.

18. II Cnut 74, in Liebermann, ed., *Die Gesetze*, I, pp. 360–1; see Pauline Stafford, 'The laws of Cnut and the history of Anglo-Saxon royal promises', *Anglo-Saxon England* 10 (1982), pp. 173–90. For Continental legislation see. Liutprand 100.v, in F. Bluhme, ed., *Monumenta Germaniae Historica Leges*, 4 (Hanover, 1868), pp. 148–9; *The Lombard Laws*, trans. Katherine Fischer Drew (Philadelphia, 1973), pp. 187–8. Legislation relating to widows has been discussed by Rivers, 'Widows' rights'.

19. Thurstan confirmed in his will a marital gift to his wife: Dorothy Whitelock, ed., *Anglo-Saxon Wills* (Cambridge, 1930), no. 31. Life-time grants have been discussed by Julia Crick, 'Women, posthumous benefaction and family strategy in pre-Conquest England', *Journal of British Studies* (forthcoming). On dower and morning-gift see Stafford, *Unification*, pp. 166–7 and 'Women and the Norman Conquest', pp. 237–9. For Continental practice see Janet L. Nelson, 'The wary widow', in Wendy Davies and Paul Fouracre, eds, *Property and Power in the Early Middle Ages* (Cambridge, 1995), pp. 87–9.

20. Sawyer, *Anglo-Saxon Charters*, nos. 1200, 1457, 1497; A.J. Robertson, *Anglo-Saxon Charters* (Cambridge, 1939), no. 63. On Sawyer, *Anglo-Saxon Charters*, no. 1457 see Patrick Wormald, 'Charters, law, and the settlement of disputes in Anglo-Saxon England', in Wendy Davies and Paul Fouracre, eds, *The Settlement of Disputes in Early Medieval Europe* (Cambridge, 1986), pp. 157–61.

It is time to look to the documentary record for examples of widowed individuals. Pre-Conquest England was not a culture which bequeathed statistical information: it produced no runs of official documents and few surveys. Even more aspects of life than usual went unrecorded, including, it would seem, straightforward transmission of property within families. The extant documentation is often private (royal or aristocratic), highly particular, puppeteered by the church, and extraordinary by its very nature. What there is – and we have 2000 land-conveyances, dispute settlements and wills – can be very revealing but it cannot claim to be in the least representative. We can anticipate that instances of remarriage and widowhood generally went unrecorded. Nevertheless, with some effort, both widows and widowers can be found.

Widowed women

For more than a hundred years now historians have been impressed by a group of propertied, apparently independent, noblewomen who feature in the vernacular documents of pre-Conquest England, especially as testatrixes. In the wills they are seen distributing land, usually multiple estates, and occasionally movable wealth of considerable value – gold and silver vessels, liturgical silver, clothing, livestock, furnishings.[21] In none of these transactions do these women act with reference to a man or make benefactions to any man identifiable as a husband – there is a separate group of wills made jointly by men and women, almost all identifiable as husband and wife. Until recently, these independent testatrixes were taken as signs of precocious sexual equality. Women, like men, could apparently offer patronage and benefaction and dispose of their property freely, that is until the Norman Conquest and the introduction of common law practices credited with restricting to wives and widows female ownership of property.[22] Certainly, the quantity and nature of the property distributed in pre-Conquest women's wills is entirely comparable with that which men are known to have bequeathed; nevertheless, predictably enough, this particular vision of English fair play – equality between the sexes – does not bear

21. Discussed by Crick, 'Women, wills and moveable wealth in pre-Conquest England', in M. Donald and L. Hurcombe, eds, *Gender and Material Culture from Prehistory to the Present*, 3 vols (London, forthcoming).

22. This point of view has been discussed by Stafford, 'Women and the Norman Conquest', pp. 221–49.

examination. First, there are strong reasons for suspecting that free bequest was nothing of the kind. Many women's grants apparently made freely simply fulfilled the terms of earlier arrangements: reversionary grants to religious houses or relatives made by husbands or fathers now dead.[23] Secondly, earlier commentators overlooked the marital status of the female donors.

Pauline Stafford has recently suggested that the women who disposed of property in bequests were, like their post-Conquest counterparts, predominantly widows.[24] My own work on the wills strongly supports this. Although twenty-three of twenty-six 'independent' testatrixes at some time had been married (i.e. they had had husbands or produced children), only one has an identifiable living spouse.[25] The remaining three women's wills offer no clues at all to marital status. Of the twenty-three married testatrixes, thirteen were certainly widowed: either the document or external information establishes this incontrovertibly. I have some evidence to think that a further six were widows: three pay inheritance tax, one has children and bequeaths the garments of a nun, others make grants for their lord's soul.[26] No conclusions can be drawn about the remaining six testatrixes; they certainly could have been widows but we do not know.

What this suggests is that the great majority of this celebrated collection of propertied women were widows.[27] Little is known of most of them beyond these documents: they represent a stratum of the aristocracy probably just out of the political limelight and therefore beyond the purview of narrative accounts of the period such as the Anglo-Saxon Chronicle. However, as widowed women, the amount of wealth which they distributed was formidable. Aside from a few royal women documented in Domesday Book, these testatrixes are among the richest attested in pre-Conquest England.[28]

23. Stafford, *Unification*, p. 175.

24. Ibid., p. 176; see also Stafford, 'Women and the Norman Conquest', pp. 236–7.

25. Thorgunnr: see W. Dunn Macray, ed., *Chronicon Abbatiae Rameseiensis* (London, 1886), ch. 107, pp. 175–6. See Crick, 'Women, posthumous benefaction'.

26. Æthelgifu, in Sawyer, *Anglo-Saxon Charters*, no. 1497; Wulfgyth, ibid., no. 1535; Leofgifu, ibid., no. 1521; Wynflæd, ibid., no. 1539; Wulfwaru, ibid., no. 1538; and Æthelgifu, in E.O. Blake, ed., *Liber Eliensis* (London, 1962), bk II, ch. 59, had adult children but their wills fail to mention a living spouse.

27. Stafford, *Unification*, p. 176.

28. Marc A. Meyer, 'Women's estates in later Anglo-Saxon England: the politics of possession', *The Haskins Society Journal* 3 (1991), pp. 116–20. For examples of women bequeathing multiple estates see Whitelock, *Anglo-Saxon Wills*, nos. 3, 8, 14–15, 21, 29, 32.

Widowed men

In comparison with the relatively familiar group of women just discussed, the widowed men of pre-Conquest England represent a totally unknown quantity. I know of no work on them of any description.[29] This neglect is understandable in that widowers were not a recognized category, legal or otherwise: they had no name, they can only be detected using highly imperfect circumstantial evidence. Nevertheless, I have identified from eighth- to eleventh-century references ten donors who have some claim on the title.[30] The sources are very miscellaneous and the stories they tell vary but all entail benefaction to the church.

Five of the ten individuals can certainly be regarded as widowers. Three of them make pious grants after the death of their wives (two for the souls of their wives).[31] The other two, most interestingly and quite improperly, act to delay their late wives' property passing to religious houses. One, Toki, *c.* 1030 negotiated with the Archbishop of Canterbury to retain a lifetime interest in an estate destined for Christ Church by his father-in-law, of which his wife had usufruct.[32] The other, Siweard, Earl of Northumbria, intervened to gain usufruct of lands bequeathed by his late wife to the monastery of Peterborough.[33] She had made the grant as a widow before she had married Siweard. A generation later, her pious gift had still not reached its destination: the property was still in the hands of her second husband's family.[34] A further four candidates are donors who make wills or grants omitting mention of two standard categories of beneficiary of men's wills – wives and sons – but all making grants to daughters. Two of these donors are almost certainly widowers (for example Ketel Alder, who goes on pilgrimage to Rome with his stepdaughter, making provision for his relatives and for the soul of

29. Although see general comments of Nelson, 'The wary widow', p. 84.

30. As Julia Smith has reminded me, they did not necessarily remain unmarried. See also Patricia Skinner on Italy, 'Re-marriage on the part of widowers seems to have been assumed': Patricia Skinner, 'Women, wills and wealth in medieval southern Italy', *Early Medieval Europe* 2 (1993), p. 152.

31. Wulfgar acts after the death of his *wif*, Æffe, in Sawyer, *Anglo-Saxon Charters*, no. 1533; Ealdorman Æthelwine mentions his wife's soul, in C.R. Hart, *The Early Charters of Eastern England* (Leicester, 1966), no. 332; Thurkill of Harringworth has just buried his wife, in Macray, ed., *Chronicon Abbatiae Rameseiensis*, ch. 107, pp. 175–6.

32. Sawyer, *Anglo-Saxon Charters*, no. 1464; Robertson, *Anglo-Saxon Charters*, no. 80.

33. Sawyer, *Anglo-Saxon Charters*, no. 1481; Hart, *The Early Charters*, pp. 107–8, no. 160.

34. Peter A. Clarke, *The English Nobility under Edward the Confessor* (Oxford, 1994), p. 69.

a woman named Sæfflæd, probably his late wife);[35] the other two probably were.[36] Candidate ten is Goding of Gretton, a wealthy benefactor of Ely who had a legitimate son and whom the house chronicle of Ely appears to style as a monk at the time of his death.[37] If he was indeed tonsured, one wonders what had become of the mother of his son by this date. She had either predeceased him or agreed to enter a religious house herself unless, contrary to the spirit of the reformed church, Goding had set her aside uncanonically.[38]

These ten individuals represent the results of an initial scan through the documentary corpus. More examples no doubt await recognition, and of course some of those listed above remain tentative identifications. Nevertheless, the ten as they stand strongly suggest certain preliminary conclusions. Most strikingly, one notices an apparent correlation between identification in the written record and irregular inheritance. In the cases of all of the five certain candidates, the transactions described look anomalous. The three pious donors granting after the death of their wives make no mention of the heirs whose claim on the property would be as great if not greater than that of a wife: children. Meanwhile Toki and Siweard revealed their widowed state when they sought to divert their wives' property. Of the other candidates for 'widowerhood', the lack of mention of sons among four forms a striking feature.

One suspects that some classes of widower need not have featured in the written record at all: those whose property passed to sons and who did not choose to enter a religious community would not necessarily have needed to have their legacies described in writing. On the other hand, men who lacked sons and did not anticipate having any, being old or widowed or pledged to celibacy, or all three, could use a will to protect direct female descendants from predatory relatives. Wulfric Spot, founder of Burton abbey, appointed a guardian to oversee his 'poor' daughter's lifetime custody of two estates pledged after her death to the abbey.[39] Ketel Alder used a will to set his affairs in order before embarking on a dangerous pilgrimage.[40]

35. Ketel Alder, in Sawyer, *Anglo-Saxon Charters*, no. 1519 and Whitelock, *Anglo-Saxon Wills*, no. 34; Ælfgar, in Whitelock, *Anglo-Saxon Wills*, no. 2.

36. *Comes* Leppa, in Sawyer, *Anglo-Saxon Charters*, no. 1254; Wulfric Spot, in Sawyer, *Anglo-Saxon Charters*, no. 1536 and Whitelock, *Anglo-Saxon Wills*, no. 17.

37. Blake, ed., *Liber Eliensis*, bk II, chs 11, 26, p. 86 n. 4; Macray, ed., *Chronicon Abbatiae Rameseiensis*, ch. 36, pp. 65–6.

38. See Brundage, *Law*, pp. 202–3.

39. Sawyer, *Anglo-Saxon Charters*, no. 1536; ed. Whitelock, *Anglo-Saxon Wills*, no. 17.

40. Sawyer, *Anglo-Saxon Charters*, no. 1519; ed. Whitelock, *Anglo-Saxon Wills*, no. 34.

This apparent connection between the written record and abnormal bequest in the case of widowers may provide an insight into the women's wills already discussed. Wills should perhaps be seen as special documents, designed to curb the usual forces of family acquisitiveness.[41] Widowed men and women who remained single could require such intervention to secure the disposal of their property as they wished, especially if the men lacked sons. Women, in particular, needed such protection. Women who, as Cnut's church-inspired legislation allowed, remained widows rather than becoming wives through remarriage, may have retained custody of a substantial part of family property; their attempts to secure its disposal using the good offices of the church would explain their entry in the documentary record. Indeed, the interests of the church and our testatrixes often coincided. In all these wills, as in almost all others from the period, the church was a beneficiary – sometimes the sole beneficiary;[42] the women bequeath religious items – liturgical silver, religious books, even a nun's habit in one case. One begins to suspect that they may be anomalous for more than their wealth. Janet Nelson has recently discussed the phenomenon of the *Deo sacrata*, the wealthy aristocratic Continental widow vowed to God, pledged to remain unmarried, and thus able to remain in control of her husband's property at least for her lifetime until it passed to the church.[43] The English testatrixes are never so styled but they, too, might be viewed as vowesses, as one product of the church's pressure against remarriage exerted directly and through royal legislation. Not only the pious nature of their bequests but the timing of their wills looks propitious: most cluster in the tenth and eleventh centuries, in the period of church reform. Further indications come from the restricted English usage of the term *vidua*.

The written representation of widowhood

If widows occupy such a secure place in the written remains of pre-Conquest England, the question naturally arises of why this was not more obvious. The answer lies in the terminology. Widows have to be prised out of the documentary record; the process is as labour-intensive as identifying widowers in other periods. The comparison

41. Stafford, *Unification*, p. 176: 'The care with which husbands provided for them in wills betokens the threat from male relatives.' Also Skinner, 'Women', p. 152.

42. See also Stafford, 'Women in Domesday', p. 84.

43. Nelson, 'The wary widow', pp. 90–3.

is instructive.[44] In pre-Conquest England, as elsewhere, men including widowers are styled by rank – earl, monk, ealdorman (a kind of exalted sheriff) – but never by marital status. When couples grant together, the man does so unstyled but the woman's role as sexual partner is signalled by terms such as *wif* (woman or perhaps wife) or *gebedda* (bedfellow). Less predictably, however, in certain Anglo-Saxon documents women, like men, almost never bear a marital style. Single testatrixes generally appear unstyled: 'I, Æthelgifu', 'This is Æthelflæd's will', 'Ælfflæd declares in this document how she wishes her property to be disposed of' and so forth. Three women are described as *comitissa* (literally, Countess) but I would see this as a badge of social rather than marital status: at least one woman used the title after the death of her husband. Widows therefore can usually be identified only by deduction, for example from references in the will to the fact of the husband's death, his soul, his date of commemoration.

We find women described as widows in only a handful of instances. My search through the documentary corpus has produced only ten vernacular documents employing terms for widow. Two words are used: *wuduwe*, which occurs twice and is obviously derived from the Latin,[45] and *laf*, meaning the one left behind (literally *relict*), which appears in all ten documents.[46] In all cases, the widows are mentioned in the third person, identified by reference to their husband, often without a personal name, X's widow, and they feature in the document as legatee. Indeed, many of these references concern either litigation over the inheritance or measures to protect it. Æthelric, for instance, asks a bishop to protect his widow and her inheritance. Note the verbal repetition 'mine *lafe* 7 þa þincg þe ic hyre *læfe*', my *widow* and the things which I *leave* her.[47] The widow is herself linguistically associated with the legacy. The Latin terminology of widowhood turns up even more rarely. *Relicta, mulier*, terms found in other medieval documents, are absent.[48] Women styled *matrona* appear in six charters of the mid-tenth century and

44. On widowers in general, see Marjo Buitelaar, 'Widows' worlds: representations and realities', in Bremmer and van den Bosch, eds, *Between Poverty and the Pyre*, p. 4.

45. Sawyer, *Anglo-Saxon Charters*, nos. 939 and 1457.

46. Sawyer, *Anglo-Saxon Charters*, nos. 1064, 1200, 1425, 1458, 1501, 1503, 1511; Robertson, *Anglo-Saxon Charters*, no. 40.

47. Whitelock, *Anglo-Saxon Wills*, no. 16.1. From *læfan* (to leave) comes *laf* (what is left, remnant).

48. See the laws of the Lombard king Liutprand AD 723 and 728, clauses 33.iiii, 100.v, 101.vi, in Bluhme, ed., *Monumenta Germaniae Historica Leges*, 4, pp. 123–4, 148–9; *The Lombard Laws*, pp. 161, 187–8. See also Patricia Skinner's chapter in this volume, 'The widow's options in medieval southern Italy'.

later.[49] *Vidua* appears in only five documents, two of which are post-Conquest creations.[50] Of the authentic pre-Conquest references, two, like the Old English examples, come from accounts of disputes over widows' property.[51] The last is a royal grant to a widow who is a nun, 'cuidam vidue sanctimonialique'. This, as we shall see, is another specialized use of the term.[52]

I am content to conclude that in contemporary wills and land-conveyances the vocabulary of widowhood appears strangely under-used and, indeed, largely confined to particular circumstances. In the final part of this chapter I want to consider the gulf between visible and invisible widows which this suggests. In this, as in other periods, men's widowhood is never made visible; but here unusually, women's widowhood likewise is identified only rarely. (For the vocabulary of widowhood in the early modern period, see below, pp. 38–43.) So in what circumstances are widows identified as such? One factor may be temporal: widows seem to become more visible as time progresses. Post-Conquest monastic writers documenting earlier bequests to their houses frequently identify widows: 'Sifled relicta Lefsii', 'quedam uidua nomine Æscwen de Stanei'.[53] A number of the female landholders reported in Domesday Book are similarly styled.[54] On the other hand, looking at earlier ecclesiastical legislation – and this is the sort of place where we would surely expect to find at least an idea of widowhood – we find the same sort of circumlocutions as in the pre-Conquest documentary sources. An eighth-century confessional guide known as the penitential of Theodore forbids a man from taking the *uxor* of a relative after his death: his wife, not his widow.[55] The same source reserves *vidua* for vowess – *vidua et virgo* – the widow and virgin pledged to religious service.[56] Two centuries later, another confessional text, attributed to Ecgbert, again uses *uxor* rather than *vidua*: 'Si mortuus maritus sit, uxor intra annum alium sumere potest . . .'.[57] Likewise, not long

49. Sawyer, *Anglo-Saxon Charters*, nos. 662, 681, 703, 754, 923, 1349.

50. Ibid., nos. 1227, 1425. 51. Ibid., nos. 939, 1481.

52. Ibid., no. 775. See above, on vowesses.

53. Blake, ed., *Liber Eliensis*, bk II, chs 11 and 18, pp. 85 and 94.

54. Listed by J.D. Foy, *Domesday Book: Index of Subjects* (Chichester, 1992), p. 270.

55. Bk XII, ch. 27, in Arthur West Haddan and William Stubbs, eds, *Councils and Ecclesiastical Documents Relating to Great Britain and Ireland*, 3 vols (Oxford, 1869–78), I, p. 201; *Medieval Handbooks of Penance*, trans. John T. McNeill and Helena M. Gamer (New York, 1938), p. 211.

56. Elsewhere, widows are called *mulier*: bk II, ch. XII.9, 10, 13, in Haddan and Stubbs, eds, *Councils*, III, pp. 199–200; *Medieval Handbooks of Penance*, p. 209.

57. 'If her husband died a wife may take another within a year': see *Penitential of Ecgbert*, ch. 33, in J.P. Migne, ed., *Patrologiae cursus completus . . . series latina*, 221 vols (Paris, 1844–64), 89, cols 402–12.

before the Conquest, in the lawcodes of King Cnut (1016–35) widows are termed *wif* (woman/wife/female partner) as often as *wuduwe* or *laf* (widow).[58]

The absence of a developed terminology of widowhood in the sources which I have investigated has various implications. First, it has caused the question of women's property in Anglo-Saxon England to be misunderstood. If it had been clear that women making bequests independently were in fact widows, then the notion of women's rights over property by virtue of social status and gender could never have flourished. As Stafford has already argued, marital status before, as after, the Norman Conquest is much more determinative.[59] Second, this lack of widows' style calls into question the existence or at least acceptance of a developed rhetoric of widowhood. Was such terminology unavailable to those drawing up these documents or simply irrelevant? Were bereaved wives only termed widows in certain circumstances? The question is the more pressing as the wills, like other pre-Conquest documents, were drafted and recorded by members of the church, although they preserve the form of a first-person declaration. Until further answers are found to what promises to be a complex question, I can offer one observation.

It is clear that even as late as the eleventh century, four centuries after the introduction of Christianity, the church had failed to impose monogamy on the English population. Concepts of legitimacy and illegitimacy, lawful and unlawful marriage were long established; nevertheless, *c.* 1020, royal legislation against concubinage was reintroduced: men who kept concubines alongside their lawful wives were to be denied the offices of a priest.[60] (Significantly no secular penalty was incurred.) I would venture that this state of affairs finds reflection in the terminology of marriage in vernacular documents.[61] Women in joint grants are styled the companion, equal or bedfellow of a man – *gemæcca, gefera, gebedda* – or more frequently they are simply his woman, *wif*.[62] This is a term which should not be

58. *wif* for widow: II Cnut 70.1, 72, 74: *laf* 1 Cnut 7; *wuduwe* II Cnut 52 (ed. Liebermann, *Die Gesetze*, I, pp. 356–61, 290–1, 346–7).

59. Stafford, 'Women and the Norman Conquest'.

60. II Cnut 54.1, in Liebermann, ed., *Die Gesetze*, I, pp. 348–9.

61. On the particular value of the vernacular see Anita Guerreau-Jalabert, 'Sur les structures de parenté dans l'Europe médiévale', *Annales ESC* 36 (1981), p. 1044.

62. *Gefera* and *gemæcca* are attested in ninth-century originals, in Sawyer, *Anglo-Saxon Charters*, nos. 1204a, 1188; *gebedda* in documents written in the tenth, eleventh and thirteenth centuries, ibid., nos. 1326, 1232, and 1234, 1481b; *wif* appears in documents preserved in manuscripts dating from the ninth, ibid., nos. 1500, 1508; and eleventh centuries, ibid., nos. 1090, 1464; and in 22 post-Conquest copies of pre-Conquest documents.

confused with its modern derivative: 'The term *wif* is basically neutral and need not refer to a woman's status as a legal wife, but it normally excludes those who have not entered into a permanent sexual union.'[63] Churchmen after the Conquest tamed these terms by rendering them into Latin as the conventional and overtly monogamous *coniunx* and *uxor*, but their pre-Conquest counterparts cannot be shown to have done the same. *Coniunx* occurs in no genuine document surviving in its original form, only in thirteenth- and fourteenth-century copies.[64] *Uxor* occurs in only two genuine pre-Conquest charters.[65] One begins to wonder whether a man's *gebedda* was indeed an exact equivalent of a *coniunx* and how closely these relationships matched the specifications of the church. Whatever the case, it seems that these documents did not employ a recognizably Christian terminology. We can identify sexual partners rather than wives.

Given that our documents yield such varied and ambivalent terms to describe the married state, perhaps it is unrealistic to expect a clear formulation of widowhood: if wives are termed simply women, why should bereaved wives be styled widows? In the medieval West the recognition of widowhood as a distinctive state suggests certain prerequisites. It clearly bears the stamp of the church's teachings on sexual continence;[66] for women, at least, it presupposes an attachment to a sexual partner which not only extends for his lifetime but beyond it.[67] This study suggests that in pre-Conquest England the disjunction between the event and the construct of widowhood had not yet healed over. Some bereaved wives were given documentary recognition as their husbands' legatees. Others gave generously to the church in their wills and perhaps retained their unmarried state with the church's protection. These, of all pre-Conquest widows, merit the designation *vidua*, especially by analogy with the Continental *Deo sacrata*. However, they lie unacknowledged in a written record on which the terminology of Christian conjugality appears to have left only a shallow impression.

63. Margaret Clunies Ross, 'Concubinage in Anglo-Saxon England', *Past and Present* 108 (1985), p. 22 n. 70.

64. Sawyer, *Anglo-Saxon Charters*, nos. 100, 513, 561, 742, 747, 866.

65. Ibid., nos. 109, 128.

66. Compare Nelson, 'The wary widow'.

67. Compare Peter Brown, *The Body and Society: Men, Women and Sexual Renunciation in Early Christianity* (New York, 1988), p. 149.

CHAPTER THREE

Finding widowers: men without women in English towns before 1700

MARGARET PELLING

Looking for widows, as the present volume attests, is one way in which recent historiography has helped to redress the historical imbalance of concentration on the male sex. Widows have a visibility within pre-industrial society which other women do not. Admittedly, the widow's visibility is also a measure of vulnerability, whatever attributes the widow herself might possess. Thus for some writers widows have been of interest simply because their powerlessness in male-dominated society, and their lack of a male protector or a male income, makes them an acid test of attitudes to dependency before the welfare state.[1] Generally, however, widows are being studied for their own sake, as a way of recovering women's experience, and of comparing this experience with the institutional, legal and prescriptive disabilities suffered by women in general.

Given that the imbalance of attention to the sexes is still far from redressed, it may seem perverse to give much attention to finding widowers. Some determination is required, since, as will become clear, widowers are remarkably difficult to find. However, as I hope this chapter will indicate, there are many ways in which the paradoxical invisibility of the widower throws light on the situation of the widow. Moreover, the widower appears to have been not so much submerged as shortlived, or hardly existent at all, and this peculiar condition suggests a number of reflections not only about how men defined themselves, but about how they wished to live, and how this affected the options left for women. In addition, justice must be done to the sense of loss felt by bereaved men. Though

1. See for example E. Hélin, in J. Dupâquier *et al.*, eds, *Marriage and Remarriage in Populations of the Past* (London, 1981), p. 251. Similar interest now attaches to the 'oldest old', who are mainly women.

society was so structured that men's losses were more personal than, as in the case of the widow, personal and material, there is adequate historical evidence to prove depth of feeling, however expressed. As we shall see, it is also possible that the social and material deprivation involved was more significant than is conventionally assumed.[2]

It is first necessary to consider the term itself. Anglo-Saxon, like the Indo-European languages in general, had no masculine form of 'widow'.[3] It seems likely that the terms 'widow' and 'widowhood', meaning bereft, void, separated, were first applied in the medieval period to men and women alike, and it is possible that this usage persisted in northern regions of Britain longer than in the south. Metaphorical as well as literal uses with reference to women developed quite early. By contrast, the term 'widower' apparently appeared belatedly as a modification of 'widow' in the fourteenth century. It is attributed to the 'clerkly' Langland, who repeatedly expressed concern for the poor (female) widow, but was also troubled by what he saw as the mercenary motives behind a spate of inappropriate marriages occurring after the Black Death.[4] By the fifteenth century, the word was apparently in common use, at least among the literate and upper classes. However, certain contexts suggest a specific usage: that is, that it was not applied to all men who had lost their wives, but rather to those about to marry for the second time. Thus, in *All's Well that Ends Well*, the King of France says of the young Bertram:

> The main consents are had: and here we'll stay
> To see our widower's second marriage day.

2. See also Chapter 14, by Pamela Sharpe. On bereaved husbands, see essays by Anne Laurence (see n. 26 below) and Pat Jalland in R. Houlbrooke, ed., *Death, Ritual and Bereavement* (London and New York, 1989). By the mid-seventeenth century, it had become possible for a husband to be chief mourner at his wife's funeral: C. Gittings, *Death, Burial and the Individual in Early Modern England* (London, 1988), p. 192.

3. The following paragraph is based upon entries in the *Oxford English Dictionary* (hereafter *OED*), and R.H. Bremmer, 'Widows in Anglo-Saxon England', in Jan Bremmer and Lourens van den Bosch, eds, *Between Poverty and the Pyre: Moments in the History of Widowhood* (London and New York, 1995), p. 59. See also Chapter 2, by Julia Crick, in the present volume.

4. *OED*; D. Pearsall, *The Life of Geoffrey Chaucer* (Oxford, 1993), pp. 27, 62, 138, 147, 245; Pearsall, ed., *Piers Plowman: An Edition of the C-Text* (London, 1978), p. 192 (Passus X, line 279). The 'exigencies of alliteration' may have inspired Langland's usage, which might not have been a neologism: the first uses of *OED* are consistently being revised by the *Middle English Dictionary*. I am grateful to Professor Derek Pearsall for his guidance on these points.

Thus, widowers were such mainly for the fleeting period just before a second marriage.[5]

There is a rationale for this in that one of the few contexts in which the state of widowerhood required formal definition was marriage licensing.[6] The basis for marrying by licence as an alternative to banns was apparently established by around 1200, with an emphasis on the need for consent from parents or guardians. However, this mode of marriage was probably uncommon until the sixteenth century, when its popularity among couples across a fairly broad social spectrum was matched by its contested status among critics of the church. In the 1590s, requirements as to (for example) evidence of consent by parents, guardians or 'governors' were made more strict, as one response to criticism of the role of bishops and their substitutes. Although the actual conduct of licensing probably never became rigorous, this development may have encouraged the adoption by bridegrooms of labels denoting marital status. It was usually the bridegroom who applied for the licence. The canons of 1604 made it clear that those 'being in widowhood' could omit the obtaining of consents.[7] Though the requirement of consent seems to have affected the woman far more than the man, even in second and later marriages, bridegrooms marrying for the second time were given some incentive to define themselves as widowers in this context.[8]

Civil legislation affecting marriage among the laity in the sixteenth century, some of it concerned with the right disposition of property, some with pronatalism, does not seem to have pinpointed widowers as it did widows and bachelors. The point at which self-definition as a widower was generally imposed, in a context implying a condition rather than a rite of passage, was the tax legislation of the 1690s. Money was raised through fines imposed not only on marriage (as an administrative process), but also on older bachelors and widowers (that is, those in certain states or conditions). Significantly, the fines on widowers were limited to those without children: an

5. Shakespeare, *All's Well that Ends Well*, V. iii. 70; Paston letter, 1477, cited by *OED*; N. Goose, 'Household size and structure in early-Stuart Cambridge', *Social History* 5 (1980), p. 378.

6. On licensing see P. McGrath, 'Notes on the history of marriage licences', in B. Frith, ed., *Gloucestershire Marriage Allegations 1637–1680*, Bristol and Gloucs. Archaeol. Soc., Records Section, 2 (1954), pp. xx–xxx. In general see E.J. Carlson, *Marriage and the English Reformation* (Oxford, 1994).

7. McGrath, 'Notes on marriage licences', p. xxviii.

8. On kin and community influence on marriage, see D. O'Hara, '"Ruled by my friends": aspects of marriage in the diocese of Canterbury, *c.* 1540–1570', *Continuity and Change* 6 (1991), pp. 9–41. For an example of influence exerted on remarriage of a widow, illustrating the multiplication of interested parties, see pp. 18–19.

apparently pragmatic distinction, reflecting the expenses borne by men with children, but also indicative of concern for national fertility according to the principles of 'political arithmetic'.[9] Bachelordom, although an honourable estate, did imply something less than full membership of the adult male community; childless widowers may have been similarly regarded, especially when male celibacy was increasingly seen as selfish.[10]

It would contradict points already made to suggest that terms denoting marital condition were constantly and consistently applied, even in the specialized contexts already discussed. In licensing, the terms 'singlewoman' and 'singleman' were apparently used to cover a range of conditions. In other contexts where it was of direct relevance, 'unmarried' seems to have been used regardless of the distinction between 'never married' and 'widowed'.[11] Parish registers rarely recorded marital status with any consistency until after Hardwicke's Marriage Act of 1754.[12] Even for women, much depended on context. For women without men, who might be expected to become a problem for the authorities, a range of descriptions were used which indicate social attitudes to this state: 'at her own hands', for example. As is well known, what mattered about a woman was that she was 'covered' by a man, who could be a father or a master

9. See T. Arkell, 'An examination of the Poll taxes of the later seventeenth century, the Marriage Duty Act and Gregory King', in K. Schurer and T. Arkell, eds, *Surveying the People* (Oxford, 1992), pp. 142–80, esp. pp. 166–7; R.B. Outhwaite, *Clandestine Marriage in England, 1500–1850* (London and Rio Grande, 1995), pp. 14–15. Paupers, bachelors under 25 and fellows and students of Oxford and Cambridge colleges were exempted.

10. This was in part a concern about urban life: see P. Griffiths, J. Landers, M. Pelling and R. Tyson, 'Population and disease, estrangement and belonging', in P. Clark, ed., *Urban History of Britain*, Vol. 2: *1540–1840* (Cambridge University Press, forthcoming). Carlson, *Marriage*, argues that celibacy was attacked less in England than elsewhere; J.R. Gillis, *For Better, For Worse: British Marriages, 1600 to the Present* (New York, 1985), reflects on celibacy but interprets early modern marriage as the exception rather than the norm, and a privilege to be earned.

11. See for example ambiguity in the bequest of Sir Thomas Gresham, who wished the professors of his College to be unmarried: M. Pelling, 'Failed transmission: the background to Gresham's professorship of physic', to appear in a volume edited by Francis Ames-Lewis commemorating the quatercentenary of Gresham College. The earlier extant documents relating to licensing use 'singleman' or nothing at all with respect to the marital condition of bridegrooms: G.J. Armytage, ed., *Allegations for Marriage Licences issued by the Dean and Chapter of Westminster, 1558–1699*, Harleian Soc., 23 (1886). Brodsky has noted that clerical dispensers of licences were less attentive to details about widowerhood: V. Brodsky, 'Widows in late Elizabethan London: remarriage, economic opportunity and family orientations', in L. Bonfield, R.M. Smith and K. Wrightson, eds, *The World We Have Gained* (Oxford, 1986), p. 132.

12. E.A. Wrigley and R.S. Schofield, *The Population History of England 1541–1871* (London, 1981), p. 258.

as well as a husband.[13] Nonetheless, many sources do not consistently ascribe marital status to the women they mention, and are often inaccurate in distinguishing the widow from the wife.[14] The 'old wife', as in 'old wives' tale', which appears to emerge as a label in the late sixteenth century, could as well have been a widow. Again, a tidy labelling of the different marital states, including specific use of 'spinster', seems to belong at the earliest to the late seventeenth century, as part of a general desire for greater certainty in social differentiation.[15]

If the term, and a sense of the condition, is sought for outside such contexts, it is hard to find. English proverbs, for example, although comparatively fertile on the subject of widows and remarriage, make very little reference to widowers. Although there is some advice literature directed at old men, there is no figure of the widower at all equivalent to the widow.[16] Old men who married late or chased women certainly attracted caricature, but the implication is usually that the old man is foolishly marrying for the first time, or that he is marrying someone too young for him, or that lust is inappropriate to old age.[17] The character-writers praised or abused all sorts and conditions of men and some women, including (in the case of Overbury) the widow; but, although their specificity reached so far as to describe 'a too idly reserved man', widowers were given no character, and the state of widowerhood does not appear in other sketches, of old men, for example. Similarly, Francis Bacon simply contrasted marriage with 'single life'.[18] Shakespeare portrays many married men without wives, but in several cases (including

13. See for example A.L. Erickson, *Women and Property in Early Modern England* (London and New York, 1993).

14. Examples are tax and other listings (C. Phythian-Adams, *Desolation of a City: Coventry and the Urban Crisis of the Late Middle Ages* (Cambridge, 1979), p. 201); or the record kept by the College of Physicians of women illicitly practising medicine in London (M. Pelling, 'Thoroughly resented? Older women and the medical role in early modern London', in L. Hunter and S. Hutton, eds, *Women, Science and Medicine 1500–1700* (Stroud, Gloucs., 1997), p. 83).

15. Marina Warner, *From the Beast to the Blonde: On Fairy Tales and their Tellers* (London, 1995), esp. chs 2 and 3; Olwen Hufton, 'Women without men: widows and spinsters in Britain and France in the eighteenth century', *Journal of Family History* 9 (1984), p. 374; Lawrence Stone, 'Social mobility in England, 1500–1700', *Past and Present* 33 (1966), pp. 16–55.

16. F.P. Wilson, ed., *Oxford Dictionary of English Proverbs*, 3rd edn (Oxford, 1982); Alan Macfarlane, *Marriage and Love in England 1300–1840* (Oxford, 1987), p. 237.

17. See for example Shakespeare's *Merry Wives of Windsor*; Simon Goulart, *The Wise Vieillard, or Old Man*, trans. T.W. (London, 1621).

18. H. Morley, ed., *Character Writings of the Seventeenth Century* (London, 1891), esp. pp. 37, 81–3, 170, 279; F. Bacon, *Essays*, Everyman edn (London and New York, 1962), pp. 22–3.

that of Bertram) the wife is not truly dead, but is lost or falsely dishonoured. In others, notably Lear, Prospero and even Shylock, the condition of widowerhood is totally submerged in the relationship between a father and his posterity.[19]

In non-literary contexts as well, we find an absence which is almost a universal. Bennett has noted for the medieval period that 'manorial records never mention male widowhood'. In fourteenth-century Florence, Henderson finds that 'men were never identified as widowers' in poor relief records.[20] Two of the most detailed listings of the households of English towns in the early modern period are those for Coventry (1522–23), and Cambridge (1619–32). In the Coventry listings, widowers are identified as such in only two instances, as compared with fourteen 'single men' (who could have children) and 46 unspecified males. In Cambridge, the word is found only once in a listing for 1632. In the most comprehensive census of poor households, that for Norwich in 1570, which covers perhaps a quarter of the English-born population of the city, the word 'widower' is used only once.[21]

These absences of widowers as compared with widows suggest the wide range of important social qualifications to which being a widower did *not* relate. The loss of a wife did not affect a man's ability to hold property, his claim on his children, his civic status, his occupational definition, or his legal status. In the case of tied housing, he did not lose his dwelling. The state of widowerhood, it seems, posed no challenge to a society's attitudes to dependency – though to this we will return. The only context in which widowers seemed to suffer some restriction was ecclesiastical, but even here the restrictions were not on widowers as such, but on those who wished to remarry. 'Widowers' existed as a class of church servant, and, as part of the medieval church's ambivalent response to remarriage, remarried men were subject to certain ecclesiastical restrictions.[22]

19. In other plays involving fathers, and children of an age to marry, the mothers are simply irrelevant: for example, *Taming of the Shrew*, *As You Like It*. For Lear-like behaviour at a humbler level of early modern society, see an example in M. MacDonald and T.R. Murphy, *Sleepless Souls: Suicide in Early Modern England* (Oxford, 1990), p. 257.

20. J.M. Bennett, *Women in the Medieval English Countryside: Gender and Household in Brigstock before the Plague* (New York and Oxford, 1989), pp. 143–4; J. Henderson and R. Wall, eds, *Poor Women and Children in the Past* (London, 1994), p. 166. I am grateful to Phillipp Schofield for his advice on medieval terminology.

21. Phythian-Adams, *Desolation of a City*, pp. 201–2; Goose, 'Household size and structure', pp. 348, 378. For Norwich, see below.

22. See *OED*; J.A. Brundage, 'Widows and remarriage: moral conflicts and their resolution in classical canon law', in S.S. Walker, ed., *Wife and Widow in Medieval England* (Ann Arbor, Mich., 1993), pp. 17–31, esp. pp. 18, 25; Macfarlane, *Marriage and Love*, p. 232.

Whether a category of person exists nominally does not of course imply anything absolute about the actual existence of that category, and for that reason the terminology has been considered separately. However, whether or not a society places a label on a category of person also helps determine visibility, and provides a focus for the accretion of meaning. 'Widower' was highly unusual among terms applied to men, in being derived from a term first applied (in the noun form) to women. In general, 'widower' seems, in spite of its derivation, entirely to lack the burden of attributes attached to 'widow': dependency, sexual avidity or availability, sexual experience, isolation, and the kind of malice associated with witchcraft. The clearest connotation of 'widower' would seem to be a kind of settled melancholy, but it is hard to be confident that the word had acquired even that much meaning before 1700.[23] Such an attribute is conventionally associated with the middling and upper classes rather than with the poor. Whatever the number of widowers actually in existence in early modern England, they were seldom defined as such. The term was available, but it was not widely used.

This lack of nominal definition was a condition normally experienced by women, with marital status the main exception. Here it is essential to remember the important part played by first marriage in men's progress to adulthood and citizenship.[24] It is not simply that marital status had no purchase at all on men's lives. The long history of the term 'bachelor', with its status as well as marital implications, is one indication of this. Thus it is even more striking that, after the point of first marriage, men were given status or occupational definitions independently of their marital standing. A woman's condition as spinster, wife or widow, by contrast, was often the only way in which she was defined over the entire course of her life. The invisibility of widowers – men who lacked wives, although not necessarily children – could of course be taken as simply another reflection of the subordinate position of women: that is, while it was important for a man to marry and to have descendants, he was not to be defined by the death of his wife, especially, perhaps, if she had borne him children. However, there are other possibilities which could modify this predictable conclusion, and it is particularly worth exploring these in the post-Reformation period, in the context of changing attitudes to men's role within marriage.

23. Robert Burton's analysis of the causes of melancholy says almost nothing about widowerhood, and couples grief with loss of temporal fortune: *Anatomy of Melancholy*, Pt I, Section 2, Memb. 4, Subs. 7.

24. For a full exploration see Lyndal Roper, *The Holy Household: Women and Morals in Reformation Augsburg* (Oxford, 1989).

Given the muted presence of the term, and perhaps the concept, it is necessary to ask to what extent widowers actually existed. Attempts to answer this question have been made chiefly by historians of demography and social structure, on the basis of population listings and reconstitutions.[25] There is frequently ambiguity in that the condition must usually be inferred. Even in reconstitutions the period of observation is seldom long enough to be sure of both marriage and remarriage of a given individual. In listings, a man with no wife but with children is probably a widower, unless the children are in fact servants or apprentices. (Desertion by wives seems hardly to come into consideration.) A man entirely on his own could be a widower, but he could also be one of the significant proportion of the English population who never married; he could also be, as we shall see, a man who had deserted his wife. Confusion also arises because of the difficulty of defining a household, and because many categories of analysis are adjusted to defining the ramifications of nuclear families, rather than households including a range of unrelated individuals. Terms like 'single' and 'alone' in different analyses have to be examined carefully for the particular meaning being applied to them.

It is easier to point to the accepted generalizations about the duration of marriage in the early modern period. Mortality rates were such that marriages had an average duration of about 20 years.[26] Qualifying this, however, is that English people married comparatively late, and that women seem always to have enjoyed greater longevity than men. For both reasons, widowers were less numerous than widows, especially at later ages. (For the twentieth century, it has been concluded that widowerhood is in itself a cause of death.)[27] However, the major factor affecting the prominence if not

25. Reference to early modern widowers is still comparatively unusual (especially in indexes), even in studies of old age, but see Phythian-Adams, *Desolation of a City*; Dupâquier, *Marriage and Remarriage*; Macfarlane, *Marriage and Love*; Goose, 'Household size and structure'; Barbara Todd, 'Widowhood in a market town: Abingdon, 1540–1720' (University of Oxford D.Phil. thesis, 1983); Jeremy Boulton, *Neighbourhood and Society: A London Suburb in the Seventeenth Century* (Cambridge, 1987); D.I. Kertzer and P. Laslett, eds, *Aging in the Past: Demography, Society and Old Age* (Berkeley, Calif., 1995); Henderson and Wall, *Poor Women and Children*.

26. Bennett, *Women*, p. 143; A. Laurence, 'Godly grief: individual responses to death in seventeenth-century Britain', in Houlbrooke, *Death, Ritual and Bereavement*, p. 64. Compare Corsini in Dupâquier, *Marriage and Remarriage*, p. 388.

27. J.E. Smith, 'Widowhood and ageing in traditional English society', *Ageing and Society* 4 (1984), pp. 430–2; M. Young, B. Benjamin and C. Wallis, 'The mortality of widowers', *The Lancet* 2 (1963), pp. 454–6. Note that the latter study concentrated on widowers rather than widows because records relating to men gave too little information about their spouses: p. 454.

the incidence of widowerhood appears to have been remarriage. Remarriage has long been regarded as an important feature of the 'European marriage pattern'. Hajnal, Süssmilch and others saw what they called successive or serial polygamy as a necessary feature, which absorbed the 'excess' of women and maintained levels of fertility.[28] The fertility rate of second marriages has been found to be as high as that of first. This is partly because widowers were less inclined to marry widows than to marry younger, never-married women. In spite of its importance, however, remarriage remains very difficult to analyse in demographic terms, for reasons already suggested.[29] For England, the consensus is that remarriage declined after the seventeenth century, but the reasons for this are much debated. Lately this debate has helped to bring to the surface major issues about human, and especially female, agency.[30] Earlier discussion was founded on a basic premise about the determining effect of sex ratios in a population, which took for granted major unstated assumptions about male and female roles in making a marriage.[31] It was assumed that if females were present, men could marry them. If widows did not marry it was because they were unable to do so; alternatively, they did not need to do so because the option existed of a system of poor relief geared to their needs.

What is puzzling for explanations of major demographic and social change based on decisions to do with marriage, is the apparent failure of certain patterns to alter in response to change.[32] In the present context, the interesting aspect of these persistent patterns is what might be called a male *longue durée*. These patterns not only have duration, they also seem to exist across a wide cultural

28. Phythian-Adams, *Desolation of a City*, p. 200; Macfarlane, *Marriage and Love*, p. 234.

29. Smith, 'Widowhood', p. 435; Kertzer and Laslett, *Aging in the Past*, p. 235. Dupâquier, *Marriage and Remarriage* is still the most usual reference.

30. See most recently Jeremy Boulton, 'London widowhood revisited: the decline of female remarriage in the seventeenth and early eighteenth centuries', *Continuity and Change* 5 (1990), pp. 323–55; Barbara Todd, 'Demographic determinism and female agency: the remarrying widow reconsidered . . . again', ibid. 9 (1994), pp. 421–50. In general see A. MacKinnon, 'Were women present at the demographic transition? Questions from a feminist historian to historical demographers', *Gender and History* 7 (1995), pp. 222–40.

31. See for example Phythian-Adams, *Desolation of a City*, p. 199: 'the most fundamental characteristic of any population is the proportion of males and females'.

32. See for example K.A. Lynch, 'The European marriage pattern in the cities: variations on a theme by Hajnal', *Journal of Family History* 16 (1991), pp. 79–96; R. Wall, 'Elderly persons and members of their households in England and Wales from preindustrial times to the present', in Kertzer and Laslett, *Aging in the Past*, pp. 81–106.

and geographical range. It seems to be something of a constant, for example, that men were more likely than women to remarry; that men remarried sooner than women after the death of a spouse; that men 'were able' to remarry at older ages than women; that widowers, as already mentioned, were less likely to marry widows than to marry younger women who had not been married before; and that widowed fathers did not often live with their married daughters. The generalizations about men and remarriage hold even when remarriage itself appears to become less common.[33] As already suggested, these persistent patterns, which are sometimes rather vaguely labelled 'cultural', are usually seen as reflecting the 'inability' of women to remarry, because of unbalanced sex ratios, the burden of children, the ineligibility of women past the child-bearing years, the effect of increasing age on women as compared with men, or the dislike of men for 'second-hand goods' even though a widow might be of proven fertility while a virgin was not. Within this framework, the impulse to remarry is taken for granted; widows become a kind of residual category consisting of those who would but cannot. The invisibility of widowers, while often unremarked, becomes unsurprising.

Although many of these features are seen as characteristic of the European marriage pattern, England appears as a special case. Recently, the modern preoccupation with dependency in old age has coincided with a certain revisionism on the part of historians of social structure. The English case, it is said, has had a disproportionate influence; the picture should be adjusted to account for the fact that co-residence of ageing parents with children was a widespread phenomenon in Europe and that the nuclear family was only part of a more complicated set of household structures.[34] The strongest claim for the peculiarity of English patterns has been that of Macfarlane, whose stress on the *longue durée* of English individualism has involved ruling out the possibility of children taking in their ageing or widowed or infirm parents. Thus for Macfarlane remarriage has a central role as the least worst option for those left alone. He points to such evidence as the lack of hostility to remarriage in English charivari (popular rituals of mockery and inversion) compared with such rituals in continental Europe.[35] For similar

33. D.I. Kertzer, 'Towards a historical demography of aging', in Kertzer and Laslett, *Aging in the Past*, pp. 373–5.

34. Kertzer and Laslett, *Aging in the Past*, Preface; Kertzer, 'Towards a historical demography', p. 369.

35. Macfarlane, *Marriage and Love*, pp. 97–8, 116, 155–8, 234–8.

reasons related to the nuclear hardship hypothesis, Boulton and others have pointed to remarriage even among poor widows, and have concluded that remarriage was something of a necessity among the poor. Writers such as Hufton, in doing justice to the work done by women within marriage, have made it clear that the loss of a wife, no less than that of a husband, could jeopardize the survival of poor households.[36]

In an earlier essay, I examined the circumstances of elderly poor people in Norwich as recorded in the census of 1570.[37] Taking all those aged 50 and over, the analysis revealed that a very high proportion of marriages among the poor were between those unequal in age, and that this feature, in the context of disability, unemployment among men in particular, and the presence of children at a late stage of the lifecycle, could be regarded as a 'symbiotic' form of marriage practised by the poor as one expedient in the struggle for survival. It also seemed plausible both that these kinds of marriages among the poor were of necessity at least tolerated by the authorities and that the association of such forms of marriage with the poor may ultimately have had some role in determining attitudes to remarriage in general, and 'unequal' marriages in particular. Hindle has recently drawn attention to repressive attitudes among parish authorities to marriage among the poor; his evidence seems to relate especially to small centres and rural areas where housing was strictly limited, but also suggests, I would argue, a predictable caution based on fears that (for example) an apparent marriage of an insider to an outsider might be a remarriage, trailing dependent children in its wake.[38] It seems less evident that parish authorities would have discouraged marriages which promised a solution to some form of dependency without cost to the parish.

36. Boulton, *Neighbourhood*, p. 131; O. Hufton, 'Women and the family economy in eighteenth-century France', *French Historical Studies* 9 (1975), pp. 18–22. The nuclear hardship model, first outlined in 1978, was formulated by Laslett to highlight 'the difficulties imposed on individuals when social rules require them to live in nuclear families', that is, with limited kin or inter-generational support: see Smith, 'Widowhood', p. 439; P. Laslett, 'Family, kinship and collectivity as systems of support in pre-industrial Europe: a consideration of the "nuclear hardship" hypothesis', *Continuity and Change* 3 (1988), pp. 153–75.

37. Pelling, 'Old age, poverty and disability in early modern Norwich: work, remarriage, and other expedients', in Pelling and R.M. Smith, eds, *Life, Death and the Elderly: Historical Perspectives* (London and New York, 1991), pp. 74–101; see also a slightly revised form in Pelling, *The Common Lot: Sickness, Medical Occupations and the Urban Poor in Early Modern England* (London, 1998).

38. S. Hindle, 'The problem of pauper marriage in seventeenth-century England', *Transactions of the Royal Historical Society* 6th ser., 8 (1998), pp. 71–89. I am grateful to Steve Hindle for allowing me to see an unpublished version of his essay.

In the course of my study of Norwich's elderly poor, it further emerged that remarkably few elderly men were without spouses, and that, among elderly men at least, the evidence suggested a 'studied avoidance' of being alone.[39] To some extent, these appearances could be attributed, especially among the poor, to the effects of the differential mortality already mentioned. For the present study, therefore, it seemed worthwhile to look again at the census to examine the condition of men of all ages. I have analysed the census and its context extensively elsewhere, and full details need not be given here.[40] However, certain of its unique qualities must be stressed. As already indicated, it recorded around a quarter of Norwich's estimated English-born population, and listed ages, occupations and relationships for a total of 2359 persons, including children.[41] Although the Norwich census-takers selected out the poor, they did so on the basis of households, not individuals, being particularly concerned to determine who was dependent upon whom (and why). Their range of summary categories for the condition of each household ranged from 'very poor' to 'indifferent'. As well as being comprehensive with respect to nuclear families, they were careful to note the presence of individuals who were unrelated, temporarily resident, or related to the head of household other than as a spouse or child. The census does not permit the conclusion that ageing and/or solitary parents were in fact taken in by their married children on anything but a temporary basis, or that the households of the poor were large rather than small. However, it does provide ample illustration of why historical demographers are now placing stress on the significant incidence of more complex (though not necessarily large) households according to local and other circumstances.[42]

39. Pelling, 'Old age, poverty and disability', p. 88.

40. See esp. ibid.; 'Illness among the poor in an early modern English town: the Norwich census of 1570', *Continuity and Change* 3 (1988), pp. 273–90; 'Older women: household, caring and other occupations in the late sixteenth-century town' (all in *The Common Lot*).

41. The full version of the Norwich census was located and edited by J.F. Pound as *The Norwich Census of the Poor 1570*, Norfolk Record Soc., 40 (1971). It is Pound's edition which is used here.

42. What I have put forward in this and earlier essays on the Norwich poor does not at all conflict with the findings of Sokoll on the complex construction of poor households, except that Sokoll challenges the accepted view of the poor household as small, and argues that the paucity of solitaries among the poor was related (at least in Ardleigh) to their being taken in by married children. However, Sokoll's conclusions derive mainly from late-eighteenth-century data, and from smaller centres. His point about the need to combine poor law records with listings is well taken, but the information in the Norwich census about family structure and housing

With respect to terminology and marital status, as already noted, the census-takers used the term 'widower' only once. The entry in question, for the parish of St Michael of Coslany, is as follows: 'John Bacon of 67 yeris, allmost blynd, & doth nothinge, widower, & lyveth of his son that kepe a skole, & dwelt here ever/Wiggetes house. No allms. Indeferent.'[43] No other poor person is noted as living in that particular house, unless it can be conflated with 'Wigites house' which is listed following an entry for 'the Colledg house'. In the second Wigget house lived a couple with a 'mayd', and a deserted wife, entered as separate households. Many of the poor lived in accommodation owned by men prominent in the civic hierarchy; Wigget was not one of these, and there were no poor living in Wigget houses in other parishes. Interestingly, the only other Bacons listed were houseowners or housekeepers rather than poor people: Mrs Bacon of St George's Colegate, apparently one of the 'select women' who helped train the poor in productive work, and a common councillor, John Bacon, who owned property rented to the poor in Colegate ward.[44] It seems fairly certain that if the almost blind John Bacon had lived with his son, then the son would have been listed (or, John Bacon would not have appeared among the poor at all). This entry illustrates the care taken by the census-takers in identifying sources of support, even if these did not derive from co-residence. On the face of it, John Bacon was, according to the calculus that misfortune enforced on the poor, quite a likely candidate for imminent remarriage; however, what is more strongly suggested here is the association of 'widower' with the (slightly) better off. John Bacon was only 'indifferently' poor in spite of his blindness and lack of any employment; he was not in receipt of the alms that preceded the Norwich poor scheme; and he had a source of support in his son.

---

is an exception to his criticisms of the limitations of poor censuses in general. See T. Sokoll, 'The pauper household poor and simple? The evidence from listings of inhabitants and pauper lists in early modern England reassessed', *Ethnologia Europaea* 17 (1987), pp. 25–42; Sokoll, 'The household position of elderly widows in poverty: evidence from two English communities in the late eighteenth and early nineteenth centuries', in Henderson and Wall, *Poor Women and Children*, pp. 207–24; Sokoll, 'Old age in poverty: the record of Essex pauper letters, 1780–1834', in T. Hitchcock, P. King and P. Sharpe, eds, *Chronicling Poverty* (Basingstoke and London, 1997), pp. 127–54. See also Kertzer and Laslett, *Aging in the Past*.

43. Pound, *Census*, p. 68.

44. Ibid., App. VIII, 81, 103; on the select women, see Pound, 'An Elizabethan census of the poor: the treatment of vagrancy in Norwich, 1570–1580', *University of Birmingham Historical Journal* 8 (1961–2), pp. 145–6.

Other terminology applied to men is relatively limited. The census is unusual in even attempting to distinguish the category of the 'never-married', but this description is applied only to women, never to men. As we shall see, there is limited scope for it to be applied to men. A good example is Margery Hyll, aged 40, whose status the census-taker first gave as 'never-married' and then altered to describe her as 'the wyfe of John Hyll, lymburner, departed from hyr a 4 yere past, & she know not wher he is'.[45] A poor man of 80, but with a wife, is called 'Father Whighthed', but a houseowner of St George's Colegate is also called 'Father'. Poor men are occasionally labelled as an 'evil husband' or 'ill husband', but only one of these was spouseless.[46] More important, as far as reflections on husbands were concerned, was the large category of deserted wives, like Margery Hyll.

If we consider marital status, the appearances are sufficiently striking. Only twelve men over the age of 20 were spouseless, that is 1.2 per cent of poor men. Of these, three lived with children: one (aged 60, 'not hable to worke for that his rybes be broken') with a daughter of eight, a second with two children at school, and a third with older children of ten and sixteen.[47] A fourth man, a cobbler in work aged 78, lived with 'his servant', another cobbler, aged 36.[48] The remaining eight, including John Bacon, lived entirely alone, although there might be other poor people living in the same building. All but one of the twelve were given an age of 50 or over. One of the solitaries, aged 50, was 'besyd hymselfe a lyttle', another, aged 72, was an 'yll husband', and a third, aged 60, was lame.[49] Bacon, it will be recalled, was almost blind. However, the presence of major disabilities and unemployment among the solitary men is balanced by the fact that several of them appear to have been owners of property, either the house they lived in or another dwelling. In addition Bacon, as we have seen, was supported by his son; the lame Richard Multon, while poor and alone, lived in a house owned by 'Heri Multon'.[50] This proximity to property ownership is far more unusual among this poor population than was physical disability. An intriguing case is that of the exception in terms of age, William Carter, a solitary aged only 22. William was 'dyseased of a sore legge', 'veri pore', and also 'withoute comforte', a description

45. Pound, *Census*, p. 36; see also the entry, also crossed out, for Eme Wode, described as both 'wedow' and 'never maried': p. 46.

46. Ibid., pp. 71, 81, 73, 80. 47. Ibid., pp. 26, 82, 87.

48. Ibid., p. 83. 49. Ibid., pp. 79, 80, 75.

50. Ibid., p. 75. No other Multons are noted, either as poor or as houseowners.

that the census-takers normally applied not to men but to women. The implication of the phrase was that someone should have been comforting the person, but was not. Nonetheless, William was found to be 'at Carters', probably the 'Ro. Carters house' mentioned a few entries before. Since William had 'dwelt ever' in Norwich, it is very possible that he was related to Robert Carter, albeit inadequately supported by him.[51] The indications are few in number, but sufficient perhaps to suggest a tendency on the part of relatives to support solitary men by providing a roof, rather than co-residence.

Besides the twelve, there are a number of ambiguous cases, perhaps five in all. These are younger solitary men, three of whom seem still to be tacked on in some way to their parents' or mothers' households. The way in which they are listed suggests that it was not they who were the household heads. The eldest of the three was aged 40. Another of the five was a Scottish labourer whose place of work was known and whose entry was later crossed out. The last was exceptional in terms of age and marital position: 'Hugh Davi of 18 yeris, gardener servant with the Deane, his wife dwell in Aylsham'. It was added that Davi, described as 'veri pore' in spite of his service with the Dean, had 'gone away'.[52]

As it turns out, analysis of the whole census, rather than just those of 50 and over and their households, produces a picture in which younger men were almost never spouseless or alone, and older men rarely so. There are almost no parallels among the men either to the solitary widow, or to the households formed by women involving such combinations as two unrelated widows, or a mother and a deserted daughter.[53] The tendency of spouseless poor men to live with their children, let alone their married children, is almost non-existent. The only way in which this proposition can be rescued for Norwich's poor population is to suppose that spouseless men were always fortunate enough to belong to, and to be taken in by, families who were well enough off to be excluded by the census-takers. An alternative proposition, that men on their own were always well enough off not to be even 'indifferently' poor, seems equally unlikely, especially given Norwich's level of male unemployment. The more likely conclusion seems to be that poor men, when widowed, married again as soon as they could.

51. Ibid., p. 43. William and Robert are the only Carters mentioned.

52. Ibid., pp. 62, 64, 77, 78, 28.

53. The ability of poor women to construct 'complex' households has been emphasized by Hufton, among others; for Norwich, see Pelling, 'Old age, poverty and disability', pp. 85–7.

A further point must be considered, and that is the legal status of the unions in question. If a man and a woman were 'keeping' together, the census-takers were apparently content to assume that the two were legally married, even though they hunted in each parish for women working as prostitutes. It is entirely possible, however, that some at least of these were 'common law' unions. The level of immigration into Norwich was such that no check could be made on the antecedents of many couples, even though the census-takers were assiduous in recording how long a household had been in the city and where it had come from. Paradoxically, the presence of common law unions is also suggested, albeit indirectly, by another feature of the census, the careful identification of deserted wives. About 49 women were described as wives with absent husbands, and where possible the census-taker recorded when the husband left, where he now was, and whether he gave any 'comfort' to his wife. Some six husbands were 'in the hospital', presumably St Giles's in Norwich. Another, Thomas Lodesman, was 'gone awaye from his wyf for dett'; the eldest son was with the father, who was in London, and the entry for the whole family was subsequently crossed out as 'Gon to London'.[54] Other absent husbands were clearly trying to work elsewhere, or to send some maintenance to their families from a distance. Most of the wives, however, had been deserted many years previously. One was Margery, aged 28, 'the wyf of Thomas Collyns, hatter, nowe dwelling at London, by whom she have no helpe'; Margery Collyns worked, had two young children, the eldest of whom (aged nine) also worked, and lived in the same house as her mother Agnes Gose, aged 68, 'a skold', whose own husband Thomas was one of those 'in the hospitall'.[55]

The number of deserted wives in Norwich far exceeds the number of solitary men, and their presence raises two questions: first, in what situation, in terms of social structure, were these absent husbands living? – those, that is, who survived for any length of time. Clearly, not all were simply vagrant; many are likely to have settled elsewhere. In any case the number of deserted wives involves *prima facie* an equal number of male solitaries elsewhere. This leads to the second question: why is there not a plausible complement of absconded husbands among the poor in Norwich? It is only sensible to assume that Norwich, the second city after London, must have

54. Pound, *Census*, p. 33. On St Giles's in this context, see Pelling, 'Healing the sick poor: social policy and disability in Norwich 1550–1640', *Medical History* 29 (1985), pp. 125–6 (also in *The Common Lot*).

55. Pound, *Census*, p. 36.

attracted its share of these from elsewhere; those heading for towns rather than for rural employment cannot all have gone to the capital.[56] One function of the census was certainly to identify those who had no right of residence in Norwich, but, as already indicated, almost no male solitaries of this kind were listed among those 'to go away'. Moreover, Norwich's policy on working immigrants was relatively open compared with other centres. As before, it seems inherently implausible that these absconded husbands of poor families should all have disappeared into the households of the better off, and thereby escaped notice from the census-takers. Nor does Norwich's poor population of this date reveal anything of the male lodger, who appears to be a phenomenon of later periods.[57] Although the argument can only be speculative, it seems reasonable to conclude that an absconding husband was most likely to set up house with (or to move in with) another woman, and to appear in this context as her spouse.

In trying to locate the widower, we have had to consider both the spouseless and the solitary male, each of which is a potentially larger category than that of the widower. Obviously, evidence based on poor populations cannot be applied universally. However, the absence of spouseless and solitary men among the poor is matched by an absence of persons identified as widowers in listings as well as literary contexts. It can be suggested that, in this period at least, widowerhood was a state which men turned away from, both mentally and otherwise. There is more than one way of defining dependency. Male solitaries are rarely if ever considered in the same way as the lone widow, but the presence of some Norwich husbands 'in the hospital' is a reminder of the fact that with respect to institutional care, English authorities of this period, at least, gave the preference not to women but to men.[58] The bishops' defence of the licensing system in the late sixteenth century cited among those likely to prefer licences to banns, men 'who have liking of mean

56. It should be noted that London, and some other large towns like York, were apparently exceptional at this period in having populations in which men outnumbered women: see Griffiths *et al.*, 'Population and disease'. On male solitaries and 'single' men in London, see Boulton, *Neighbourhood*, pp. 123–8. Single male householders in the London suburbs were a very small proportion; solitaries were even fewer, and likely to be poor.

57. See Pelling, 'Old age, poverty and disability', p. 88, and references there cited; Wall, 'Elderly persons'.

58. See for example Todd, 'Widowhood', p. 228. Boulton, *Neighbourhood*, p. 131, is unusual in suggesting poor law support as a factor affecting remarriage by men, rather than women.

persons, so sometimes the rich have of poor, and old of young . . . parties in disparity of each other . . . Likewise sometimes it may fall out, that a lame or impotent man, for comfort; a man who hath lived loosly many years of his life with some one woman, may be desirous even in the very point of death to marry her.'[59] Perhaps then, as now, spouseless men died earlier. The importance of remarriage is confirmed in the tendency of men to remarry (formally or not) as soon as possible. The imperative was probably strongest for poor men. Nonetheless, the English context can be seen as one in which both culture and ideology placed as few obstacles as possible in the way of male remarriage among all social orders, and in particular remarriage to younger, unmarried women. This is compatible not so much with individualism as with recent work stressing community norms respecting marriage.[60] In their harping on widows, men were in part expressing fears for their own mortality, but they may also have been distancing themselves from the widowed state.[61] If women, especially younger women, married widowers, it may not necessarily have been that they were desperate to do so, but rather that the full weight of contemporary ideology and social circumstances was required to persuade them to do so.

59. McGrath, 'Notes on marriage licences', p. xxv.

60. For example, O'Hara, 'Ruled by my friends'; Hindle, 'Problem of pauper marriage'. Compare D. Levine, ' "For their own reasons": individual marriage decisions and family life', *Journal of Family History* 7 (1982), pp. 255–64; R. Houlbrooke, 'The making of marriage in mid-Tudor England: evidence from the records of matrimonial contract litigation', ibid., 10 (1985), pp. 339–52.

61. Pictorial representations include the tendency to memorialize all wives and children, the well-known deathbed portrait (1635–36) of the Astons by Souch (in which the widower Sir Thomas Aston and his surviving son both hold the cross-staff), and the 'death-in-life' marriage portraits. In the 'Judd Marriage' (1560), both man and wife touch the skull, but it is the man who points downwards to the (male) corpse; this could however be interpreted principally as a gesture of moral authority (the wife is shown looking across at her husband). See N. Llewellyn, *The Art of Death* (London, 1991), figs 2, 33, 77.

PART TWO

Models and Paradoxes

CHAPTER FOUR

The widow's options in medieval southern Italy

PATRICIA SKINNER

This chapter addresses the economic and physical maintenance of the widow, and how these intersected.[1] Economic welfare might depend on the maintenance of widowed status for a woman in a way that it certainly did not for a man. Widowhood itself was a gendered status – the charter evidence, that is, written documents recording property transactions, is far more explicit about widows than widowers, simply because women's marital state was recorded as a legal condition. Indeed, in the sample under discussion here, it is only the mention of a second wife or children by two women in cases from Naples, Bari and Salerno that reveals men who may – or may not – have been widowed. It was, after all, perfectly acceptable for a man to have children outside marriage in this early period, and for provision to be made for such offspring. The idealization of the chaste widow in ecclesiastical prescription is not mirrored by equally positive male images. Widowers, in effect, disappear from the evidence unless they had some residual claim to their late wife's property, in which case she might be named in a document. Widows,

1. The primary sources used in this chapter are all published. For Naples see B. Capasso, ed., *Regesta Neapolitana*, in *Monumenta ad Neapolitani Ducatus Historiam Pertinentia* (Naples, 1885), II i. For Salerno and its region see M. Morcaldi *et al.*, eds, *Codex Diplomaticus Cavensis* (Milan, Naples, Pisa, 1873–93), I–VIII, and S. Leone and G. Vitolo, eds, *Codex Diplomaticus Cavensis* (Badia di Cava, 1984, 1990), IX and X. For Amalfi see R. Filangieri di Candida, ed., *Codice Diplomatico Amalfitano* (Naples, 1917), I; *Codice Diplomatico Amalfitano* (Trani, 1951), II; J. Mazzoleni, ed., *[Le] Pergamene degli Archivi Vescovili di Amalfi e Ravello* (Naples, 1972), I; C. Salvati, ed., ibid. (Naples, 1974), II; B. Mazzoleni, ed., ibid. (Naples, 1975), III. For Gaeta see *Codex Diplomaticus Cajetanus*, 2 vols (Montecassino, 1887–91). For Bari and other Apulian cities see the many volumes of the *Codice Diplomatico Barese* (1899–), continued by the *Codice Diplomatico Pugliese*. A comprehensive list of these sources can be found in the bibliography of Patricia Skinner, *Health and Medicine in Early Medieval Southern Italy* (Leiden, 1997).

on the other hand, are highly visible, more so than any other group of women in the charter evidence. Even in boundary clauses relating to pieces of land, their status is carefully recorded.

The tenth-century St Nilus of Rossano, visiting his home city in Calabria, is said to have re-founded the convent of St Anastasia there. Having introduced a complement of virgins into the newly refounded house, he admonished the citizens to look after them, as they were the weaker sex. The reason he gave for doing so was this:

> If any one of you dies, and his widow wants to remain chaste for the rest of her life, if she has nowhere to seek refuge she will be forced to enter into a second marriage – and you will be to blame because you didn't ensure that such an important city has a convent.[2]

This episode, of course, derives from numerous patristic examples of withdrawal from the world being preferable to carnal relations within marriage. St Nilus's close contemporary, St Fantinus, built a monastery and a convent so that his parents and siblings could withdraw from the world as he had. But Nilus's speech made several assumptions: first that widowed status was created by the death of the husband; secondly that the widow would wish to remain chaste; thirdly that she would wish to do so in monastic surroundings; and finally that failing this remarriage was inevitable.

In Nilus's view, or at least that of his almost contemporary biographer, claustration was by far the best outcome for a widow. How far are these assumptions reflected in contemporary southern Italian society? And does the prescriptive nature of the hagiographic text imply that exactly the opposite was happening? Fortunately, this region has a considerable amount of evidence surviving, in the form of charters and other written materials, to begin to attempt to answer this question.

The sample under examination consists of charter material from all parts of southern Italy. There are considerable regional differences in widows' lives here, and nuances of class and relative wealth. The majority of the charters concern property-owners, often aristocratic ones. It could be suggested that the norms visible for wealthy women might not apply to their less well-off sisters. Moreover, two legal traditions, Roman and Germanic (Lombard in this case), coexisted in the peninsula. They cannot be clearly defined, nor assigned to tightly-delineated territories, but their differing effects

2. *Vita di San Nilo*, trans. G. Giovanelli (Grottaferrata, 1966), p. 46.

are visible in the charter material, in particular where the status and property of women were concerned. For example, Lombard women, for the most part, were unable to enter into property transactions without the permission of a male *mundoald*, or legal guardian, usually a member of the woman's family. Women living according to Roman law, on the other hand, did have a separate legal identity and therefore more liberty in their choice of transactions.

The evidence produces 215 documented widows up to AD 1100, a sample large enough for it to be possible to compare how the evidence of practice corresponds with the assumptions in ecclesiastical texts like Nilus's *Vita* about widows and their maintenance.

The first premise was that widowhood resulted from the husband's death. What was 'widowhood' in medieval Europe? A perhaps rather startling fact was that a woman's husband did not have to die for her to be designated a widow. He might instead enter the church. After all, retreat to the monastic vocation meant in effect that a man was 'dead to the world'. In 1053 we see just such an arrangement, when Letitia, who designates herself the widow of John 'who is now a monk', sold off a well to the monastery of St Benedict in Conversano in Apulia. It is highly likely that this church was where her husband was now living.

A second route to widowhood was if the husband was away for longer than a prescribed period (often three years). The laws of the Lombard king Liutprand, which were observed, albeit imperfectly, in large areas of southern Italy, include provision number eighteen that a father absent three or more years lost all his property to his children and could not claim it back.[3] His wife, too, was allowed to assume his death and seek permission from the royal authorities to remarry. A widow's options were circumscribed in different ways by the nature of her 'widowhood'. Also, very importantly, her choices were dependent on whether she had children. We shall return to this issue presently.

Nilus's preaching had assumed that a widow would wish to remain chaste. This again does not appear to be borne out by the empirical evidence. Of 215 recorded widows in total there are twenty recorded cases of remarriage, almost 10 per cent of the entire sample. Medieval ecclesiastical prescriptive sources suggest that the remarriage of widows was, for the most part, discouraged,[4] but secular sources

3. The laws are most easily accessible in translation in Katherine Fischer Drew, *The Lombard Laws* (Philadelphia, 1973).

4. James A. Brundage, *Law, Sex and Christian Society in Medieval Europe* (Chicago, 1987), provides a comprehensive survey of the relevant primary texts on remarriage.

from the Mediterranean reveal an expectation that it would take place, either through choice or coercion. Lombard law, for example, allowed for a widow wanting to remarry: Rothari's law 182 states that she could go to another husband or remain in the power of her *mundoald* or male legal guardian. A will that survives from Salerno, dated 996, even contains a bequest of cash for the widow to remarry and names her future husband! More surprising still is a document recording the permission given to a free woman named Leni to remarry by the abbot of the church of St Maximus in Salerno in 1010: in this case, however, class won over clerical idealism, as Leni and her new husband would be bound to labour for the church.

The law in Lombard areas circumscribed women's options when becoming a nun as well. Liutprand's law 100 stated that a widow might not become a nun within a year of widowhood except with the king's permission, because her *mundoald* or legal guardian had influence over her when grief was new and could incline her to any action – then, 'when she has returned to herself and the desires of the flesh return, she may fall into adultery and behave as neither nun nor laywoman should'. The very next clause stipulated what should happen to her property if she chose to take the veil. If she had children she could give up to a third of her property to the church she was entering; if not, that amount rose to a half, and the rest was to be disposed of by her *mundoald*. The effects of this law are visible in a document of 883 from Salerno, in which Teoperga stated that she wished to take the veil and leave all her goods to the church for her own soul and that of her dead husband and son. 'But the law says in this case that a woman may only give a third of her goods and the rest must go to her *mundoald* (guardian)' – note here the error slipping in. However, all her relatives were dead and so she petitioned Drogo the *gastald* (the local public official) for permission. He allowed her to donate all her goods because as a woman with no relatives her *mundium* (legal guardianship by the *mundoald*) fell to the palace. It may be no coincidence that the beneficiary of this transaction was the church of St Maximus in Salerno, itself the recipient of numerous princely donations.

Nilus's speech had presumed that a widow would wish to enter a nunnery. It is extremely difficult to see much evidence for this. Of the fifteen cases we have of nuns, only three can definitely be placed in religious houses, one at Salerno and two in Naples. Liutprand's law explicitly allows for the widow remaining chaste at home. This law left the woman in a somewhat liminal state and it may explain a rather strange document from Bari, dated 1054. In it, five men testified that they had seen Bella, the widow of Bisantius, *laica vestita et ligata caput* – that is, in lay clothing with a bound head. Had Bella decided to take the veil at home? And was her appearance in lay clothing a slip-up? Unfortunately, we do not have the outcome of whatever case was being pursued using this document. Nevertheless, evidence from eleventh- and twelfth-century Salerno suggests that remaining chaste at home was becoming a popular expression of piety among Lombard women.[5]

Nilus's final assumption was that remarriage was inevitable for the uncloistered widow. Although we have seen legal provisions for the remarriage of widows, King Rothari's law 182 provides for the woman who does not wish or is not able to have another husband. And there is plenty of evidence in the charter material for widows who had neither remarried nor entered the church. The general problem of the evidence of course is that it is a snapshot – the moment after a document records a woman on her own, she might have remarried. However, there are sufficient documents to suggest that being on her own was not merely a temporary status in the lives of many women.

If, therefore, it was not an automatic choice for a widowed woman to take another husband or enter the church, how did widows fare in early medieval southern Italy? A common feature of historiography about widows is the pressure that they might come under from family members and outsiders over the future of the property that they held (and indeed about their own futures).[6] This, however, does not appear to be a strong feature of the southern Italian material, where there were only sixteen cases of widows embroiled in disputes – although it is worth remembering that only those cases requiring a public settlement may have ever come to written evidence. Of these, seven are with family members. It is interesting to note that four of these family disputes arise from remarriage of one of the partners. A particularly informative case is that of Gemma of Salerno. In 954 she was trying to sort out a dispute between her second husband, Mirandus, and her former father-in-law over a piece of land. Her father-in-law agreed to allow Mirandus to keep the land in exchange for the return of the quarter of her first

5. G. Vitolo, 'Primi appunti per una storia dei penitenti nel Salernitano', *Archivio Storico per le Province Napoletane* 17 (1978), documents this phenomenon.

6. Patricia Skinner, 'Gender and poverty in the medieval community', in Diane Watt, ed., *Medieval Women in Their Communities* (Cardiff and Toronto, 1997), surveys the evidence.

husband Richard's property which Gemma and Mirandus now held. By 982 Mirandus had died, but the dispute resurfaced, and three documents of that year culminate in Gemma, with the permission of her son, giving up more contentious property and receiving a settlement payment.

If widows came under pressure to remarry, there is little evidence of it in the charter material, although the bitterness of the language in a dispute between a certain Calomaria and her second husband Caloiohannes in Bari in 1003, where she ascribed the dispute to 'the hatred that had come between them', may suggest that she found herself in a marriage that she would have preferred not to have entered.

Many of the disputes are in charters from regions where Lombard law was current, and may have arisen because of the rights that this law gave to wives and widows. A particular problem, it seemed, was the fact that marriage was accompanied by the permanent transfer of *morgengab* or morning-gift from the husband to his wife. This could be up to a quarter of his property, landed and movable. Thus, when the husband died, his widow irrevocably retained a substantial amount of his property. In addition, husbands frequently made provision in their wills for their widows to manage the rest of the estate as well.

In theory, therefore, a widow stood to gain by remaining unmarried after the death of her first husband, although Lombard law, by assigning her a legal guardian or *mundoald*, ensured that she was subject to some check on her activities. (Indeed, the provision in Liutprand's laws against abuses of the *mundoald*'s position reveal how oppressive such control could be.) For her former husband's family, however, her retention of part of the estate in perpetuity was something of an irritant. Although there are no documented cases of a family challenging the right of a woman to retain her *morgengab*, widow's documents do reveal that women were acutely conscious of the tensions that surrounded their property. For example, they frequently ensured that their children could redeem any property that they donated to the church by stipulating a cash sum to be paid: in 997 the widow Guiselgarda of Salerno gave her *morgengab* to her sons, retaining the use of it until her death. In 1019, Senda, the widow of Iaquintus, having handed over half of a piece of land that her husband had co-owned with her brother-in-law, succeeded in securing a cash payment from the latter in lieu of her *morgengab* portion of the property.

In areas of Roman law, too, the quarter appears to have been a traditional portion for the widow to take, and widows again are seen attempting to allay fears that the land was permanently lost. Thus in 1010 Anna, the widow of the duke of Gaeta's son, returned her quarter of his property back to his family through a sale to the then duke. Widows' discretion in areas of Roman law in managing their estates was considerable. This is reflected by the fact that the overwhelming majority of the forty-one documents in which widows are actively managing land (as opposed to selling it off or donating it to the church, which we shall come to in a moment) are from Amalfi, Gaeta, Naples and Calabria. In these areas, although many of the women mentioned were acting with adult children, it appears to have been assumed that they had the ability and judgment to transact business on their own and family members' behalves. (The remainder, from supposedly 'Lombard' areas, warn us against making any hard and fast generalizations.) Transactions include sales on behalf of absent sons; confirmations of documents; leases out to cultivators; divisions; wills and their execution; purchases; agreements; and exchanges. It took a great deal to persuade a widow to give up these responsibilities, as a document of 1012 illustrates. In that year, the widow Sillecta handed over land she had managed after her husband's death to the church, prompted by the onset of war against the Lombards.

However, of the 215 documents recording widows' actions, over half reveal them alienating property. Eighty are records of sales, a further 33 are donations to the church. What are we to make of this significant disposal of land by widows?

In 46 transactions, the recipient is the church, either as purchaser or the recipient of gifts. A further seven documents almost certainly show widows selling off property to family members. As in the case of *morgengab*, the transactions are often 'tidying up' the aftermath of a remarriage. For example, in 1029, Roma of Salerno and her son by her first marriage received permission from Roma's second husband to give property to her former brother-in-law, probably restoring to his family what she had previously received as *morgengab*. The remainder of widow's alienations, however, fall outside these two categories of recipients, and are to individuals whose relationship to the widow cannot be ascertained.

Why were these sales happening? If we pick apart some of the documents, some reasons become apparent. Legal provisions allowed for donations to the church, whereas alienation to laymen was not permitted, especially where it harmed the interests of the widow's offspring. Thus entering into a transaction with the church allowed a widow a certain amount of discretion over her property, and piety was of course a strong motivation for donations.

Sometimes, widows cite poverty as the reason for their transaction. These charters are all from areas of Lombard law, and reflect the legal requirement that poverty had to be cited in any sale of children's lands. Other alienations were made with extremely specific reasons given. For example, the widow Wiletruda cited her hunger during a Saracen siege of Salerno in 882 as the reason for her sale. War was also a factor in a sale of 1063, when the widow Theodonanda, her son and her daughter-in-law sold land to raise a ransom payment to the Normans for her other son.

A considerable number of Lombard widows are seen selling off their *morgengab*, perhaps in reaction to pressures from their late husbands' families, discussed earlier, or perhaps simply to raise money to support themselves. Were the alienations a sign of financial difficulties? In certain cases, the sales might be seen as a rationalization of agricultural estates now that the main cultivator was no longer alive. In 1041, for example, Maria, widow of Constantine, and her sons sold off half the land in Salerno they had previously received to cultivate. Relatively few cases are this explicit, however.

One major impetus for land donations by widows, in particular, was the commemoration of their deceased partner (widowers, too, make such provisions). Often, donations might be made to family members or apparently unrelated laymen in return for a promise of commemoration of either the dead or living partner or both. Commemoration appears to be one area where widows and widowers behaved in very similar ways. It is also perfectly possible to find isolated examples of widowed men entering the church, and having some provision made for them in their deceased wife's will as they might make for their widows. A case in point is that of one Fermosano, son of Gregory of Gaeta, whose wife had left half of a house to the church for her soul. In 1061 Gregory donated the other half, but retained the property to live in until his death, a clause which must also have been in his wife Maralda's original document. Whether the wife's provision was appropriate was another matter: in 987 we see Peter the spinner of Naples rather sheepishly donating to the church a selection of movable goods, including a frying-pan and a lectern, left to him by his wife. Rather more valuable was the castle donated in 1052 to the monastery of St Maria Tremiti by Gualbert son of Gisbert, of Veterana in Apulia, who stated he had inherited it from his wife.

Nevertheless, it is true to say that widows negotiated a far greater number of restrictions on their actions than their male counterparts in this period of southern Italian history. Nilus's speech to the inhabitants of Rossano may be setting up an ideal to which few women actually aspired or achieved in reality. The documents of practice and legal codes do seem to reflect the main message that Nilus was trying to get across: that widows were, in effect, the responsibility of their male relatives and needed provision making for them. In areas of both Lombard law, like Salerno and Apulia, and even Roman law, corresponding to Nilus's Calabria, we find examples of widows whose business affairs were conducted on their behalf by male relatives. In this sense, therefore, ecclesiastical prescription may have had relevance to the everyday life of the widow, and contributed to the maintenance of her often restricted position.

CHAPTER FIVE

The virtuous widow in Protestant England

BARBARA J. TODD

In the last scene of the play *The Puritaine* the unnamed Nobleman (who has just saved Lady Plus from remarrying unwisely) offers one view of the nature of widowed women:

> Such is the blind besotting in the state of an unheaded woman that's a widow! For it is the property of all you that are widows . . . to hate those that honestly and carefully love you . . . such is the peevish moon that rules your bloods.[1]

Prescribing behaviour for these unheaded widows challenged early modern theorists of woman's place. Understanding how ordinary widows survived bereavement and then constructed their own new role in the face of such assumptions likewise challenges the historian of widowhood. This chapter will comment on both these subjects.

To begin with some familiar premises. A fundamental idea of early modern social theory was that all women were to be under the headship and control of men, living in obedience within a family unit. In many kinship systems widows were passed from their dead husbands to the control of a son, father or new husband. But in England, because of the cultural preference for elementary conjugal households, widows could not easily be put under control of another male. Long-standing tradition supported the contrary notion that the widow should if at all possible be encouraged to head her own household, either as successor to her husband or in a new home. Only in cases of unusual necessity did English widows retire into the households of married children. Meanwhile, in contrast to societies practising levirate (the marriage of the woman to her deceased husband's brother), remarriage of widows was strongly

1. *The Puritaine: or the Widow of Watling Street* (1607).

discouraged. Tradition thus forced English widows to be 'un-headed' and out of control.

One response to the resulting patriarchal dilemma was the common negative image of the widow in pre-modern England. Certainly some treatises and sermons did take a positive view, acknowledging biblical injunctions to honour widows, but even there honour was often diluted by the vulnerability implied by parallel references to texts that demanded protection for the 'widow and orphan'.[2] Popular literature was almost unremittingly negative. Pathetically eager to remarry, the sexually-experienced widow was assumed to be even more insatiable in her sexual demands than younger married and unmarried women. Equally threateningly, as a woman wise to the ways of men, she was seen as a subversive counsellor of young married women, teaching them how to undermine their husbands' control.

All early modern widows lived with these deleterious expectations. They encountered them first at a time of great stress when, coping with the emotional and financial shocks of losing a partner, they most needed to be courageous and secure. Painfully trained 'to live under obedience',[3] suddenly they had to unlearn that difficult lesson, and instead take control. How did women negotiate this aspect of entry into widowhood? In thinking about this question I have taken the perspective (difficult for a sceptic like myself) that widows sometimes responded to the prescriptive advice directed to them, and further that in interpreting early modern widows' lives one must understand them in spiritual as well as sexual and economic terms.

To prescriptive writers fell the task of reintegrating the widow into the patriarchal order. They concluded that so long as she was unheaded, she must be taught to control herself. Positive exhortations employed two strategies to encourage that self-control. Like most works of advice to women, works on widowhood either celebrated women's virtues as different from but complementary to men's, or stressed women's comparability to men and their equal virtues.[4] The former emphasized the mutual responsibilities of husband and wife. When this model was extended into widowhood, the woman's responsibilities to her dead husband continued to be the central theme: a widow was merely perpetual wife. On the other

2. See for example A. Fawkner, *The Widowes Petition* (London, 1635).

3. See L. Pollock, '"Teach her to live under obedience": the making of women in the upper ranks of early modern England', *Continuity and Change* 4 (1989), pp. 231–98.

4. Constance Jordan, *Renaissance Feminism* (Ithaca, NY, 1990), pp. 7–8.

hand, in the group of writings which saw women as equal human beings, widowhood became a unique stage in a woman's life, a time of female virility when legal independence gave her an opportunity to demonstrate her equality of virtue. The agenda of self-control was easily met in works of the first type: the widow was to see herself as still under the headship of the husband and to follow his expectations just as she always had. In the second group, the widow was taught that self-control, despite her male-like prerogatives, was her greatest virtue. On the English scene the first approach is best represented by the section on widowhood in the 1529 translation by Richard Hyrde of Juan Luis Vives' *Instruction of a Christian Woman* (published in Latin in 1523),[5] probably the best-known early modern text on widowhood. The second group is represented by the only early modern English treatise devoted exclusively to widowhood, William Page's 'The Widdowe Indeed', written about 1620.[6]

Defending the proposition that each of these works was representative and influential is a challenge. One can hardly argue that Vives, a Spanish humanist of Jewish descent writing in Latin for the princess Mary Tudor, represented traditional English values or spoke to ordinary English widows' lives. But the many reprintings of his work[7] and the fact that his premises were reiterated and his words echoed a century later in Richard Brathwaite's *The English Gentlewoman* (1631), suggest that Vives' ideas were long perceived as relevant on the English scene. Page's work, written by a man of middling status for the use of his mother, was clearly more English in its origins.[8] Yet Page used many Continental sources and, further, his treatise of itself could hardly have been widely influential since it was never published. Nonetheless, Page's work, firmly based in Protestant doctrine, provides the best insight we have into the frameworks within which the Protestant widows of seventeenth-century England interpreted their lives.

Vives' Instruction

Vives' advice for all stages of women's lives emphasized the fundamental premise of most Renaissance prescriptions for female

5. Juan Luis Vives, *A Very Frutefull and Pleasant Boke Callyd the Instruction of a Christen Woman*, trans. Richard Hyrde, facsimile reprint in D. Bornstein, ed., *Distaves and Dames* (Delmar, NY, 1978). All citations are to this unpaginated edition.

6. Bodleian Library, Oxford, MS Bodl. 115.

7. STC lists eight reprintings to 1592.

8. *Dictionary of National Biography* (hereafter *DNB*). See below for more detail on Page's career.

behaviour: chastity (that is, the reputation for sexual purity) was the central defining characteristic of the virtuous woman. He summed it up succinctly: 'a woman hath no charge to see to but her honesty and chastity, wherefore when she is informed of that she is sufficiently appointed'.[9] Because the widow was apparently at liberty her task was even harder: 'She is chaste indeed that may do evil . . . and will not.'[10] Far from recognizing widowhood as a unique time when a woman could exercise her virtues in independent action, Vives thought that such freedom was illusory and absurd, observing by analogy that 'the ship is not at liberty that lacketh a governor'.[11]

Instead Vives' chaste widow was to continue to follow her husband's wishes, in fact living as if he were not dead. Even her mourning was shaped by this premise. Ironically the widow, who had suffered what modern studies have shown to be the most devastating human loss, had, according to Vives, little reason to mourn: 'a good widow ought to suppose that her husband is not utterly dead, but liveth both with life of his soul, which is the very life, and beside with her remembrance'.[12] Therefore,

> let her live and do so, as she shall think to please her husband, being now no man but a spirit purified, and a divine thing . . . let her take him for her keeper and spy, not only of her deeds but also of her conscience . . . let her not behave herself, so that his soul have cause to be angry with her, and take vengeance on her ungraciousness.[13]

Thus Vives transformed the Christian commonplace of the continued life of the soul into a sort of patriarchal spiritualism, leaving little opportunity for a widow to move through the processes of separation and closure described in modern studies. Rather he counselled what some theorists of bereavement now regard as a pathological suspension of grief.[14]

Preserving chastity was of course harder for the widow.[15] Without the protection of a husband she could only defend her honour by a withdrawal from public contacts even more complete than the separation Vives prescribed for the wife. Protecting chastity came

9. Vives, *Instruction*, preface. 10. Ibid., bk iii, ch. 4. 11. Ibid., bk iii, ch. 1.

12. Such advice was common: see for example Erasmus, *De Vidua Christiana* (1529), trans. J.T. Roberts, *Collected Works of Erasmus*, Vol. 66 (Toronto, 1988). Christianity's messages of salvation and immortality of the soul, of course, discouraged exaggerated mourning in all cases.

13. Vives, *Instruction*, bk iii, ch. 3.

14. See for example Paul Rosenblatt, *Bitter, Bitter Tears: Nineteenth-Century Diarists and Twentieth-Century Grief Theories* (Minneapolis, 1983), pp. 34–8.

15. Vives, *Instruction*, bk iii, ch. 5.

before any activity in public. Even if legal and economic problems arose, chastity came first: 'in courts and i[n] resort of men . . . a widow should not meddle . . . [for] abroad and afore many mens eyes and handlings . . . honesty and chastity commeth in jeopardy'.[16] 'Chastity requireth solitariness', no matter what the cost. In the end, Vives himself seems to have recognized how impractical his advice was. His solution, however, was not to admit that the widow as independent household head had to act in the world. Rather he balanced loyalty to the husband with chastity, and concluded that the only sure protection of the latter was remarriage to a sober, careful, mature man who would relieve the widow of the responsibility of protecting her honour herself. Materially successful but chaste widowhood was virtually unimaginable for the Spanish humanist.

Widowhood as desolation and salvation: a Protestant model

We know that in the century following the first publication of Vives' work English widows did continue to engage vigorously in economic affairs, and indeed became even more numerous amongst those involved in litigation.[17] They were also increasingly less likely to remarry.[18] They played the man's part. If they were going to be controlled it would have to be by self-restraint, balancing feminine virtue with public virility. How should they be taught to control themselves? The English writer William Page offered a strategy more relevant to northern Protestant cultures than Vives' Mediterranean fixation on chastity. Building on the other tradition of humanism, the celebration of the virile woman as the equal of man,[19] he acknowledged that the practice of public activity gives the widow the

16. Ibid., bk iii, ch. 6.

17. See Maria Cioni, *Woman and Law in Elizabethan England with particular reference to the Court of Chancery* (New York, 1985); Tim Stretton, *Women Waging Law in Elizabethan England* (Cambridge, 1998); Amy Erickson, *Women and Property in Early Modern England* (London, 1993), and Laura Gowing, *Domestic Dangers: Women, Words and Sex in Early Modern London* (Oxford, 1996).

18. See B. Todd, 'The remarrying widow: a stereotype reconsidered', in M. Prior, ed., *Women in English Society, 1500–1800* (London, 1985), pp. 54–92, and J. Boulton, 'London widowhood revisited: the decline of female remarriage in the seventeenth and early eighteenth centuries', *Continuity and Change* 5 (1990), pp. 323–55.

19. See Ruth Kelso, *Doctrine for the Lady of the Renaissance* (Urbana, Ill., 1956), pp. 126–33.

opportunity to demonstrate her talents.[20] But Page added to this another emphasis. At the core of his work lies a metaphor for the Protestant salvation experience: widowhood represents the affliction and loss of self every Christian must endure to achieve justification by faith.[21] The widow who most completely experiences the true desolation and deprivation of widowhood will be the closest to achieving the triumph of salvation. By realistically praising the public virtue of the virile widow, Page stressed even more the private achievement of self-control by the woman herself through God's grace in face of opportunities to grasp the pre-eminence of a man.

Page was born in Middlesex in 1590, attended Balliol and later was appointed Fellow of All Souls where he composed two treatises on women: a defence entitled 'A Woman's Worth, or a treatise proving by sundry reasons that women doe excel men' (part of the flurry of replies to Swetnam's *Arraignment*)[22] and his 'Widdowe Indeed'. Rather than publishing these works Page deposited manuscript copies in the Bodleian Library with the proviso that they not be made available to readers during his lifetime. Later he published works of vigorous religious controversy and then wrote more gently on the theme of toleration. He became schoolmaster at Reading, and later rector of East Locking, Berkshire, where he died in 1663.[23]

How did this young Protestant academic go about composing a work on widowhood for the use of his mother? Page drew his title from the text of 1 Timothy where St Paul enjoins the church at Corinth to honour those who are 'widows indeed'. Following a

20. In this Page's 'Widdowe Indeed' can best be compared with Horatio Fusco's *La Vedova* (Rome, 1570). Erasmus' *De Vidua* generally takes the same perspective. Giovanni Giorio Trissino (*Epistola del Trissino de la vita, che dee tenere una donna vedova* [Rome, 1525]) seems to have been more conservative in his understanding of the role of the virile widow: see Jordan, *Renaissance Feminism*, pp. 71–2.

21. On affliction and suffering as part of the salvation experience and the language used to describe it, see J. Sears McGee, *The Godly Man in Stuart England* (New Haven, Conn., 1976), ch. 2; neither McGee nor Barbara Lewalski (*Protestant Poetics and the Seventeenth-Century Religious Lyric* (Princeton, 1979), pp. 147–78) discuss this use of widowhood as a metaphor for affliction. For a brief reference to women's evaluation of affliction see Diane Willen, '"Communion of the Saints": spiritual reciprocity and the godly community in early modern England', *Albion* 27 (1995), p. 39 n. 91.

22. Joseph Swetnam, *The Araignment of Lewde, Idle, Froward and Unconstant Women* (London, 1615).

23. *DNB*; a response to William Prynne published at Laud's request, a translation of Thomas a Kempis' *Imitatio Christi*, and several other tracts, including *The Peace Maker or a Brief Motion of Unity and Charity in Religion* (1652). I have not been able to discover a sustained discussion of widowhood by an author clearly identified with the Puritan perspective to compare with that of Laudian Page.

common device,[24] Page defined three categories: the detestable or evil widow (who lives for pleasure), the miserable or worldly widow (who is either poor and comfortless or 'liveth honestly and intendeth not to marry'), and the good widow, who is his 'widow indeed'.[25] To describe the latter Page again followed other authors in using the etymological connection of *vidua* with emptiness. Thus the 'widow indeed' is the most honourable because in spite of her freedom she has been able to achieve the greatest desolation or emptiness. But the woman who remains a widow because of the worldly freedom that her independence gives her cannot qualify as the 'good widow', even though Page praises that independence. Nor can the widow who succeeds in sustaining her reputation for chastity, although that too is an important component of Page's idea of the good widow. Rather the role he prescribes for a true widow is far more demanding than the mere successful exercise of chaste independence.

> Where the honour is great . . . so the labour and striving cannot be small . . . for not only she who hath buried her husband, no nor she who can live chastely and contentedly without an husband (although it be a singular victory to conquer that affection) is the widow I have spoken of, but there is also required unto a widow indeed many inward virtues and heavenly endowments of the mind.[26]

The first half of Page's work is devoted to describing the acts by which a widow acquires these inward virtues, essentially an intensified version of the duties required of any Christian, shadowed here by the bereavement and material hardships of living as a widow. Since affliction is Page's central theme, not surprisingly the widow's first duty is 'Desolation' and it is the 'foundation of all the rest'. Any widow is to a degree desolate through bereavement: 'this is a hard condition which followeth her estate whether she will or no'. The 'widow indeed', however, experiences not merely passive desolation, but achieves a higher, active desolation by patiently enduring her afflictions and, most importantly, accounting them 'an exceeding joy'.[27] Page's version of widowhood is thus akin to the Protestant conviction of sin without which there can be no salvation: 'so should all Christian souls be desolate'.[28]

24. Used by St Augustine (*de bono viduitate ad Julianan viduam*) and Savonarola (*Libro della vita viduale*, 1495) among others, who in turn were inspired by St Paul. The 'good' and the 'ordinary' widow were also commonly contrasted in Theophrastian books of characters.

25. 'Widdowe Indeed', p. 9. 26. Ibid., p. 12.

27. Ibid., pp. 15–16. 28. Ibid., p. 21.

Page inventories the problems facing a widow: already desolate at the loss of her husband, her children also 'will be for the most part forward and stubborn for want of a father'; 'her friends and neighbours now begin to forsake her'; 'her enemies wrong and despise her'. Even if by chance she has wealth, friends and obedient children, a widow is still to strive for desolation by not trusting in any of those things. One might assume that a poor widow had little enough of things in which to place her hope; seemingly for her desolation would be easily achieved. But merely making a virtue of the normal poverty of widowhood is not enough; the woman who is desolate *in spite of* worldly possessions is closest to the widow indeed.[29]

The requisite sense of desolation achieved, Page prescribes the spiritual duties for the true widow: hope in God (just as the convicted sinner had only hope in God to cling to, so the widow), prayer and fasting.[30] Then come duties of daily life. Solitariness is first, 'for if every good woman should be like a snail hid within her house . . . then much more should my widow keep within doors'. Staying at home will also help the widow to avoid gossiping women, and that thought leads Page to the next duty, Taciturnity. Too much talking leads to 'busyness' with men's affairs.[31]

Finally Page enjoins active duties, the 'works' required of good Christians. These include duties to kindred and care of 'the saints', care and education of the widow's own children,[32] and of all those in need. No matter how small the widow's resources she is to use some charitably. Thus the most obvious material obligations of the widow are acknowledged, but only within the context of universal Christian duties at the secondary, Protestant level of 'works'. Given all these strictures and responsibilities, most widows probably would have eagerly concurred with the sentiments expressed in the prayer Page prescribes for his mother at the end of his work: 'Lord thou has taught me by experience how vile and contemptible, how desolate

29. Ibid., pp. 17–20.

30. The last is described as an aid to prayer and almost incidentally, 'a sovereign preservative of chastity', for 'unruly and headstrong motions are by no means better quelled and subdued', ibid., p. 37. Thus in one of his few bits of material advice Page betrays the common awareness of the widow's sexuality.

31. This aspect of the work might also be read as a response to the fear of the widow as a subversive adviser of young married women, but Page encourages conversation between women: 'I wot very well that the company and conference of modest and discreete matrons is a great comfort and recreation the one to the other', ibid., p. 46.

32. Ibid., pp. 65–74. Compare Erasmus, *De Vidua*, p. 202.

and comfortless, how hard and almost impossible to be sustained my condition of life is.'[33]

Nothing could seemingly be farther from a 'feminist' vision of free and empowered widowhood than the affliction and self-abnegation that is at the core of this young man's advice. Yet, quite unexpectedly, the second half of Page's work turns to a celebration of the freedom of widowhood albeit with the negative intent of discouraging remarriage. Unlike Vives, who finally prescribed it to preserve chastity, Page was uncompromisingly opposed to remarriage. His reasons are not the obvious patriarchal ones of loyalty to the deceased husband or interests of children.[34] Rather they savour of egalitarian feminism:

> If it be true which the Philosopher [Aristotle] sayeth that a woman naturally desireth to be a man, then see I no reason why a woman should not be content to be a widow seeing in this estate she cometh nearest to the preeminence and prerogative of a man, for what is the privilege of a man above the woman but to bear rule and when can a woman be liker unto a man in this than when she is a widow.[35]

Although the freedom and opportunities of widowhood were sometimes used by authors to criticize the contrasting repressive situation of women as daughters and wives,[36] Page's agenda was different. His purpose was to set the limitations that he expected the widow to impose upon herself while 'at liberty'. She may have been physically released from a husband's control,[37] but Page's free widow was not a liberated individual in the modern sense. Not only would that have been foreign to early modern ideas but it would also have contradicted the thrust of the rest of the treatise. His intention was to channel the woman's energy under her own self-discipline towards two universally desirable goals: order and salvation. By focusing on the desolation of bereavement as the central

33. 'Widdowe Indeed', p. 233.

34. He might, of course, have had a personal agenda; I have not been able to discover more about Page's mother or whether her remarriage might have harmed his interests.

35. 'Widdowe Indeed', p. 119.

36. Fusco does that, for example.

37. At p. 194 he observes: 'My widow is . . . not subiect to the command of an husband. . . . she liveth peaceably in the day, and she sleepeth quietly in the night, she goethe to bed when shee list, and she riseth when shee list, shee goeth abroad when shee will, shee cometh home when shee will.' These phrases echo Robert Copland's satirical *The Seven Sorrowes that Women have when theyr husbandes be deade* (1568); the author of *The Lawes Resolution of Womens Rights* (London, 1632, pp. 231–2) also addresses the practical consequences of the freedom of widowhood.

distinguishing characteristic of widowhood, Page's model allowed for both female agency and social control. The freedom of widowhood was important precisely because it uniquely gave a woman the 'Christian liberty' to perform the duties Page had so carefully outlined in the preceding section of his book, that is to follow the path that could lead to salvation. True widowhood created a peculiarly female context for the working of free will.

Influence and consequences of these doctrines

How effective were these two prescriptive models in practice? Here one turns to widows' own experience of bereavement. Women's written accounts of course over-represent women of property and privilege, and, since personal writing was often a religious exercise, tend to emphasize a spiritual response. We might well discount this work as atypical. Yet property entailed pressing responsibilities on wealthy widows no less than poverty did on the poor. Nor do we have any grounds for assuming that most widows in this great crisis of their lives did not find consolation and courage in religion. Rather the contrary. Turning to religion in affliction is so obvious a pattern that it is easily overlooked as unimportant, yet without acknowledging things of the spirit we cannot begin to understand women of the past.[38] Though we cannot expect to find Page's unpublished treatise specifically acknowledged in these widows' writings, the principles it articulated were widely shared in Calvinistic culture.[39]

Space allows only for a brief suggestion of the responses of a few well-known widows, and of one woman hitherto unknown, Thomasin

38. The case for attending to gender in evaluating spirituality is well put by Diane Willen in 'Godly women in early modern England: Puritanism and gender', *Journal of Ecclesiastical History* 43 (1992), pp. 561–80 and ' "Communion of the Saints" ', pp. 19–41.

39. See McGee on the doctrine of suffering (n. 21 above); and on the commonplace notion that grief and mental suffering were spiritual afflictions solvable by spiritual remedies see Michael MacDonald, *Mystical Bedlam: Madness, Anxiety and Healing in Seventeenth-Century England* (Cambridge, 1981), pp. 176–7. Many widows were doubtless familiar with Jeremy Taylor's discussion of affliction in *Holy Living* (the London widow Katherine Austen paraphrased his ideas in her meditational journal, British Library, Add. MS 4454, f. 36). The same notions were also sometimes articulated in attenuated versions in funeral sermons, praising widows who followed patterns espoused by Page. See for example Ignatius Fuller, *A Sermon at the Funerals of Mrs. Anne Norton* (London, 1672) and John Collinges, *Par Nobile* (London, 1669) on Lady Frances Hobart.

Head. Although self-examination is most associated with Puritans, reflections on widowhood survive from the pens of women whose views ranged across the religious spectrum of conforming Protestants. However even the most prolific of female memorialists and letter writers were remarkably reticent on the subject of bereavement. Only a handful of women's memoirs and journals span the time of a husband's death or recall the immediate period afterward.[40] There is a common pattern: grief dissolves at first into guilt, and then through guilt into acceptance of God's will as just punishment of sin, and then through empowerment by God's will to action.[41] This appears for example in the prayer that Ann Fanshawe inserted into the narrative of her married life after her account of the death of her husband. The passage is unique in her work. She recorded the deaths of children with sadness, but the passing of her husband in 1666 while ambassador to Spain was a devastating tragedy.

> O all powerful Lord God, look down from heaven upon me, the most distressed wretch upon earth. See me with my soul divided, my glory and my guide taken from me, and in him all my comfort in this life. See me staggering in my path . . . Have pity on me, O Lord, and speak peace to my disquieted soul now sinking under the great weight which without thy support cannot sustain itself. See me O Lord, with . . . a distressed family . . . the want of all my friends without counsel, out of my country, without any means to return with my sad

40. Elizabeth Freke's memoir is unique in seventeenth-century women's writings in print in its intense description of the moment of her husband's death: 'at the fattall houre of my Life and his death, Noe Mortall was with him butt my wretched selfe. In my Arms He Lay Dyeing, which quite distracted me; he bid me nott stirr from him, but . . . my crying out soon filled the house . . . to be A Witnes of My unhappy and deplorable Fate.' Although she reports herself as being 'distracted for my loss & nott (able) to support myself in itt' she does not discuss how she overcame her grief: the next entries made several weeks later deal with the problems of settling the estate. ('Mrs. Elizabeth Freke, her Diary, 1671–1714', *Journal of the Cork Historical and Archaeological Society*, 2nd series, 17 [1911], 105.) Discussion of the death of the husband is rare in the autobiographical writings discussed by Sara Heller Mendelson ('Stuart women's diaries and occasional memoirs' in M. Prior, ed., *Women in English Society, 1500–1800* [London, 1985]). The present essay is largely based on materials in print; no doubt other records of widows' grief survive in manuscript form.

41. This is a commonplace of seventeenth-century doctrines of suffering. It contrasts with modern studies, which generally discount religion as a factor and also conclude that while guilt is one of the emotions experienced by bereaved people, anger is the stronger and more common reaction (see for example Beverley Raphael, *The Anatomy of Bereavement* (New York, 1983), pp. 184–6). Rosenblatt's analysis in *Bitter Tears* relies on a secular post-Freudian idea of 'grief work' although several of the nineteenth-century diaries that he uses construct the experience of bereavement in metaphors of sin like those used by seventeenth century widows.

family to our own country... But above all, my sins, O Lord, I do lament with shame and confusion, believing it is them for which I receive this great punishment.... O God, forgive whatsoever is amiss in me; break not a bruised reed. I humbly submit to thy justice. Do with me and for me what thou pleasest, for I do wholly rely upon thy mercy, beseeching thee to remember thy promises to the fatherless and widow, and enable me to fulfil thy will cheerfully in the world.[42]

Similar passages appear in Rachel Russell's letters,[43] while the testing of faith in early widowhood is reflected at second hand in the correspondence of the Puritan Joan Barrington, and in a reconstruction of the thought of Viscountess Falkland by her chaplain.[44] The pattern appears with almost painful intensity in a set of meditations composed by an obscure seventeenth-century woman, Thomasin Head, whose life and writing, so far as I know, are entirely unknown to early modern historians and literary critics.

Thomasin Head's story can be reconstructed partly from the preface to her *The Pious Mother; or Evidences for Heaven written in the Year 1650... for the benefit of her Children* (a work not published until 1790), and partly from the fictionalized autobiography of her son, Richard Head, *The English Rogue*, published in 1663.[45] According to her son, Thomasin Head was a gentleman's daughter who married a young cleric in a runaway match in the mid-1630s. The young husband took a post in Ireland. There the family suffered hardships as they were displaced first by Catholic rebels when they fled in 1640 from Knockfergus to Belfast and then by radical Protestant parishioners in Belfast who found the senior Head's adherence to Anglican ritual unacceptable. They became refugees yet again when in 1641 they were finally driven from Ireland to the Isle of Man.[46] Either in Ireland or shortly after their departure Thomasin's husband died. Richard says he was 'barbarously murdered by the rebels for being a protestant preacher'; he also recounts the death of one

42. John Loftis, ed., *The Memoirs of Anne, Lady Halkett and Ann, Lady Fanshawe* (Oxford, 1979), pp. 185–6.

43. See for example *Letters of Lady Rachel Russell: from the manuscript in the library at Wooburn [sic] Abbey*, 6th edn (London, 1801), pp. 10–11; Lois Schwoerer, *Lady Rachel Russell: 'One of the Best of Women'* (Baltimore, 1988), p. 147.

44. Arthur Searle, ed., *Barrington Family Letters 1628–1632*, Camden 4th ser. (London, 1983), Vol. 28, p. 15; John Duncon, *The Returns of Spiritual Comfort and Grief in a Devout Soul* (London, 1649).

45. Richard Head, *The English Rogue: described in the life of Meriton Latroon, a witty extravagant, being a compleat history of the most eminent cheats of both sexes* (London, 1665). Head was actually author of only the first part. He earned a *DNB* entry which does not mention his mother's work.

46. *English Rogue*, pp. 1–20; *Pious Mother*, p. 19.

brother.[47] Thus in 1641 or 1642 Head brought her family back to England. After living for a while with kin in Plymouth, they were forced to fend for themselves. Like so many other women, Head adopted the makeshifts that lay to hand, in her case capitalizing on her learning and piety. According to her son she learned to shape her theology to suit the expectations of her current hosts.

> We being here [in Plymouth] altogether unacquainted both with the people and their profession, my Mother having an active brain casts about with her self how she should provide for her charge, but found no way more expedient than the pretention of Religion. Zeal now and Piety were the only things she seem'd to prosecute, taking the litteral sence of the Text; without doubt Godliness is great gain: But she err'd much in the profession and seasonable practise thereof; Hers being according to the mind of the true Church, the Church of England, whereas the Plymotheans were at that time Heterodox . . . Finding how much she was mistaken she chang'd quickly her Note and Coat; a rigid Presbyterian at first, but that proving not so profitable, instantly transform'd her self into a strict independant. . . .

Moving from village to village, the family received aid from pious clergy and parishioners.

> No matter wither we went . . . we found . . . some or other that gave us entertainment for those good parts they found in my Mother she being very well read both in Divinity and History, and having an eloquent tongue, she commonly apply'd her self to the Minister of the town; who wondering to see so much learning and perfection in a Woman, either took us to his own house for a while; or gathered some contributions to supply our present necessities, with which we travelled to the next Town: And in this manner we strouled or wandered up and down being little better than mendicant Itinerants.[48]

Thomasin Head's resourcefulness allowed her family to survive. Her own version of these years recorded in the group of meditations later published as *The Pious Mother* is much more painful than her son's lighthearted portrait, although one might perhaps wonder if her meditations were also part of a genteel theological con perpetrated by a mother supporting her children by her wits. But even if they do not represent her genuine beliefs they show how one widow constructed an understanding of God's working in the world by

47. *English Rogue*, pp. 8–9, 17.

48. Ibid., pp. 18–20. I have been able to discover nothing further as to the rest of her life. Her eighteenth-century editor records that she also left works (never published) entitled 'The Vanity of the World' and 'Glories of Heaven' which were 'remarkable for a judicious application of historical facts'.

stressing how His chastisements demonstrate His love for the sinful Christian. As William Page prescribed, Head experienced the affliction of her dramatic widowhood as a step toward the experience of God's mercy. She certainly effectively expresses the desolation of widowhood:

> Alas! why should I love the world! It hates me, and casts me off as one dead and out of mind. Am I not crucified to the world? The World loves its own, but me it cannot love, because I am not of the world . . . I have lost that precious friend, who was the companion of my life, the joy of my heart, and the cause of my earthly contentment. And who would esteem the world, that hath lost in one person all that it can give?[49]

Like Page's widow she feels isolated from friends:

> How hath the false friendship of the world deceived me! How firm and erect have those reeds stood in the calm and sunshine of my prosperity! . . . [yet] I have never leaned on these reeds, but they have either bended or broken. They have been like an old ruinous house – when I have come to them for shelter and protection against a storm, they have fallen upon me, and crushed me to the ground.[50]

But, just as Page would have urged, Head asserts that the suffering of bereavement is the basis for salvation:

> Who would refuse to be tried in this furnace of affliction when he knows, with certainty, that it will not consume him, but only purify him from the dross of sin and corruption? . . . Now what have my afflictions wrought in me? Truly the peaceable fruits of righteousness.[51]

This pious widow, then, experienced the desolation of bereavement as the evident basis of God's will and the first step to salvation. Despite her remarkable achievements in meeting the material challenges of her situation, when she re-created that experience the metaphors of sin and salvation provided the language through which she could understand her bereavement, as it gave her the courage to confront its consequences.[52]

49. *Pious Mother*, pp. 88–9. 50. Ibid., p. 86. 51. Ibid., pp. 76, 78, 81.

52. The trope of bereavement as a testing affliction from God also appears in Rachell Russell's letters to John Fitzwilliam and in his replies to her, although in this case Russell's sin is too much grief while her eventual recovery from the grief is equated with salvation. Gilbert Burnet's letters to Russell offered more 'modern' counsel (turn your attention to something else: educating your children 'will be a noble entertainment to you, and the best diversion and cure of your wounded and wasted spirits', *Letters*, p. 17), but she reported that Fitzwilliam's message of widowhood as desolation suited her the best of any she had received (*Letters*, p. 23).

The surviving volume of the meditational diary of the London widow Katherine Austen does not record the immediate period of her husband's death, but long sections reflect on the nature of widowhood. Although Austen never attained the same despairing desolation described by Head and others she certainly effectively exploited the trope of affliction as a sign of God's promise: 'Many women have had great afflictions. Yet sometimes I think mine out goes them all. But then I turn on t'other side to the favour and conduct of my Heavenly Guardian his sweet converting every rebuke to a blessed love token.'[53]

The words of a handful of widows scarcely prove that this doctrine of widowhood as a metaphor for Christian sin and salvation was widely shared. But a completely different genre, theatrical comedy, suggests widespread awareness of the affliction model of true widowhood. William Rowley's *A New Wonder, A Woman Never Vex'd,* first performed in 1632, based its whole comedic premise on the assumption that the audience would understand that widows believed that affliction was the key advantage of their state. Rowley's satire of 'Puritan' intensity was commonplace, but the play provides a complex exception to the usual negative depictions of widows in Jacobean comedy. The central character is a rich widow who, typically on the stage, is seeking a husband. But her purpose in doing so is not the common one of sexual satisfaction: rather she seeks a husband because she seeks affliction. She is cursed with good luck and a happy disposition and is thus deprived of the desolation required for successful widowhood. As she explains to the clergyman from whom she seeks advice:

> How think you then, is not this a wonder?
> That a woman lives full seven and thirty years
> Maid to a wife, and wife unto a widow,
> Now widow'd and mine own, yet all this while . . .
> Did never taste what was calamity?
> I know not yet what grief is, yet have sought
> An hundred ways for its acquaintance
> . . . even those things that I have meant a cross,
> Have that way turn'd a blessing.
> . . .
> I have heard you say, that the child of heaven
> Shall suffer many tribulations . . .
> Then I that know not any chastisement,
> How may I know my part of childhood?

53. British Library, Add. MS 4454, f. 70.

The clergyman's 'comic' reply is not too far from consolations addressed to real-life widows:

> 'Tis a good doubt, but make it not extreme.
> 'Tis some affliction that you are afflicted
> For want of affliction; cherish that . . .
> . . . Pray let me question you:
> You lost a husband – was it no grief to you?

But not so, as the widow takes up another commonplace of contemporary thought on bereavement:

> It was; but very small. No sooner I
> Had given it entertainment as a sorrow,
> But straight it turn'd into my treble joy:
> A comfortable revelation prompts me then,
> That husband (whom in life I held so dear)
> Had chang'd a frailty to unchanging joys;
> Methought I saw him stellified in heaven,
> And singing hallelujahs . . .
> . . . it was a sin for me to grieve
> At his best good, that I esteemed best:
> And thus this slender shadow of a grief
> Vanish'd again.[54]

Building on the lesson taught in so many other comedies that remarriage brought dishonour on a widow and danger to her fortune, Rowley's widow strives for affliction by seeking a spendthrift suitor who will not only make her life miserable but will dispose of her fortune as well. But she is frustrated yet again, for no sooner has she married the perfect ne'er-do-well debtor than he turns into an ambitious, loyal and honest husband, whose careful management of her estate increases it to the benefit of the couple, his kin and London society as a whole. By adopting the desolation model of widowhood, as well as the commoner trope of the remarrying widow, Rowley successfully satirizes both versions.

That widows responded to Page's ideas does not mean that they did not also sometimes guide themselves by their husbands' wishes as Vives advised,[55] or worry about issues of chastity and personal honour. The Yorkshire gentlewoman Alice Thornton was bitterly

54. 'A New Wonder, A Woman never Vext' reprint, in R. Dodsley, ed., *Select Collection of Old English Plays*, 4th edn, rev. W.C. Hazlitt (London, 1874), Vol. 12, pp. 112–14, Act I sc. i.

55. See for example Lady Grace Mildmay's meditation on the corpse of her husband, in Linda Pollock, *With Faith and Physic* (London, 1993), pp. 40–2.

disturbed by the rumour spread shortly before her husband's death that she would quickly marry the young clergyman Thomas Comber.[56] The London widow Katherine Austen was much concerned about the dishonour an unsuitable marriage would impute to herself and her family;[57] but while Austen had doubts about pursuing public activities, her concern did not arise from fear of harm to her reputation for sexual purity, but rather from the sense that public affairs took time away from her spiritual pursuits.[58] No paramount concern about chastity pervades the rest of the accounts of either of these two women; if it concerned them it was so internalized that it no longer bore commenting upon.

Another prolific Protestant writer, Lady Anne Halket, used a brief meditation to comment on the meaning of the retired widowhood advocated by Vives.

> Widows in this Country are called . . . mens Relicts. And Relicts in the Romish Church, are seldom exposed to publick view, and when they are, they are look'd upon with veneration, and stir up peoples affections, to imitate the Vertues of these Holy Saints, to whom, its pretended, they belong: From this their Superstitious practice, If I can learn, to live Devotely and retiredly, never seen abroad but when the offices of Piety, Charity or such like call me, and then my Behaviour, and example be such, as to excite all that behold me to say, God is in her of a truth, then shall I in reality, answer the name to better purpose, than their Imaginary Relicts.[59]

But although Halket desired privacy as Vives prescribed, her Protestant widow is very far indeed from the dangerous helpless ship without a master.

After the guilt, or paralleling it, the process of mourning and recovery as defined by modern studies leads to rebuilding. Circumstances rarely gave early modern widows much time for the transition. With or without the formality of probate most had to manage the family's affairs through the crisis. Even without their 'head'

56. Charles Jackson, ed., *The Autobiography of Mrs. Alice Thornton of East Newton, County York*, in Publications of the Surtees Society, 62 (1873), pp. 221–7, 234–9.

57. British Library, Add. MS 4454, ff. 94^{v}–95^{v}.

58. Compare Peter Lake's study of John Ley's account of Jane Ratcliffe's spiritual emancipation in widowhood: 'Feminine piety and personal potency', *The Seventeenth Century* 2 (1987), pp. 143–61, esp. 153–4.

59. Lady Anne Halket, *Pious Reflections and Observations . . . Occasional Meditations*, in *Works* (Edinburgh, 1701), p. 77. Halket is best known for the narrative of her coming of age (see n. 42 above), but she continued to write throughout the rest of her life. Her manuscripts listed in the biography published with her selected *Works* include twenty-two volumes (some hundreds of pages long) of unpublished meditations and other essays.

they executed these responsibilities competently. Indeed, some widows recorded the passage through financial and legal crises with pride. The Countess of Warwick and Lady Rachel Russell, for example, responded to the challenge of arranging marriages and defending property interests even in the midst of intense grief.[60] Fanshawe's agony of bereavement is followed by an account of how she settled her husband's affairs in Spain and managed the daunting logistics of getting his body and her household back to England safely.[61]

Paradoxically, from a twentieth-century perspective at least, these women used models of just punishment for guilty sin to give them strength to meet the immediate demands of widowhood. Not only did taking guilt upon themselves help early modern widows to pass through bereavement, it was also the means by which they justified and reconciled themselves to the contradiction of becoming independent women in a patriarchal world. 'Desolation' aided them in seeing themselves as 'good widows' despite the calumnies of a literary tradition that assumed they were 'evil' or merely 'ordinary' widows when they became involved in worldly activities or married again. Affliction put the stamp of God's approval on their subsequent independent lives. The woman who became the triumphant Christian through God's grace rather than her own striving succeeded spiritually (and sometimes materially) as a result of widowhood. And in their world this was the success that mattered most. The paradox of Page's simultaneous desolation and pre-eminence created a model of virtuous widowhood in which English widows found consolation and courage in the greatest crisis of their lives.

60. On Rich see Sara Heller Mendelson, *The Mental World of Stuart Women: Three Studies* (Brighton, 1987), pp. 110–15; on Russell, see Schwoerer, *Lady Rachel Russell*, pp. 137–63.

61. Ann Fanshawe shepherded a household of 30 back to England, travelling together with her husband's body in its coffin. Virtually the last thing she records in the memoir of his life written for her children reports her pride at her achievement: see *Memoirs*, p. 189.

CHAPTER SIX

Widows, widowers and the problem of 'second marriages' in sixteenth-century France[1]

LYNDAN WARNER

The second half of the sixteenth century in France was a time of change and restriction for widows and, to a lesser extent, widowers. In 1559 when King Henri II died after a jousting accident, Catherine de Medici became a public widow in black and a power behind the monarchy as three of her sons succeeded to the throne over the following decades. Her eldest son, Francis II, introduced the Edict of Second Marriages in 1560, which, as we shall see, restricted the actions of remarrying widows and addressed the anxiety that widows might act foolishly and lasciviously by giving away the family inheritance to a future husband. The magistrates in the Parlement de Paris registered this royal edict 'with great Applause'. But that was not the end of the story. As the sixteenth-century writer Jacques-Auguste de Thou recalled, the edict 'at first enacted against the Women, was afterward extended to Men by a Decree of Parliament'.[2] This chapter examines the extension of this law from widow to widower by exploring the court case between a widow and her stepchildren that prompted this decree. However, to understand this landmark interpretation of the Edict of Second Marriages, we must first examine the edict and the idea of widowhood in France at this time.

1. I would like to thank the participants at the University of Warwick History Research Seminar as well as the Social and Cultural History 1500–1800 Seminar at All Souls College, Oxford for their comments on versions of this chapter. I am especially grateful to Sandra Cavallo, Tim Stretton and Hugh Stretton for their suggestions on earlier drafts.

2. Jacques-Auguste de Thou, *Monsieur de Thou's History of His Own Time*, 2 vols (Eng. trans. London, 1730), II, p. 526.

The Edict of Second Marriages

The preamble to the 1560 Edict of Second Marriages explained that 'Because widows with children or grandchildren are often solicited to remarry, and as these widows do not recognize that they are more sought after for their wealth than for their persons, they abandon their wealth to new husbands. Under the cloak of marriage, the widows make excessive gifts to these new husbands, and forget their natural duties to their children.' The edict went on to say that at the death of their fathers, children are left 'destitute of paternal succour and aid', hence widows should take on the duty or 'office' of both father and mother. The edict emphasized how remarriage and gifts to new husbands could inspire quarrels and lawsuits and result in the 'desolation of good families' and a 'diminution' in power of the 'public state'. Because of the consequences of this problem for the strength of the state, the edict described how Roman Emperors, zealous to maintain civil government, peace and tranquillity among their subjects, provided several good laws and decrees on this question.

> And we [the French state] for the same consideration understanding the infirmity of the [female] sex, praise and approve these [Roman] laws and ordinances and in so doing declare, enact, and order that all widows [*femmes veufves*], with children or grandchildren, who remarry cannot and will not be able to give their movable goods, *acquests* [property acquired by the current generation; not lineage property] or *propres* [personal property from an ancestor; lineage property] to their new husbands, or the father, mother or children of these men. And if there is an unequal distribution of goods between the widows' children or grandchildren, the gifts made by widows to their new husbands will be reduced and measured according to the inheritance of the child[ren] who received the least.[3]

The Edict of Second Marriages thus clearly linked a widow's conduct with her ability to govern her household and her children. Failure to govern her desires or to care for her children, the edict implied, could undermine the very foundations and government of the state. An important second clause required widowers as well as widows to preserve gifts received through the generosity of a spouse for their children by that spouse. As the sixteenth-century lawyer

3. Antoine Fontanon, *Les Edicts et Ordonnances des Rois de France Depuis Lovys VI dit Le Gros iusques a Present: Avec les verifications, modifications, & declarations sur iceux*, 4 vols (Paris, 1611), I, p. 751.

Antoine Fontanon tells us in his commentary on the royal ordinance, the edict of 1560 was subject to numerous 'interpretations'. Some pretended that the edict did not apply to husbands, and there was such a 'diversity of opinions' that the question was hotly disputed.[4]

René Filhol has noticed the intriguing way in which the edict inverted both its Roman models. The first Roman rule, the law on gifts of movable goods and certain types of real property, applied to both men and women under Roman law but the French edict applied it only to women. The Roman law against transferring gifts from a deceased spouse to a new spouse applied only to remarrying women but the 1560 edict adapted this second law to apply to both men and women.[5]

What prompted the French crown to take such measures against the remarrying widow? Some early modern commentators suggested that the extravagance of a rich Parisian widow to her young second husband at the expense of her seven children had triggered the intervention of the state.[6] But was the remarriage of widows a problem in France at this time? From Guy Cabourdin's research on the sixteenth and seventeenth centuries and André Burguière's studies of the eighteenth century, it appears that between roughly one-fifth and one-third of all marriages involved a remarriage. As elsewhere in Europe, widowers actually remarried more frequently and with a

4. Ibid.; two appeal cases were heard by the Parlement de Paris in July 1577: see the comments of advocate Le Maistre on the judgment given in the case three days earlier, Archives nationales (hereafter AN), X/1a/5071, f. 489ʳ. Louet's *Recueil* cites the two cases from 1577, a further case from 1599, and another from 1639: see Georges Louet, *Recueil de Plusieurs Arrets Notables du Parlement de Paris*, 2 vols (Paris, 1742), II, p. 212.

5. See the Code of Justinian on second marriages (*C. de secundis nuptiis*), V, 9, 6, *hac edictali* and V, 9, 3, the law *feminæ quæ*; René Filhol, 'L'application de l'édit des secondes noces en pays coutumier', *Recueil de Mémoires et Travaux Publié par la Société d'Histoire du Droit et des Institutions des Anciens Pays de Droit Écrit* 11 (1974), p. 295. There remains the question of whether the Edict of Second Marriages applied in the south of France where written law or Roman law still held sway. The 1560 edict would have conflicted with the Roman law which included both men and women in the law on second marriages. Some royal edicts such as the inheritance law, the *Edict des Mères* in 1567, were not registered by the Parlement de Toulouse for its jurisdiction in southern France. See the legal commentary of Geraud de Maynard, *La Seconde Partie des Notables et Singulieres Questions du Droict Escrit. Decidees et Iugees Par Arrests Memorables de la Cour Souveraine du Parlement de Tholose* (Paris, 1606), pp. 488–90.

6. *Monsieur de Thou's History*, p. 526; Louet, *Recueil*, II, p. 637 n. 8: 'Sur quoi a été tracé l'Edit des secondes nôces, selon l'opinion de Monsieur Cujas'; Barbara Diefendorf, *Paris City Councillors in the Sixteenth Century: The Politics of Patrimony* (Princeton, 1982), p. 289; Filhol, 'L'application', p. 295.

shorter delay than their female counterparts. Burguière estimates that approximately three out of five remarrying partners were widowers and about one in two widowers remarried, whereas only about one in five widows remarried. The likelihood that a widow might remarry was dependent on her age at the death of her spouse and may also have been susceptible to the attitudes of the church and the community.[7] The church, for example, refused to bless second marriages with a widow bride although it would bless widowers marrying for a second or third time. Burguière has concluded that this may have contributed to the village charivari and popular attitudes against the remarrying widow.[8] It is perhaps not so surprising, therefore, that the state introduced a law aimed at the remarrying widow, but early modern French attitudes to remarriage among widows and widowers are certainly worth further investigation.

In an excellent pioneering study on widowhood and remarriage in sixteenth-century France, Barbara Diefendorf studied marriage contracts of the Châtelet in Paris to determine whether, as the Edict of Second Marriages feared, widows did disadvantage their heirs when they married for a second or third time. When Diefendorf compared Parisian marriage contracts of widows with those of first-time wives, she found that almost one-third of widows' contracts were disadvantageous to the existing heirs, whereas no first wife made a donation to a husband which might disadvantage lineal relations. On the other hand, in only five out of 58 remarriage contracts did the husband give the widow bride properties that should have gone to his heirs. It appears from this small sample that the heirs of widows did have some reason to fear their mothers' remarriages.[9] However, Diefendorf detected a change in the patterns of remarriage after the introduction of the edict. The proportion of widows' marriage contracts signed and negotiated in the

7. André Burguière, 'Réticences théoriques et intégration pratique du remariage dans la France d'Ancien Régime – dix-septième–dix-huitième siècles', in J. Dupâquier *et al.*, eds, *Marriage and Remarriage in Populations of the Past* (London, 1981), p. 42; Guy Cabourdin, 'Le remariage en France sous l'Ancien Regime (seizième–dix-huitième siècles)', in Dupâquier *et al.*, *Marriage*, pp. 278, 282.

8. Burguière, 'Réticences', p. 45; Martine Segalen, 'Mentalité populaire et remariage en Europe occidentale', in Dupâquier *et al.*, *Marriage*, p. 74. On the charivari and remarriage, see A. Burguière, 'The charivari and religious repression in France during the Ancien Regime', in R. Wheaton and T. Hareven, eds, *Family and Sexuality in French History* (Philadelphia, 1980), pp. 84–110.

9. Barbara Diefendorf, 'Widowhood and remarriage in sixteenth-century Paris', *Journal of Family History* 7 (1982), p. 392. Of the 58 Châtelet contracts involving the remarriage of a widow, eighteen contracts were disadvantageous to the legitimate heirs.

presence and 'with the counsel of relatives' jumped from approximately one-third prior to 1560 to two-thirds after the restrictive legislation came into effect.[10]

To put this 1560 edict in context it is helpful to recall that it was one of a series of restrictive edicts on the family, which Sarah Hanley has argued stretched from 1556 to 1639.[11] Other measures included the 1556 edict against clandestine marriage and the 1567 *Edict des Mères* which prevented mothers from inheriting from their children. In sixteenth-century France, when a woman married she became a legal minor under her husband's control and the husband managed the couple's marital community of goods, although he could not alienate his wife's lineage property without her consent. A woman only gained legal independence when she reached 25 as a single woman or when her husband died: in these two legal states she could control her financial affairs, sign contracts, dispose of her property or seek justice in a civil lawsuit.[12] A son usually gained legal independence from his parents when he married or when he reached the age of majority. In practice, however, many first- and second-time brides and grooms would have lost at least one parent and have been guided by the counsel of a widowed mother or father. In the absence of both parents, and sometimes in the absence of a father, a paternal or maternal uncle or older brother would act as guardian or supplement the mother's role by acting as 'substitute tutor'. Some French noble women, for example, found to their detriment that a brother might be willing to marry them off cheaply to a *roturier* or non-noble husband and, because a wife shared the status of her husband, these women lost their nobility.[13]

10. Ibid., p. 393. In the period 1540–60, twelve out of 23 contracts were signed in presence of witnesses. From 1570 to 1580, eighteen out of 25 contracts were signed in presence of witnesses.

11. Sarah Hanley, 'Engendering the state: family formation and state building in early modern France', *French Historical Studies* 16 (1989), pp. 4–27. She has subsequently altered her argument to suggest that the process of state-building coincided with a process of family formation: Sarah Hanley, 'The monarchic state in early modern France: marital regime government and male right', in Adrianna Bakos, ed., *Politics, Ideology, and the Law in Early Modern Europe* (Rochester, NY, 1994), p. 112 n. 14.

12. The Ordinance of Blois 1579 introduced a new law stating that widows under 25 would also be considered minors who needed to seek parental consent before remarriage, a point of law reiterated in 1639: see no. 327, art. 2 in F.A. Isambert, *Recueil Général des Anciennes Lois Françaises depuis l'an 420 jusqu'à la Révolution de 1789*, 29 vols (Paris, 1822–33, facsimile edn 1966), XVI, p. 520.

13. See Gayle Brunelle, 'Dangerous liaisons: *mésalliance* and early modern French noblewomen', *French Historical Studies* 19 (1995), pp. 75–103.

The 'widow' and 'widower' in sixteenth-century writing

The edict was concerned with inheritance and family property, but its language and focus reveal moral issues, such as the temptation to remarry, which resurface as common themes in sixteenth-century French literature. The topic of widowhood can be found across the genres of printed satires, dialogues, paradoxes, discourses and even private letters and *mémoires*. Most of the satires and prescriptive literature tend to come from male pens and depict moral conventions, stereotypes and caricatures. The lusty widow was a favourite target. She personified the concern expressed in the Edict of Second Marriages: that the widow was ready to be consumed by a new passion and would forget her responsibilities to her children and her duty of fidelity to her late husband.[14]

On the other hand, plays and satires also parodied the male – the late husband, the widower and the new lover. What could a dying husband expect for his reputation and the reputation of his household after his death? Who was the new husband who wooed or, in the words of the edict, 'solicited' the widow? What could a second husband expect when he married a widow? Upon widowhood the sixteenth-century woman emerged from legal tutelage to enter a time of legal autonomy. Moralists and legislators worried that she would enter a time of sexual freedom as well. If by some miracle a husband hadn't been cuckolded during his lifetime, wrote one anonymous satirist in the sixteenth century, his widow would surely be encouraged to roam once set free by his death: 'Et bien souvent, de liberté esmue / mort son mary, femme le cul remue'; that is, stirred up by the liberty of widowhood, a wife shakes her ass! While a widow lived, she would continue to spread 'misery' for her husband and 'dishonour' his name after his death.[15]

In his essay 'On three good wives', Montaigne celebrates the constancy and fidelity of wives such as Paulina who, in Roman times, committed suicide or attempted to die with their husbands. He contrasts these Roman examples with the false mourning and hypocrisy

14. Pieter Heyns, *Le Miroir des Vefves: Tragedie Sacrée d'Holoferne & Judith Representant, Parmi les Troubles de ce Monde, la Pieté d'une Vraye Vefve, & Curiosité d'une Follastre* (Amsterdam, 1596) contrasts the lusty 'worldly widow' who wants to meet 'young lovers' with the pious Judith.

15. *La Louënge des Femmes, Invention extraite du Commentaire de Pantagruel, sus L'Androgyne de Platon* (Lyon, 1551, facsimile edn, Ruth Calder, ed., 1967), pp. 25–6 or sigs b 5^r–b 5^v.

of widows in the 1580s: 'Moreover, take no notice of those moist eyes and that pitiful voice: but do note the way they carry themselves and the colour of those plump cheeks beneath their veils.'[16] Widowhood, Montaigne implied, was a welcome prospect for women. The same idea of liberation through widowhood could also be found in literature about marriage, men and husbands. In some sixteenth-century satires and paradoxes the death of a wife was a welcome prospect. Whatever type of wife a man chose he could be certain that the happiest man is the bachelor 'who lives and dies without a wife'. A husband, meanwhile, could expect only two happy days in marriage – his wedding night and the day he put his wife 'in the grave'.[17] These ideas were perhaps most boldly phrased in Charles Estienne's 1553 paradox: 'Against the widower who laments the death of his wife. Declamation that a dead wife is a useful thing to man.'[18]

And what of the widower or unsuspecting bachelor who married a widow? In her study of popular attitudes to remarriage, Martine Segalen suggests that the widower had learned the importance of a wife to his household so that in the popular imagination and according to proverbial sayings an experienced husband would be likely to treat a second wife better than his first. '"La première épousée est la servante, la seconde la maîtresse" (Bordelais), "La première a les pleurs, la seconde les fleurs" (Provence).'[19] But the portrayal of the widow in most print literature was not so flattering: she would be a 'maîtresse', a bossy widow who ruled the roost. In a scene from a late sixteenth-century play a married man warns his bachelor brother not to marry and describes the specific inconveniences of marriage to a widow. 'Don't you know, poor man, the torment spread by wives? This widow for the slightest displeasure you might cause her, will scold you and say my other husband never did such a thing. He never contradicted me, and he would have been very sorry to have displeased or offended me.'[20]

16. Michel de Montaigne, 'On three good wives', in *The Complete Essays* (1588; Eng. trans. Harmondsworth, 1991), bk II, ch. 35, p. 843.

17. *Louënge*, pp. 42 and 45.

18. Charles Estienne, *Paradoxes ce sont propos contre la commune opinion: debats, en forme de declamations forenses: pour exerciter les ieunes advocats en causes difficiles* (Poitiers, 1553), pp. 144–54. These paradoxes were meant to be exercises for young lawyers to practise arguments against the common opinion.

19. Segalen, 'Mentalité', p. 74: 'The first wife is the servant, the second the mistress' (Bordelais); 'The first wife has tears, the second flowers' (Provence).

20. Pierre de Larivey, *La Vefue Seconde Comédie*, in *Les Six Premières Comédies Facétieuses* (Rouen, 1601), pp. 117 and 120. Gratien Dupont, a *Querelle des femmes* writer, told the potential husband of a widow that 'even if you are an angel and her previous husband the devil himself', the second husband could only expect a series of reproaches by a remarried wife, in Gratien Dupont, *Controverses des sexes masculin et*

Contre le ſexe Femenin. 175
De Ialouſies, de peines & tourmens
De grans deſpences, & de gros couſtemens
De tant de maulx, qui les uouldroit compter
Que fort faſcheux, ſeroit les racompter.

De prendre femme veufue.

QVi ueufue prend, ſe fait quaſi infame
De droit eſt dit, ſe me ſemble bigame
Le priuiliege, il pert de la coronne
Que de mourir, garde mainte perſonne
Et maintes autres, fort belles choſes pert
Ainſi que plus, clerement uous appert
En ce beau tiltre, des bigames uous ditz
Ou ſont eſcriptz, maintz treſexcellens ditz.
Et dauantage, qui quen ſoye marry

FIG. 1 *De prendre femme veufue*, 'On taking a widow as a wife'. Gratien Dupont, *Controverses des sexes masculin et feminin* (1537), © Bodleian Library, University of Oxford, 8°C.91 Art. Seld., fo. 175r.

feminin (Paris, 1541), ff. 148v–149r. Nicholas de Cholières' dialogue voices the same complaints and worse ones such as husband-beating in 'De l'inegalité de l'aage des mariez. Si un vielard doit prendre une jeune fille, ou une vieille chercher un jeune homme', *Les Matinées* [1585] in E. Tricotel, ed., *Œuvres de Seigneur de Cholières*, 2 vols (Geneva, 1969), I, pp. 272–3.

To marry the widow, a suitor had to woo her and it was precisely this 'solicitation' of the widow by potential husbands that worried the legislators of the 1560 edict. Would the temptation lead her to forget her children and late husband? Pierre de Larivey's 1579 comedy *The Widow,* adapted from an Italian play, focuses on this 'solicitation' of a chaste widow by two suitors. The widow remains faithful to her husband's memory after more than fifteen years, and it is her good reputation and her well-governed household which make her a target for 'solicitation' by an old bachelor and a widower. Although the widow is comfortably off, with a servant and a good marriage arrangement for her daughter, both suitors seek her for her 'person' and not, as stereotypes suggested and the edict feared, for her riches. She is vigorously sought after. An acquaintance tells the old bachelor he will have a struggle to win her as his wife: 'She has been asked to marry several times by many gallant men, but they have always been refused.'[21] Like the bachelor, his rival the widower employs an agent – a priest – to persuade the widow Clemence to remarry. He tells the priest that since the death of his first wife he has had no desire to remarry and this widow alone has 'warmed his soul and made him lusty again'.[22] The widow, worried about the visitors to her house, explains to the priest that the woman who lives withdrawn from the world 'sets tongues wagging' and can't allow the 'slightest cause for suspicion'. The priest proposes a remedy. 'A husband', he tells the widow, 'is a better guardian of your honour, than the walls of a house.' 'Follow my advice,' he counsels her, 'after such a long widowhood you have already shown your honour to everyone.' When the widow protests that she likes her solitude, the priest insists that it is impossible for her to be content because 'widowhood is a continual and hopeless war' against the desire to remarry, although she can honourably deliver herself from the dangers to her reputation by taking a new husband. She replies that time and vigilance have overcome these dangers and, instead of consoling her, his advice grieves her and opens the wounds caused by her husband's death. The priest, chastened and almost moved to tears by her speech, scurries off to tell her suitor of 'this virtuous woman, I would to God that all widows were like her'.[23]

21. Larivey, *La Vefue*, pp. 123–4. 22. Ibid., pp. 109 and 141.

23. Ibid., pp. 141–3. It turns out that 'widow' and 'widower' were in fact not widowed at all, but married to each other. They had lost contact after a shipwreck, each believing the other to be dead.

Larivey presents a range of characterizations from the bossy widow to foolish old men in love, and the contemporary expectation that widows would prefer remarriage to solitude. But his portrait of the virtuous widow faithful to her late husband hints at the ideal that real widows espoused in their private writing. Widows such as Philberte de Feurs, Gabrielle de Coignard and Marie Le Gendre all expressed grief, distress, constancy, fidelity and the loneliness of widowhood, in ways reminiscent of the ideal widow of Larivey's play.[24] Sixteenth-century attitudes to the situation of the widow reveal numerous tensions and contradictions – for some, especially satirists and moralists, widowhood was a liberation, while prescriptive literature and private writing on the experience of bereavement stressed fidelity to the memory of a first husband and the need to rebuff solicitations to remarry. Some commentators could see both sides of the coin. While Montaigne complained that '[i]n our century wives usually reserve their displays of duty and vehement love for when they have lost their husbands', in praising the constancy of a particular widow he reiterated the concerns of the 1560 edict:

> Anyone who knows how young you were when your husband Monsieur d'Estissac left you a widow; the proposals which have been made to you by such great and honourable men (as many as to any lady of your condition in France); the constancy & firmness of your purpose with which you have for so many years and through so many difficulties, carried the weight of responsibility for your children's affairs . . . will readily agree with me that we have not one single example of maternal love today more striking than your own.[25]

While the widow's dilemma of fidelity to her late husband or remarriage to a new one may have been familiar to a sixteenth-century reader, we know less about the suitors, the many 'great and honourable' bachelors and widowers trying to tempt widows into remarriage. The Huguenot Charlotte Arbaleste's account of her widowhood written for the son of her second marriage gives us a glimpse of the courtship of a widow. A bride at seventeen, two years later she was a widow and the mother of an infant daughter. Her first husband Jehan de Pas 'gave up his soul to God' in May 1569

24. Philberte de Feurs, 'Soupirs de viduité' in Rigoley de Juvigny, ed., *Les Bibliothèques françoises de La Croix du Maine et de Du Verdier*, 6 vols (Paris, 1772–73), V, pp. 195–6 or sig. BB ij^{r}; Marie Le Gendre, 'Stances à M. de Rivery' and 'Stances à luy-mesme' in the forthcoming edition by Colette Winn (Champion).

25. Montaigne, 'On three good wives', bk II, ch. 35, p. 843 and 'On the affection of fathers for their children', bk II, ch. 8, p. 433.

'to the great regret of honest men who knew him' and left her with 'very happy memories' of him. 'I was then 19 years old . . . away from my native land and much grieved.'[26] Several years later a bachelor suitor, 'Monsieur du Plessis', and his two brothers began to pay her daily visits and she enjoyed their 'honest conversation'. 'Nevertheless, having lived alone for the five years of my widowhood, and wishing to continue this way of life, I deliberately sounded his intentions by remarking how strange I thought it for those in the war to think of marriage during such calamitous times.'[27] Du Plessis-Mornay's thoughts seemed 'far away from marriage' so she began to enjoy his visits, and took great pleasure in her solitude and in the study of painting and arithmetic. Called away on business, du Plessis-Mornay wrote to her in his absence, and on his return spent two to three hours a day with her over a period of about eight months. She began to worry about this 'familiarity' and planned a voyage of her own to lessen the strength of the friendship, when du Plessis-Mornay proposed to her. She tells her son she felt honoured by his father's proposal but that she could not respond without knowing the wishes of his family. The couple sought the consent of both their families and she reports that they also asked the advice of the 'relations of her late husband', so that it was June 1575 before she felt able to accept his offer of marriage.[28] Aged 25 and a widow for six years, Charlotte could legally contract a marriage on her own without consulting her relatives but she is careful to point out to her son the level of family consultation in her remarriage to his father.

A widow such as Charlotte Arbaleste knew the prescriptive codes and social expectations she had to negotiate in her widowhood and remarriage. As a widow she enjoyed her solitude and worried about her suitor's 'solicitations', but in the preparations for her remarriage she prudently set out to preserve her good reputation and the honour of her family, her first husband's family and her new husband's family. Her concern echoes the impulse behind the edict that the conflict between widowhood and remarriage was not the widow's alone. For his part, Philippe du Plessis-Mornay had ventured to marry a widow despite legal restrictions and satirical warnings and the couple went on to enjoy a long and happy marriage. When

26. Charlotte Arbaleste, *Mémoires de Madame de Mornay*, 2 vols (Paris, 1868–69), I, p. 58; Charlotte Arbaleste, *A Huguenot Family in the Sixteenth Century*, trans. Lucy Crump (London, 1926), p. 120. My translation.

27. Arbaleste, *Mémoires*, I, p. 83; Arbaleste, *A Huguenot Family*, pp. 140–1.

28. Arbaleste, *A Huguenot Family*, pp. 143–4.

Charlotte died after more than 30 years as his wife, du Plessis-Mornay wrote on several occasions of his 'affliction'. He told a friend that he tried to swallow his bitterness as much as he could by seeking to 'adoulcir' or sweeten his thoughts in God. In another letter he wrote that while the loss of his only son made him scream, the death of his wife left him speechless – 'm'a osté la voix' – and he was merely able to 'sigh' and submit to God's will.[29] He remained a widower until his death.

To judge by the du Plessis-Mornay/Arbaleste marriage the edict was doing its work. But not all matches were so considered. Although at first glance it would seem that women bore the brunt of the Edict of Second Marriages by having their actions restricted, men too sometimes found themselves caught in the net of increasingly interventionist state legislation on family matters. For, as we have seen, widowers were far more likely than widows to remarry. Because the remarriages of both widows and widowers affected family fortunes and patterns of inheritance it was perhaps predictable that about fifteen years after its introduction the 1560 royal ordinance on 'second weddings' inspired a flurry of court cases disputing whether the edict applied to widowers or husbands as well as widows. And here we come to the particular case, an appeal to the Parlement de Paris, whose decision changed the law.

The widow and widower in the courtroom

In 1568 François Chabot's first wife died after the couple had had at least four surviving children together and seen two of them marry. In her last will and testament Chabot's wife, apparently in the belief her husband would not remarry because he was about 60 years old, had given him her movable goods, her acquired property and a third of her lineage property. After about a year of widowhood and on the last day of 1569, Chabot, Sieur de Pimpelinière, signed a marriage contract with Catherine Viault, a widow with four children of her own. It was a 'second wedding' for both. Chabot died in 1574 after five years of marriage. Within months his children, led by his eldest son, an official or *lieutenant particulier* in the court of justice of Niort, faced their stepmother in the local court over

29. Philippe du Plessis-Mornay, *Mémoires et Correspondance*, 12 vols (Paris, 1824–25), X, pp. 176–7, 181; 'Codicile de Monsieur du Plessis', in Joachim Ambert, *DuPlessis Mornay ou Études Historiques et Politiques sur la Situation de la France de 1549 à 1623* (Paris, 1848), p. 533.

the gifts their father had given to her during his second marriage.[30] The *sénéchal* of the Poitou jurisdiction, or his lieutenant in the small town of Niort, decided that the restrictive 1560 edict applied equally to widows and widowers. The verdict allowed the second wife some of the disputed inheritance, but ruled that the Edict of Second Marriages entitled her to no more than the amount inherited by each child of the first marriage bed.[31] Both the stepmother and her opponents in the case – the widower's children – appealed against the Poitou verdict to the highest sovereign court in France, the Parlement de Paris, which heard the appeal in July 1577. The First President of the Parlement, Christophe de Thou, presided. The historian and lawyer Estienne Pasquier pleaded on behalf of the widow. Jean Le Maistre, from a dynasty of *Parlementaire* advocates, represented her second husband's children.[32] This landmark case and verdict, reported and reprinted in numerous law books of ordinances, famous cases and 'notable decisions' from the sixteenth into the eighteenth century, clarified the application of the Edict of Second Marriages to men and to women 'convolant en secondes noces'.[33] If the law included men as well as women, then the edict applied to the gifts a remarrying widower gave to his second wife in addition to, as the law explicitly stated, the gifts a widow might offer her second husband. The edict explicitly prevented a widowed spouse of either sex from giving to a new partner any wealth or gifts received from the first spouse. But only widows were barred from giving other movable goods, acquired property and lineage property to a new husband. The case was to decide whether widowers too must obey that rule.

Le Maistre and Pasquier argued the case on several complex legal grounds: on customary law, on the adaptation of a Roman law

30. By the time of the case in 1575, only two of the Chabot children were still living. But the deceased children had left grandchildren with an interest in the disputed inheritance: see AN, X/1a/5071, f. 476^r.

31. AN, X/1a/5071, f. 470^v; Jean Chenu, *Cent Notables et Singulieres Questions de Droict, Decidées par Arrests Memorables des Cours Souveraines de France* (Paris, 1603), Question 64, pp. 396–7.

32. Another advocate pleaded for the Bourguignon family (a granddaughter of the widower Chabot and his first wife), but his speech is not reported in the Archives nationales records.

33. Chenu, *Cent Notables*, pp. 395–408; Fontanon, *Les Edicts*, I, pp. 751–2; Louet, *Recueil*, II, pp. 211–13; Louis Le Caron, *Responses ov Decisions dv Droict François Confirmées par Arrest des Covrs Sovveraines de ce Royaume et Autres* (Paris, 1605), ff. 78^r–82^r; Louis Le Caron, *Memorables ov Observations dv Droict François Rapporté av Romain Ciuil & Canonic* (Paris, 1603), ff. 91^r–92^r; Pierre Néron, *Recueil d'édits et d'Ordonnances Royaux sur le fait de la Justice et Autres Matières. Augmenté sur l'Édition de P. Néron et E. Girard*, 2 vols (Paris, 1720), I, sig. aiiij^r and II, p. 600.

for contemporary French use, and on the nature and the timing of the gifts exchanged by the widow and widower during their second marriage. In the context of this volume, we shall not dwell on the technical legal arguments but focus on the cultural assumptions and characterizations of widowhood in the lawyers' pleadings before Parlement.[34] As Cicero explains in the *De inventione*, a prosecuting lawyer attempts to discredit the defendant in court by describing the 'circumstances', past actions and the 'attributes of persons', and to do so the orator gathers arguments or proof by means of the 'attributes of persons or of actions'.[35] By examining the 'attributes of persons' put forward by the advocates Pasquier and Le Maistre and by comparing these arguments with the characterizations of widows and widowers found in contemporary literature we can begin to get a sense of early modern perceptions of widowhood both inside and outside the courtroom, and see how closely a lawyer and client followed the 'common opinions' in praise and blame of widows or widowers. Regardless of which arguments actually swayed the judges, it is fascinating to observe how the advocates deployed images of widowhood identical to those found in literature.

Pasquier reviewed the proceedings in the local court in Niort. The widower's children had claimed that although the Edict of Second Marriages referred only to women – 'ne parle que des femmes' – the edict was written for the 'preservation of the rights of children and as such applies both to fathers and mothers'.[36] Pasquier countered that before the introduction of the edict, husbands and wives entering second marriages could give 'whatever they pleased' to each other in their marriage contracts and in their wills. The new law 'explicitly prohibited a widow from giving to her new husband' *more* than the smallest portion the mother intended to give to any one child. 'Consequently', Pasquier told the court, the law permitted a husband to give 'whatever he liked to his future wife'. He argued that it was 'not necessary to extend the law from woman to man' because of the 'great difference of reason' or judgment between the two sexes. On behalf of the widow, Pasquier argued that woman's nature had always been considered to be more 'imbecile' than man's, and one of the contemporary reports of the

34. I shall be discussing legal arguments about customary law and the French adaptations of Roman law in a forthcoming book, *Renaissance Man and Woman: Morals and Government in French Print*.

35. Cicero, *De inventione*, trans. H.M. Hubbell (London, 1949), II.X.32–4 and I.XXIV.34.

36. AN, X/1a/5071, f. 479r; Chenu, *Cent Notables*, pp. 396–7.

case highlights this point by printing 'On the imbecility of women' in the margin.[37] This reputation for weakness meant that the Romans could place women 'in perpetual tutelage', something they 'never did to men'. Pasquier reminded the court that in Rome and ancient Gaul, husbands even had the power of life and death over their wives. The Bible, he said, 'teaches us that man commands woman'. Moreover, he indicated that 'almost all French laws favour the male'. Although the Romans sometimes 'put men and women on an equal footing', the male was never included or understood to be covered by the feminine laws. Therefore, Pasquier contended, it would be a 'ridiculous thing' that in France, where 'our laws are all masculine and not feminine', one would now 'extend this edict to males' despite the fact that the relevant passage of the law never mentions men.[38]

Pasquier stressed how at all times his client's second husband, François Chabot, Sieur de la Pimpelinière, had been careful to 'advance' his children, whether with gifts of land or through good and advantageous marriages. But, according to Pasquier, after his first wife died in 1568 Chabot began to push for a marriage with Catherine Viault for the 'benefit of his children'. Moreover, when he began to seek her hand in marriage Viault was 'more than 25 years old' and had no thought or 'desire to remarry'.[39] But because she was 'rich' and 'opulent in both movable and immovable goods' and had at least 15,000 or 16,000 livres, Chabot enticed her into marriage. Chabot even made use of the authority of the governor of the region of Poitou, and through this agent Chabot made such 'solicitations' that the widow was 'constrained' to 'change her mind' and marry him.[40] Pasquier stressed the general idea that men 'solicit' women to marry, exactly as, he claimed, the widower Chabot and his various agents assiduously 'solicited' the widow Viault – though Chabot seems to have had more powerful allies than his fictional counterparts in Larivey's play *The Widow*. In his speech before Parlement, Pasquier repeated the words of the edict to the effect that widows are 'often enticed and solicited to remarry' without realizing that they are sought after more for their wealth than their persons.[41] He reminded the court that the king introduced the edict to 'bridle' widows 'caught up in a violent and passionate

37. Chenu, *Cent Notables*, p. 399.
38. AN, X/1a/5071, f. 480^r; Chenu, *Cent Notables*, pp. 398–9.
39. AN, X/1a/5071, ff. 476^v–477^r.
40. Ibid., f. 477^r.
41. Chenu, *Cent Notables*, pp. 399–400.

new love' who, in their haste to remarry, make gifts to the new lovers in the marriage contract.[42]

Knowing that her future second husband had provided well for his own children by giving them portions of his goods, Viault as a 'good mother' did the same for her children the day before her second wedding. Pasquier stressed that despite these gifts to her children, the widow brought some 25,000 livres to Chabot in silver, plate and goods and, in stressing her contribution to the marital community, he noted that the couple made several 'purchases' or *acquests* together. Two references in Pasquier's speech indicate that the couple or at least Viault may have been aware of the dispute over inheritance which lay ahead. In acknowledging a mutual gift the couple made to each other in accordance with regional customary laws, he noted that they were careful 'not to defraud the children'. Secondly, he described the property arrangements the couple made so that the 'heirs could not trouble their stepmother Viault'.[43] Apart from these misgivings about the widow's situation, Pasquier implied that the law was in place to protect the children of the rich widow Viault from the grasping hands of Chabot who had solicited her in marriage. Like the 'virtuous widow' of Larivey's play and Charlotte Arbaleste's representation of herself in her memoirs for her son, Pasquier's pleadings characterized the widow Viault in ideal terms, stressing the length of her widowhood and her lack of desire to remarry.

The lawyer Le Maistre, who represented the widower's adult children and grandchildren, not surprisingly told the court a very different story and stressed the vices or 'attributes of persons' opposite to the virtues Pasquier had sketched for the widow Viault.[44] Instead of the 'good mother' of Pasquier's portrayal, a widow reluctant to marry and forced into remarriage by Chabot and his agents, Le Maistre portrayed Viault as a 'crafty and fraudulent stepmother', in fact the craftiest stepmother 'that ever was', ready to employ 'artifices' or deceit and well able to 'extract' a lion's share of her second husband's goods even to the point of depriving his children of their proper inheritance. Le Maistre suggested that after the death of

42. Ibid., p. 400. 43. AN, X/1a/5071, f. 477^{v}.

44. Le Maistre summarized Pasquier's pleading in three points: (1) that the Edict of 1560 only applied to gifts made by widows to their husbands; (2) that if the edict applied to men and women it could not apply in this case, because of the type of property in dispute; (3) the edict could not apply in this case because of the timing of the gifts, for example, that a 'donation mutuel' or mutual gift made during the marriage was not subject to the edict.

Chabot's first wife, Pasquier's client began to inform herself of the goods in Chabot's household. Through 'plots and conspiracies' she made the widower Chabot 'yield to her' and 'promise to marry her'. As a widow with four children, Viault sought this remarriage to benefit herself and her children – to the 'ruin' of her stepchildren.[45] Le Maistre noted the beneficial terms the widow arranged for the marriage contract, including her gift of property to her children the day before the contract was signed in December 1569, which ensured this wealth did not enter the marital community of goods.

From the opening words of his pleading before the court, Le Maistre's rhetoric characterized the 'bossy widow' familiar from vernacular literature. The widow Viault he portrayed to the court was not a widow in need of protection from the edict or from eager suitors, but the type of wife that generations of potential husbands had been warned about in moralist literature and in the debate on the nature of women known as the *Querelle des femmes*. Le Maistre directed a whole series of accusations against the widow and her treatment of her second husband, all with the underlying message that 'she made him do it', beginning by forcing him into marriage. '[I]f she began this marriage much to the profit of herself and her children, she accomplished more during the marriage and continued until the death of the deceased.' According to Le Maistre, she 'defrauded' her stepchildren and her husband by repeatedly forcing him to sell some of his lineage and personal property in order to 'convert' it into a type of property that he would be able to dispose of in her favour.[46] In order to 'make' property 'enter into the [marital] community' of goods, Viault 'made him sell' certain lands and mills acquired during his first marriage. To further 'deceive her stepchildren', 'she made him declare' his intentions about money and goods.

Le Maistre suggested that Chabot was aware of the 'wrong he was committing to his children' so he ensured that a certain amount of cash proceeding from a sale would be granted to them, and not enter the community of goods. Le Maistre argued that this enrichment of the marital community was not enough for the widow – 'lappellante non contante de cela' – who pushed for another gift in December 1571 after two years of marriage. This time 'she made the deceased give her' all his movable goods, and the use of his

45. AN, X/1a/5071, f. 483^{v}.

46. Le Maistre comes back to this point at the end of his speech: ibid., f. 488^{r-v}.

'acquests', and forced him to renege on his declaration to the children. Later, when he was sick with his terminal illness, 'she made him draw up a contract' to confirm all the donations or gifts and as he approached death he made a division of their joint purchases.[47] On the subject of Viault's contribution to the marital community, which Pasquier had stressed made her a target as a 'rich and opulent' widow, Le Maistre suggested that to 'give a pretext' to her 'benefits' she made the contract between herself and her husband specify that he had released her from certain financial obligations in 'consideration' of the 'grandz biens' or 'substantial riches' she had brought to the marital community.[48] Le Maistre implied that Viault had forced her husband to acknowledge her contribution, and insinuated that this contractual statement was 'false' because it was well known that she had 'given all her goods to her children' the day before the marriage contract. Finally, Le Maistre alleged that after Chabot's death in 1574, his widow had 'seized' all of the remaining movable and immovable property.

Thus, according to the children's advocate, the widow Viault sought out the widower Chabot, obtained a favourable marriage contract and then continued to control her husband after their wedding vows. Le Maistre's depiction of the domineering widow and her hen-pecked husband could have been found in Gratien Dupont's *Controversies of the masculine and feminine sexes*, the *Praise of women*, Charles Estienne's paradox and countless other examples of sixteenth-century literature. Warnings to the groom *before* the wedding were a common source of humour. The bachelor had to worry about taking a rich wife, a poor wife, a beautiful wife, an ugly wife or a widow, because each one posed her particular inconvenience. But once he married, any accusations about the behaviour of a wife implied that the husband could not govern her and could not govern his own household.

There is a certain irony in this extraordinary case. Quite remarkably both advocates represented their clients by undermining them. To advance the cause of the widow Viault, Pasquier argued the incapacity of her sex, while salvaging her role as a 'good mother'. But the children's advocate made allegations about the terms of the second marriage which were ruinous to the reputation of their father as a husband and head of household. As we have seen, popular wisdom suggested that the second wife was the 'mistress' or 'dame' rather than the servant and these proverbs gave the impression that

47. Ibid., ff. 484^r–485^r. 48. Ibid., f. 485^r.

the second wife found a more compliant husband than the first. But Le Maistre had to make such characterizations believable to the courtroom and to the presiding judges.

To understand why Le Maistre pleaded as he did, we must consider what beliefs the magistrates may have held or encountered about 'man' and his roles as bachelor, husband, father and widower. Challenges to the dignity of man or the superiority of man were not uncommon in Renaissance literature. The weakness of man, his pride and his vices of gluttony, sloth, ambition and sensuality were commonplace targets of satirical and moral literature, backed by biblical stories. God had made Adam from the dust of the earth to remind man of his vile origins. In the *Querelle des femmes,* the defenders of women praised those females who had played a role in the downfall of great and powerful but vicious men. When Holofernes tried to corrupt the chaste widow Judith, she saved her virtue and released a nation from tyranny by beheading him with his scimitar. Even Larivey's play *The Widow* highlights the antics of foolish old men chasing after a constant and virtuous widow. Sixteenth-century writers mocked the idea that man was superior to animals because he was the only creature capable of reason. 'I firmly believe that if the philosophers who considered the human condition so great and precious, had known the errors and follies of our age, instead of declaring man alone capable of reason, they would have given him an entirely different definition, or said that most men have nothing but the form and effigy of the reasonable creature.'[49] Jacques Tahureau's mid-sixteenth-century *Dialogues* mock a long list of learned men, including Plato and Aristotle. Montaigne follows this precedent in his *Essays.* He suggests that it would be far too easy to target the folly of the 'ordinary man', so instead he considers a select group, the 'small number of excellent men' who have taken humanity 'to the highest point of wisdom that it can attain'. He finds it ridiculous that such a 'miserable and puny creature' as man, who cannot even claim to be 'master of himself', should be paraded as the 'master and emperor of the Universe'.[50] While it might be commonplace to mock the folly of man in the abstract, it was a more difficult enterprise to question the roles particular men might fill as fathers, husbands or widowers – roles which conferred authority on men.

49. Jacques Tahureau, *Les Dialogues: Non Moins Profitables que Facetieux* [1565] Max Gauna, ed. (Geneva, 1981), p. 15.

50. Montaigne, 'The Apology for Raymond Sebond', bk II, ch. 12, pp. 559, 502. My translations.

When Montaigne was writing the *Essays* in the 1580s, the lawyer Jean Dagoneau published a series of dialogues under the pseudonym of Nicholas de Cholières. In his books, two of which he named *Matinées* and *Après Disnées* after the morning and afternoon sessions of the court of Parlement, Cholières broached many thorny questions of law, such as the problem of second marriages, by presenting both sides of the argument. In Renaissance paradoxes and dialogues each participant argued from opposite sides – *argumentum in utramque partem* – and while no party had a monopoly of the truth, each participant's speech suggested an element of truth. In a similar way, the judicial rhetoric of Le Maistre and Pasquier tended to appeal to 'common opinions' about types of characters in order to discredit opponents or to persuade the judges of the elements of truth in their clients' stories. So we should not be surprised to find that in a Cholières dialogue, the anti-woman speaker suggests that second marriages are very odious to 'Legislators' because of the 'infinity of inconveniences' which evolve from the imperfection and fragility of this sex (women) whose 'incontinence' leads them to cease mourning their first husbands. The defender of women takes the opposite stance and points to the unfairness of blaming the remarriage problem on women alone: 'Ah, don't you reason well? To hear you talk, one would think that only women remarry. How many thousands of men do we find remarrying several times. And I by no means rebuke them for these remarriages, preferring to approve the path permitted by divine law than to subject them to the yoke of a law which would throw them into lechery, adultery or other impieties.' Then the defender of women adds a very interesting point. If second weddings were so outrageous against the duty to honour and virtue, he asks 'why were males not included in the penalties prescribed against second marriages'?[51] This was precisely the question faced by the judges in the case argued by Le Maistre and Pasquier before the Parlement de Paris. Only the first clause of the edict explicitly mentioned widows, 'les femmes veuves', and here Le Maistre turned the tables to show the court that in this case the widower and his children needed the law to protect their property and patrimony from a clever remarrying widow.

While moral and satirical literature warned the groom against marrying a bossy widow, what attributes characterized the remarrying widower? Le Maistre countered Pasquier's description of the

51. Nicholas de Cholières [Jean Dagoneau], *La guerre des masles contre les femelles: representant en trois dialogues les prerogatives et dignitez tant de l'un que de l'autre sexe. Avec les melanges poetiques du sieur de Cholieres* (Paris, 1588), ff. 73^{r}–74^{v} or sigs N^{r}–Nii^{v}.

'weak and imbecile' female sex by pointing out the follies and weaknesses of men. Men, Le Maistre argued, are more susceptible to losing their passions in a new love. The children's advocate considered that Pasquier's speech was rather 'laboured and inflated' in its attempt to demonstrate that the only reason for the 1560 ordinance was the 'infirmity of the female sex' ('l'infirmité du sexe') as if this weakness could not be found in men. While anyone would recognize that 'a man considered in all his liberty could in no way approach the infirmity of a woman', Le Maistre cited St Jerome to assert that the 'passionate man in love' 'loses his liberty', is stripped of his 'virile countenance' and acquires instead a 'female weakness'. 'Experience shows us that more husbands are passionately in love with their wives, than the contrary' so that a second wife acquired far more advantages from her husband than second husbands received from their wives, partly because, as Le Maistre told the courtroom, 'a man would stop at nothing to achieve his ends in love', whereas the woman's 'natural avarice' prevents her from giving too much even if she is in love.[52] Le Maistre seemed to admit the dedication with which men solicited or pursued their objects of desire, even though he argued that in this case it was the widow who forced the widower into marriage. Clearly, men in love could behave just as foolishly as women, and widowers needed the protection of the law just as widows did.

Le Maistre disagreed with Pasquier that the fragility of the female sex was the 'principal' and 'utmost' cause for the ordinance. In his view the principal purpose of the edict was to protect the 'children of the first marriage bed' because of 'the fear' that they might be 'defrauded of their maternal or paternal patrimony'. Le Maistre focused the court's attention on the preamble to the edict which stated that through remarriage the surviving parent deprives the children of all 'succour and aid', and at the very moment when the widowed spouse should perform the duties of both mother and father, the gifts to the new spouse bring about the 'desolation of good families'. Instead of emphasizing the danger posed to the weaker sex, Le Maistre contended that 'it is certain these reasons behind the edict apply more to gifts husbands make to their second wives than gifts offered by wives to their second husbands'. Goods which should have been inherited by the first family were diverted

52. AN, X/1a/5071, f. 486^{r}. One of the contemporary law reports of the case even highlighted the 'L'homme amoureux passionné' argument with a note in the margin: see Chenu, *Cent Notables*, p. 401.

instead to the second wife who 'has no kin relation to her husband's family leaving the paternal family utterly ruined'.[53] Le Maistre remarked that even if the edict mentioned only widows ('les femmes veufves'), the terms husband and wife were 'co-relatifs'; for example, a husband's status or 'personal privilege' is always conferred upon his wife, but not always inherited by his children.[54] Citing Jason among other doctors of law, Le Maistre argued that to apply a law to both husband and wife 'is not to extend the law' but to 'interpret' the law.[55] He suggested that if the edict was not applied to husbands, the most 'unjust situation in the world' might arise: a widower with several children, overcome by love for a new wife, could benefit his second wife and send his children to the local orphanage. 'Is there anything more wicked than that?', he asked the court.

To argue for the weakness and folly of man was a commonplace, which Le Maistre executed with great flourish, but the lawyer's most difficult task was to transfer this folly to a man's role as husband, father and widower. As we have seen, although Pasquier echoed the words of the edict disparaging the weakness of the female sex, he still maintained his client's reputation as a good wife reluctant to remarry and as a 'good mother' who protected her children's inheritance. Attacks on 'man' were as common as those on 'woman', but once 'man' stepped into a role as husband, father or widower this mockery tended to lapse into silence. Astonishingly, the children's advocate was willing to damage the reputation of their dead father by alleging that he could not govern his second wife and that widowers, equally subject to passion, irrationality and weakness, needed to be regulated in remarriage. This widower's folly had carried through from courtship into marriage. To preserve family honour a husband's control over the household could not be questioned, as the presiding judge Christophe De Thou revealed in his summary of the case before he sent it to the Conseil for a verdict.

> The court understands from the speeches in this lawsuit that often in the contracts of second marriages husbands are not as well advised [*avisés*] as their wives. As we see in this case, although both parties

53. A point echoed in one of Nicholas de Cholières' dialogues by one of the interlocutors who asserts that because women are 'easily deceived' they allow themselves to become 'stepmothers' and forget the children of the first marriage bed, so that the goods of the first husband fall into the hands of someone who has 'neither the family name nor the arms of the deceased', see Cholières, *La guerre*, f. 43^{r}.

54. AN, X/1a/5071, f. 486^{r-v}; Chenu, *Cent Notables*, p. 402.

55. AN, X/1a/5071, ff. 486^{v}–487^{r}; Chenu, *Cent Notables*, pp. 403–4.

> had children from the first marriage bed, the remarrying wife gave her movable and immovable goods to her children so that nothing would enter the [marital] community of goods except for the profits of a farm to which she kept the right of use. By contrast the husband, to benefit his wife and to the prejudice of his children from the first marriage bed, gave to his future wife the use of his properties for her lifetime, and sold some of his [personal] property so that if the said husband was deceived or cheated it was because he wanted to be.[56]

De Thou concluded that 'si ledit mary a esté trompé cest quil a voullu estre' – 'if the said husband was deceived or cheated it was because he wanted to be'. As the head of the household the patriarch was expected to control his household, and if he succumbed to the wiles of his wife, then, as the judge implied, he must have done so by choice. Certain anxieties, certain doubts about the authority of the father could not be expressed, and De Thou could not question the husband's command over his household although he seemed to accept that a suitor wooing a wife and negotiating a marriage contract might lose his faculties of reason. Although all parties seemed to agree, as the edict stated, that women in general were irrational and weak, the judgment in this particular case extended that irrationality to men in love, and made it clear that the second wife acted 'advisedly' while her husband had been a fool. The stability of the state was predicated on a model in which a husband and father governed his wife and children and the edict explicitly linked these 'good families' with the strength and foundations of the state. But what happened when this model was breached? The edict should have protected, and was designed to protect, the children of the widow Viault from the grasping hands of Chabot, who 'solicited' her and pressured this rich widow to marry, but in this remarriage the wily widow got the better of her second husband at his children's expense. Her triumph did not last long. In May 1578, the President of the Parlement de Paris announced the verdict that 'for the past and for the future' the restrictions of the Edict of Second Marriages applied 'as much to husbands as to wives entering a second marriage'.[57]

The verdict applied the restrictions, as the Romans had done, to widows and widowers with children from a previous marriage who then embarked upon a second or third marriage. When the legislators of the 1560 edict adapted the Roman law and imposed the restrictions of the first clause on widows only, they did not foresee,

56. AN, X/1a/5071, f. 489^{r-v}. 57. AN, X/1a/1659, f. 289^{r-v}.

or they could not bring themselves to contemplate, that men might 'forget their natural duties to their children' and squander the family inheritance for the love of a new wife. For sixteenth-century contemporaries, the idea of the father governing his household was strong enough to overcome even the most glaring inconsistencies. Yet widowers were more likely to remarry. And in their haste to get to the altar for a second time, they were capable of losing their reason and jeopardizing the family inheritance. But it took eighteen years for the state to admit that widowers might pose more of a threat to family stability than the stereotypical merry widow.

CHAPTER SEVEN

Marrying the experienced widow in early modern England: the male perspective[1]

ELIZABETH FOYSTER

The remarrying widow was a common sight in early modern England. Even though widowers rather than widows were more likely to remarry, and with greater speed, studies of remarriage rates in early modern England show that from the male perspective, widows were popular choices as marriage partners.[2] Vivien Brodsky has calculated that nearly one-third of single men aged 30 to 34 who applied for marriage licences in London from 1598 to 1619 married widows.[3] Although the rate of remarriage gradually declined through the early modern period, Jeremy Boulton estimates that even by 1685 to 1689 in the parish of Stepney, around 30 per cent of all brides had been married before.[4] In rural areas, where marriages were less likely to be interrupted by the premature death of a spouse, remarriage rates were generally lower. Nevertheless, B.A. Holderness's survey of parishes in Yorkshire, Lincolnshire and Norfolk between *c.* 1665 and *c.* 1730 still suggested an aggregate rate of remarriage

1. I would like to thank Keith Bartlett, Alan Dyer, Anthony Fletcher, Margaret Pelling and Ceri Sullivan for their helpful comments on this chapter.

2. See for example, V. Brodsky, 'Widows in late Elizabethan London: remarriage, economic opportunity and family orientations', in L. Bonfield, R.M. Smith and K. Wrightson, eds, *The World We Have Gained: Histories of Population and Social Structure* (Oxford, 1986), p. 122, and J.D. Griffith, 'Economy, family, and remarriage: theory of remarriage and application to preindustrial England', *Journal of Family Issues* 1 (1980), pp. 486–7.

3. Brodsky, 'Widows', p. 130; E.A. Wrigley and R.S. Schofield have estimated that in the mid-sixteenth century about 30% of all marriages were remarriages: *The Population History of England 1541–1871* (Cambridge, 1989), pp. 190, 258–9.

4. J. Boulton, 'London widowhood revisited: the decline of female remarriage in the seventeenth and early eighteenth centuries', *Continuity and Change* 5 (1990), p. 329; Wrigley and Schofield confirm this decline: *The Population History*, p. 351; the reasons for this decline have been debated by Barbara Todd, 'Demographic determinism and female agency: the remarrying widow reconsidered . . . again', *Continuity and Change* 9 (1994), pp. 421–50.

of 11.2 per cent.[5] Despite the relative frequency of these marriages, we still know little about their quality. What were the experiences of these couples who remarried, and how did their relationships differ from those in which both partners were wedding for the first time? What particular difficulties did couples face when one or both partners had been formerly married?

While remarriage was frequent, it was also subject to suspicion and disapproval. Ironically, this criticism of remarriage within early modern culture ran parallel to the negative portrayals of widows who did not remarry, and were likely to be stereotyped and sometimes slandered as whores, bawds or witches.[6] English society was perhaps more tolerant of remarriage than French society as the targets of charivari were rarely remarrying couples.[7] But there is still a wealth of English literary material, ranging from advice books to ballads, plays and medical tracts, which mocks and condemns widows and widowers who remarry. As the ideal of the companionate marriage was gaining momentum in this society, in which Puritan writers of marriage conduct books and the authors of popular fiction concurred that marriages should be made on the basis of mutual affection, the marriages of those wedding for a second or further time were represented as the very opposite of this ideal. Instead of marrying for love, for example, the authors of conduct book literature all assumed that the motivation behind remarriage was either material gain or to satisfy sexual appetite. When it was widely agreed that the key determinant to happy and stable marriage was parity in condition, the stereotypical remarrying couple were portrayed as disparate in wealth and age. Men who married widows were motivated by financial gain and therefore were portrayed as of lesser status than the women they married. 'Let him that is poor and to wealth would acquire, get some rich old widow and grow

5. B.A. Holderness, 'Widows in pre-industrial society: an essay upon their economic functions', in R.M. Smith, ed., *Land, Kinship and Life-Cycle* (Cambridge, 1984), p. 430.

6. For examples of widows slandered as whores see Lambeth Palace Library, Court of Arches (hereafter CA), Case 2987 (case numbers taken from J. Houston, ed., *Index of the Cases in the Records of the Court of Arches in Lambeth Palace Library, 1660–1913* (London, 1972)), (1664), Deposition (hereafter Eee), 1, ff. 287–8; Case 4171, (1668), Eee3, ff. 200–3; for examples of widows being slandered as bawds see Case 5945, (1668), Eee3, ff. 214^{v}–222^{r}; Case 7620, (1669), Eee3, ff. 281^{v}–283^{r}; for widows being accused of witchcraft see A. MacFarlane, *Witchcraft in Tudor and Stuart England* (London, 1970), p. 164, and J.A. Sharpe, 'Witchcraft and women', *Continuity and Change* 6 (1991), pp. 182, 184.

7. E.P. Thompson, *Customs in Common: Studies in Traditional Popular Culture* (New York, 1991), pp. 493–8; Holderness, 'Widows', p. 433; for French examples see N.Z. Davis, *Society and Culture in Early Modern France* (London, 1975), pp. 100, 105–6.

wealthy by her', the playwright Thomas Dekker advised.[8] 'Wherefore did I marry', Fainall jokes in *The Way of the World*, 'but to make lawful prize of a rich widow's wealth'.[9] Widows, on the other hand, were thought to remarry because they were driven by lust and therefore chose men younger than themselves.

While some writers believed that disparity of age was a feature of the remarriages of both men and women, it was generally widows who were the targets of the harshest criticism.[10] Juan Luis Vives, in the early sixteenth century, thought it was widows 'inflamed with vicious lust' who neglected their children's futures by remarrying; Joseph Swetnam thought that no widow, if given the opportunity, could possibly 'forbear [the] carnal act'.[11] Fears that widows too often remarried hastily to the detriment of their children's maintenance and inheritance were expressed throughout this period.[12] The novelist Samuel Richardson could not see that remarriage would bring any benefits to children of the previous match. In 1741 he published a book of letters 'to and for particular friends' which he thought his readers could copy and send as the occasion arose, as well as read to obtain general guidance 'in the common concerns of human life'. Several letters were addressed to widows. The idea of 'a Woman all hoary and grey-goosed over by Time, or who will be soon so', exposing herself 'to the Embraces of a young Fellow' filled Richardson with so much disgust that he thought it 'next to a Degree of Incest'.[13] That widows were typically thought to determine who to remarry only on the basis of their partner's sexual prowess

8. As cited in C. Carlton, 'The widow's tale: male myths and female reality in 16th and 17th century England', *Albion* 10 (1978), p. 118.

9. W. Congreve, *The Way of the World* (London, 1700), Act II, sc. i, lines 180–1.

10. W. Gouge, *Of Domesticall Duties* (London, 1627), p. 110; S. Richardson some one hundred years later condemned both remarrying men and women who were disparate in age: see S. Richardson, *Letters Written To and For Particular Friends* (London, 1741).

11. J.L. Vives, *The Instruction of a Christian Woman* trans. R. Hyrde (London, 1529?), as cited in J.L. Klein, ed., *Daughters, Wives and Widows: Writings by Men about Women and Marriage in England, 1500–1640* (Urbana, Ill., 1992), p. 120; J. Swetnam, *The Arraignment of Lewd, Idle, Froward and Unconstant Women* (London, 1667), as cited in A. Fraser, *The Weaker Vessel: Woman's Lot in Seventeenth-Century England* (London, 1993), p. 99.

12. See for example Vives, *Instruction*, as cited in Klein, *Daughters*, pp. 120–1; Gouge, *Of Domesticall Duties*, pp. 234, 276–7; *Sir Walter Raleigh's Instructions to his Son and to Posterity* (London, 1632), in L.B. Wright, ed., *Advice to a Son: Precepts of Lord Burghley, Sir Walter Raleigh, and Francis Osborne* (Ithaca, NY, 1962), p. 22; M.R. Sommerville, *Sex and Subjection: Attitudes to Women in Early-Modern Society* (London, 1995), p. 120; S. Collins, 'British stepfamily relationships, 1500–1800', *Journal of Family History* 16 (1991), pp. 331–44, has shown that these fears had little basis in reality.

13. Richardson, *Letters*, p. 210.

was reflected in the contemporary proverbs, 'He that woos a maid, must fain lie and flatter, But he that woos a widow, must down with his breeches and at her', and 'He that woos a maid must come seldom in her sight, But he that woos a widow must woo her day and night'.[14]

The speed with which these lusty widows sought remarriage also provoked criticism. The opposite to the virtuous widow which Sir Thomas Overbury portrayed in 1614 was a widow for whom 'the end of her husband begins in tears, and the end of her tears begins in a husband', a reflection which has similarities with another contemporary proverb, 'the rich widow weeps with one eye and casts glances with the other'.[15] Two ballads in Pepys' collection mock widows who marry young bachelors within a month of their husband's death, for 'they cannot live single they'le marry therefore, with any young man though he's never so poor'.[16] The desire of widows to resume sexual relationships could even be portrayed as a medical necessity. At a time when popular medical lore held that both women and men produced the seed which was required for conception, its accumulation within the body was thought to cause illness. Women were believed to suffer from illnesses known as 'greensickness' and 'the frenzy of the womb' if they did not have regular sex.[17] The author of the most widely read advice book on sex in the period, *Aristotle's Masterpiece*, declared that all widows had an urgent desire to remarry since that would avoid greensickness, and Nicholas Culpeper's 1662 *Dictionary for Midwives* held that widows had wombs that were so frenzied by excess seed that they were 'mad for lust, and infinite men'.[18] 'An old woman's appetite is depraved like that of a girl – 'tis the greensickness of a second childhood', remarks Mirabell of the widow Lady Wishfort in *The Way of the World*.[19]

14. As cited in J.A. Sharpe, 'Plebeian marriage in Stuart England: some evidence from popular literature', *Transactions of the Royal Historical Society* 36 (1986), p. 74; G.L. Apperson, *English Proverbs and Proverbial Phrases: A Historical Dictionary* (London, 1929), p. 708.

15. Sir Thomas Overbury, *A Wife* (London, 1614), as cited in N.H. Keeble, ed., *The Cultural Identity of Seventeenth-Century Woman* (London, 1994), p. 254; a later version of Overbury's observations was printed in *The Gentleman's Magazine* 8 (1738), p. 38.

16. 'The Wiving Age' (*c.* 1627), in W.G. Day, ed., *The Pepys Ballads,* 5 vols (Cambridge, 1987), I, p. 384; 'The Cunning Age' (*c.* 1625), in Day, ed., *Pepys,* I, p. 413.

17. P. Crawford, 'The construction and experience of maternity in seventeenth-century England', in V. Fildes, ed., *Women as Mothers in Pre-Industrial England* (London, 1990), pp. 6–7.

18. *Aristotle's Masterpiece: Or, The Secrets of Generation Displayed* (London, 1694), p. 3; N. Culpeper, *Dictionary for Midwives* (London, 1662), as cited in Keeble, *Cultural Identity,* p. 29.

19. Congreve, *The Way of the World,* Act II, sc. i, lines 282–3.

Not only were these matches distasteful, without any regard to 'common Decency', as Richardson put it, but in the minds of contemporaries they bore the seeds of marital disharmony.[20] Marriages where there was an inequality 'between Age and Youth', *Aristotle's Masterpiece* warned, would end in 'Jealousies and Discontents'.[21] These unions were ill-fated because they were ill-matched. Within marriage, a wife was expected to be subordinate to her husband, but William Gouge warned that 'if a rich woman marry a poor man, she will look to be master, and to rule him'.[22] Some one hundred years later, Richardson wondered if a widow who married a man of 'meaner Degree' would be willing or able upon remarriage to relinquish the 'power' which she had held since her former husband's death. Would she 'communicate any part of that Power' to her new husband and give him 'a Right to control' herself and her children?[23]

What were the realities of remarriage? The work of historians such as Brodsky, Boulton and Barbara Todd has revealed that early modern culture provides us with a distorted and exaggerated picture of remarriage. Despite the persistent stereotype of the wealthy widow in popular literature and drama, in fact wealthy widows who considered remarriage were notable because of their rarity. Most gentry widows valued their economic independence too highly to risk remarriage. At the other end of the social scale, those who were very poor, especially women who lived in urban areas and had no rights to land, were viewed by men as an economic burden. Instead widows within the middling sorts were most likely to receive and accept a proposal of marriage.[24] Widows did tend to marry men who were younger than themselves. In Brodsky's study of late Elizabethan London widows were on average 4.5 years older than the men they married.[25] In Boulton's work more than a quarter of remarrying widows in Stepney in the seventeenth and early eighteenth centuries were five years older than their husbands.[26] What

20. Richardson, *Letters*, pp. 207, 210. 21. *Aristotle's Masterpiece*, p. 63.

22. Gouge, *Of Domesticall Duties*, p. 110. 23. Richardson, *Letters*, p. 134.

24. Brodsky, 'Widows', p. 128; Barbara Todd, 'The remarrying widow: a stereotype reconsidered', in Mary Prior, ed., *Women in English Society 1500–1800* (London, 1985), pp. 68–72; A.L. Erickson, *Women and Property in Early Modern England* (London, 1993), pp. 196–7.

25. Brodsky, 'Widows', p. 127.

26. Boulton, 'London widowhood revisited', p. 336; M. Pelling's study of the 1570 Norwich census has revealed greater discrepancies between the ages of the poor who married, but it is not possible to be certain of how many of these marriages were remarriages: 'Old age, poverty, and disability in early modern Norwich: work, remarriage, and other expedients', in M. Pelling and R.M. Smith, eds, *Life, Death, and the Elderly: Historical Perspectives* (London, 1991), pp. 88–90.

these studies have shown is that although remarrying widows did tend to be older than their new partners, the age gap was not as disproportionate as popular culture might lead us to think.

Just as the historian Charles Carlton has shown that there was a male-created mythology about the status of widowhood, so also there were male fictions about remarriage.[27] What function did this literature serve? It is clear from the statistics we have of the numbers of remarriages in the early modern period that the warnings to avoid marrying a widow were largely unheard, although some may have been deterred from marrying a partner who was widely different in age or economic status. While there was a mass of advice on the relative merits and demerits of remarriage, contemporary literature fell silent about how couples who did embark on remarriage should readjust to their new marital roles and duties. Yet a wedding which involved the remarriage of one or both of the partners marked the beginning of a significant change in lifestyle and behaviour. For a widow who was remarrying, it represented the relinquishment of a position of relative freedom and even power over her own affairs, to one of subordination under a new husband. Instead of forming a new household, for one party remarriage could mean moving into a household which had already been established and maintained by a spouse's previous partner. New relationships might have to be formed with stepchildren and their kin. For the remarrying party, these new relationships would need to be balanced with commitments to the children and kin of the former marriage. It is immediately apparent that remarriage could bring with it a complex web of kin relationships which would need to be negotiated, and which in turn could place pressures and tensions upon the marriage. Most importantly, a remarriage represented a union of individuals and their family units which had formerly undergone different experiences or histories which, unless reconciled, could act to set them apart. As we have seen, contemporary advice and fictional literature warned that remarriages were troublesome and likely to be unsatisfactory, but in reality, when these marriages did break down, to what extent was the fact that the relationship had been a remarriage to blame?

Between 1660 and 1700 the Court of Arches heard ninety-two cases of marriage separation in which parties gave 'personal answers' to libels and allegations and/or witnesses were called to give statements known as 'depositions'. Out of these ninety-two cases,

27. Carlton, 'The widow's tale', pp. 118–29.

only twelve were cases where one or both spouses had been married previously. It seems probable that it would have been in the parties' interest to state whether they had been married and widowed before, since if a woman's suit was successful her husband would be ordered to pay alimony, with her inheritance from any previous marriages taken into account in its calculation. So it would appear from this court evidence that marriages which involved remarriage were not particularly prone to breakdown. Only two of the twelve cases were brought on the grounds of adultery: the other ten cases involved accusations of cruelty. Nine cases involved marriage breakdown in which the women had been formerly widowed, three cases where both parties had been widowed. There were no separation cases brought in which the husband alone had previously been a widower. Although their witnesses could be servants, because of the cost of pursuing a case into an appeal court like the Court of Arches, the social status of litigants tended to be middling to upper. Even though the statements of husbands and wives and their witnesses cannot always be taken as literal accounts of married life, what we do gain from them are detailed stories of marriage breakdown, and female accounts of remarriage, which we miss by concentrating on the prescriptive and fictional literature composed largely by men. Adultery and cruelty as the most obvious signs of marital breakdown were common to all stories given in separation suits at this time but, as we shall see, contemporaries attributed quite different causes to broken marriages when they had been remarriages.[28]

Money is a central issue of contention in these marriages. A widow's previous marital experience could make her extra cautious before she consented to embark upon any new match. A man who courted a widow could find his economic status and prospects under intense scrutiny, and his marriage proposals rejected if these did not match up to the widow's expectations.[29] In legal theory, upon remarriage a widow surrendered all the goods she had inherited from her previous husband; by the doctrine of coverture everything

28. For details of marriage separation procedure in this period see M. Ingram, *Church Courts, Sex and Marriage in England, 1570–1640* (Cambridge, 1987), ch. 5, R. Phillips, *Putting Asunder: A History of Divorce in Western Society* (Cambridge, 1988), and L. Stone, *Road to Divorce: England 1530–1987* (Oxford, 1990); for the procedure of the Court of Arches see M.D. Slatter, 'The study of the records of the Court of Arches', *Journal of the Society of Archivists* 1 (1955), pp. 29–31, and Stone, *Road to Divorce*, pp. 33–41.

29. L. Gowing, *Domestic Dangers: Women, Words, and Sex in Early Modern England* (Oxford, 1996), pp. 158–9, 167, 169–71, 173.

she possessed became her new husband's. However, Amy Louise Erickson has concluded that a 'second-time bride was older, perhaps wealthier, and wiser at least in the ways of legal coverture than she had been first time round'.[30] Widows who remarried were roughly twice as likely as maids to make a settlement, by which separate estate was preserved in a woman's name.[31] Widows who remarried 'seldom put their estates out of their own reach', lamented Francis Osborne in 1656, 'perverting so far the course of nature as to make [their new husband] . . . thrash for a pension who ought to command all'.[32] Of making arrangements prior to remarriages which will deprive new husbands, ' 'tis the way of the world, sir, of the widows of the world', explains Mirabell in Congreve's play.[33]

Once marriage had begun, from the male perspective, there was immediate frustration or problems if the widow with some property or estate then refused to give her husband what he believed had been promised at the wedding. Stephen Bolton, a major in the militia, claimed in the adultery suit brought against him in 1667, that before his marriage to Hester a settlement was made in which he was promised two houses his wife had inherited from her previous marriage. But he said that since the marriage Hester had endeavoured to 'obtain the possession and inheritance to herself', so that when he hit upon hard times, he was forced to rent the houses, instead of selling them. In her statement to the court, Hester denied that she had ever made a settlement or deed to her husband which gave him rights to the houses, and accused him of financial incompetence. According to her side of the story, he rented one of the houses without ever telling her, and handled the business so badly that her friends had to intervene to alleviate the situation. Her servant, Mary Shirwin, who had worked for Hester for twenty years, during the lifetime of Hester's first husband and then through her remarriage, told the court how Stephen was given to gambling, drinking and whoring. According to Mary, despite the fact that Hester was 'used to things handsome and decent about her', Stephen failed to provide for his wife, and when he left her in London to flee the plague, Hester was so poor that she was forced to borrow money from friends and even servants.[34]

30. Erickson, *Women and Property*, p. 123. 31. Ibid., pp. 80, 103, 132–5, 149.

32. F. Osborne, *Advice to a Son* (Oxford, 1656), in Wright, ed., *Advice to a Son*, p. 68.

33. Congreve, *The Way of the World*, Act V, sc. i, lines 500–1.

34. CA, Case 1001, (1667), Personal Answer (hereafter Ee), 3, ff. 119^{v}–124^{v}; Eee3, ff. 96^{r}–100^{r}; for ease of comprehension all spellings from the Court of Arches have been modernized.

The marriage between William Culliford and the widow of John Mitchell in 1681 was to follow a similar course. Elizabeth had already been married twice when she married William Culliford and was at pains before the marriage to arrange a settlement which gave her a 'distinct Estate' of houses, goods and chattels to remain for her 'sole benefit', and which her husband was 'not to intermeddle therewith'. But when the marriage fell apart, and Elizabeth successfully sued her husband for separation on grounds of cruelty, William was to dispute the amount he had to pay her in alimony by telling his version of events in the marriage. William, like Stephen Bolton, claimed that his wife made promises on their marriage which never materialized. He said that he should have had £3000 upon marriage with her. According to William what followed, though, was a marriage in which the couple quarrelled over who should pay for lodgings, food and the maintenance of Elizabeth's two daughters from a previous marriage, while she stubbornly refused William access to any of her separate estate.[35]

Even if their wives did allow them to become the managers of the household estate and income, husbands could find themselves criticized if they did not keep their wives in the manner which they had experienced in their former marriage. John Beverley was accused of cruelty by his wife in 1669. Instead of telling the usual tale of beatings and assaults, Catherine Beverley's two female witnesses claimed that John had been cruel because he had not fed or clothed her as she was accustomed under her former husband, described as 'a very rich man' who 'left her a very good estate'. In contrast, her next husband, John Beverley, was 'a Frenchman', used to a 'diet of herbs and other slight eating'. Witnesses claimed that John made no provision for Catherine, who was an Englishwoman accustomed to eating meat and who 'by this diet of herbs' had frequently been forced to go to her neighbour's house to eat meat, where she complained of her 'great hunger'. Her standard of clothing had also declined. Under her previous husband she had been 'a woman of very good quality and fashion', but now her clothes were 'very much worn', and 'very much below her quality and condition'. Both in a consistory court and in the appeal court of the Arches, Catherine was able to pursue a marriage separation case in which she claimed that these sources of deprivation amounted to life-threatening cruelty,

35. CA, Case 2476, (1684), Ee5, ff. 166–176^{r}; for another example of a remarrying widow making a settlement see CA, Case 14, (1671), Eee4, ff. 331, 364–5; for examples earlier in the seventeenth century of remarrying widows and financial disputes leading to marital breakdown see Gowing, *Domestic Dangers*, pp. 214–15, 223–5.

meaning that she could only lead a 'very unquiet life' with her husband. These claims only bore significance if her witnesses compared her former condition of 'good quality and fashion' with her decline in status since remarriage.[36]

Discord in the Charnock marriage during the 1670s was partly blamed on the disparity of wealth between Ellen and John, her second husband. John admitted that he was 'advanced in his Estate and Fortune' by marrying Ellen, a fact that is confirmed by several witnesses. But, according to John, Ellen drew attention to the superior status and wealth that she held before marriage to shame and humiliate him. She told him that if it had not been for her, he would not have had 'a shirt to his back and might have worn a livery', and that his family 'lived upon her'. She also told others that she did not have enough to eat, and that he gave her clothes to his sister. This was a period in which a wife's dress and the quality of hospitality offered to guests directly reflected her husband's status or honour. But Ellen refused to dress appropriately, wearing an old waistcoat or vest, even though, according to a servant, Mary Woolley, she had a chest full of better clothes. John told her that she chose to wear the old clothes to his 'disgrace'. Ellen also bought poor cuts of meat so that the boy who waited at table said that his master 'was often angry at the poorness of the provisions made by his wife'. John Charnock may have increased his wealth by marrying Ellen, but Ellen's behaviour ensured that the wealth he gained would not be matched with an increase in male status, power or authority. According to his version of events, Ellen was determined that in one way or another he would remain indebted to her. Furthermore, no matter how Ellen behaved, neighbourhood opinion was weighted in her favour because of her former economic status. When neighbours learned of the discord in the Charnock household, one of them later told the court that they mostly passed 'their verdict' against John, because of the good estate that Ellen had brought with her in marriage.[37]

The experience which women had gained managing their legal and financial affairs during their widowhood, however short, meant that in men's eyes they could make formidably assertive marriage partners. Within their new marriages widows could unsettle the dynamics of power which had traditionally given men the upper hand. This was not just because some widows were wealthier than

36. CA, Case 842, (1669), Eee3, ff. 544^{v}–547^{r}.
37. CA, Case 1813, (1673), Ee4, ff. 118^{v}–129^{r}; Eee5, ff. 13^{v}–29^{r}.

their husbands, as the case of Ellen and John Charnock has illustrated, or as advice books suggested, but also because, at a time when some were debating John Locke's theories on the nature of the marriage contract, widows who remarried, such as Hester Bolton, Elizabeth Culliford, and Catherine Beverley, were already negotiating their own terms of marriage.[38] They were more likely to establish settlements which allowed them to continue to exercise control over at least some of their inheritance, independent of their new husbands. Furthermore, the expectation held by remarrying widows, their neighbours and servants, that husbands should maintain their wives at a standard established by the previous spouse, predetermined the level of expenditure on diet and clothing which these husbands should devote to their wives. In other words, the freedom of men who married widows to deploy money how they wished was restricted, and the power which traditionally accompanied that freedom, diminished. What is more, it is possible that the experienced widow had more confidence to call her husband's behaviour into question if she believed he was not fulfilling his obligations. The duty of a husband to give 'provident care' for his wife, and to 'keep her in sickness and in health' was an essential of advice literature and of the church wedding service.[39] Just as the contracts between apprentices and masters could be broken if masters did not provide adequate diet and clothing, so also widows could claim in the church courts that deficiencies in care meant they should no longer be tied to their duties of marriage.[40]

While arguments over money and the payment of portions and jointures could follow when men married maids, a further difference of marriages to widows was that there was a higher probability that the father of the bride would have died. Instead of disputes being negotiated and settled with the involvement of others, the onus was on the couple themselves to reach compromise. It may well be significant that *A Viewe of Man's Estate*, a conduct book written specifically for a widow considering remarriage in 1576, was written by the widow's brother and not her father.[41] Indeed, the absence

38. M.L. Shanley, 'Marriage contract and social contract in seventeenth century English political thought', *Western Political Quarterly* 32 (1979), pp. 79–91; C. Pateman, *The Sexual Contract* (Oxford, 1988).

39. See for example F. Dillingham, *Christian Oeconomie, or Household Government* (London, 1609), p. 18; W. Gouge, *Of Domesticall Duties* (London, 1634), pp. 400–10; *The Book of Common Prayer* (1662), 'The Form of Solemnization of Matrimony'.

40. M. Pelling, 'Apprenticeship, health and social cohesion in early modern London', *History Workshop Journal* 37 (1994), pp. 42–3.

41. A. Kingesmill, *A Viewe of Man's Estate* (London, 1576).

of parents upon their daughter's second or further remarriages is apparent in some of the court records. Elizabeth Culliford claimed that the details of her marriage settlement were agreed between her and William 'and their friends'; no parents are mentioned.[42] Although Erickson has found that most suits which contested a widow's separate estate when she remarried were not pursued in the Court of Chancery until after her death, during her lifetime disagreements between a widow and her new husband over goods became centred within the conjugal unit, sometimes with disastrous consequences for the marriage.[43]

It appears that if a woman felt she was being mistreated in her second marriage, the network of friends, kin, children and even servants which she had established in her former marriage could be called upon for help and support.[44] This could be particularly important if a second husband proved violent. On one occasion when Margaret Etheridge was beaten by her husband in the 1620s, her daughter from a former marriage ran to a neighbour 'crying they were undone for her father in law'.[45] Elizabeth Hardwicke's son from her previous marriage, and his wife, were the two witnesses who spoke on her behalf when she brought a cruelty suit against her second husband in 1669; and the two sons from the previous marriage of Mary Morgan of Montgomeryshire provided important evidence to support their mother in her cruelty suit in 1680.[46] Joseph Brook accused his mother's new husband, Daniel Citty, and his son of beating and abusing his mother in their house in Shoreditch, but his story was denied by Daniel's son from his former marriage, who also acted as a witness in the marriage separation case.[47] Of course, there may have been an element of self-interest behind the involvement of a woman's kin in her marriages. There was always property and income at stake which could be lost if her suit was unsuccessful.[48] But children who probably would not have dared to have testified against their natural father were prepared to protect their mother against a violent stepfather. In other cases more distant relatives could also come to the assistance of a woman who

42. CA, Case 2476, (1684), Ee5, f. 171^{v}.
43. Erickson, *Women and Property*, pp. 123–4.
44. For servants see CA, Case 1001, (1667).
45. As cited in Gowing, *Domestic Dangers*, p. 216.
46. CA, Case 4177, (1669), Eee4, ff. 167^{r}–169^{v}; CA, Case 6397, (1680), Eee6, ff. 440^{v}–445^{r}.
47. CA, Case 1865, (1669), Eee4, ff. 212^{r}–214^{r}; 279^{v}–280^{v}.
48. For children's concern about inheritance when their parents remarried see Collins, 'British stepfamily relationships', pp. 334–7.

remarried.[49] Margaret Hunt has concluded in her study of domestic violence in the early eighteenth century that 'for women, embeddedness in a community of friends, neighbors, relatives, and workmates was the most effective way to counterbalance the overwhelming power of men both in the family and in society'.[50] What was most dangerous for married women, Susan Amussen has shown, was being isolated from that community support.[51] Most women who were marrying for a second or further time would have formed those all-important friendships and kin ties which could be enlisted for protection and help if their husbands became violent.

Widows may have had both economic and community know-how which could prove troublesome to men, but it was their sexual experience which was most threatening. Thomas Whythorne was a musician in Elizabethan England, whose account of his life working in households of wealthy, and sometimes widowed, women has been skilfully analysed by the historian Katharine Hodgkin. It was not unusual for female pupils to seek sexual favours from Thomas, but when he declined one widowed employer, she retaliated by saying that he was 'but a huddypick, and lacked audacity'. A huddypick, Hodgkin tells us, was an insult which suggested sexual simplicity.[52] The sexual assertiveness and confidence that Thomas Whythorne had encountered could have disastrous consequences if a widow remarried. Ellen Charnock not only caused her husband, John, to be 'laughed at and scorned abroad' because of her unwillingness to wear decent clothes and prepare adequate food, but because by her behaviour and her words she questioned his sexual competence. When John learnt that when he was absent on business Ellen 'was usually taken up by Strangers in the Fields and thereby had the reputation of a Common Strumpet', he upbraided her for her 'scandalous actions'. But in reply Ellen was reported to have asserted that John 'was no man, notwithstanding she was assured to the Contrary by having her hand in his Codpiece before the Marriage', declaring that, 'had she not had two husbands before she should not have known what belonged to man'. She claimed all John's 'strength', which would have allowed him to have an erection, was drained out of an issue in his back which he had to prevent apoplexy.

49. CA, Case 4688, (1690), Eee7, ff. 121^{v}–124^{r}.

50. M. Hunt, 'Wife beating, domesticity and women's independence in eighteenth-century London', *Gender and History* 4 (1992), p. 23.

51. S.D. Amussen, '"Being stirred to much unquietness": violence and domestic violence in early modern England', *Journal of Women's History* 6 (1994), p. 81.

52. K. Hodgkin, 'Thomas Whythorne and the problems of mastery', *History Workshop Journal* 29 (1990), p. 33.

From their courtship Ellen had established herself as the dominant partner in this relationship, and her behaviour as a widow anticipated what was to come within marriage. Her sexual experience gave her the confidence to explore John's codpiece in a seemingly unabashed manner, and to declare that he was 'no man' if he did not sexually satisfy her within marriage as her previous two husbands had done. 'He that wooeth a widow must not carry quick eels in his codpiece', Thomas Whythorne warned his readers after his encounter with the widow, 'but show some proof that he is stiff before'.[53] If John Charnock had achieved an erection when his wife had her hands in his codpiece before marriage, Ellen's behaviour since their marriage seriously questioned his potency. Unable to control his wife sexually, John found himself without any power to rule Ellen. In a period when the key to female subordination was thought to lie with sexual domination, there was a close link between female lack of chastity and scolding. A whore was also likely to be a scold, and vice versa.[54] And so Ellen is described as 'a woman of a very high and insolent spirit and demeanour continually scolding and brawling', always behaving 'very disobediently' towards her husband. She laughed at his weakness, telling him that he 'was too young to catch her', by which she indicated that his youth and therefore sexual inexperience meant that he would be unable to lay claim to her as his own. That this lack of sexual proficiency could be so disastrous as to render John effeminate is powerfully shown by Ellen's words to the servants that, 'if she had not married him . . . he must have worn a Frock'.[55]

Surprisingly, this story of male impotence and female adultery is taken entirely from John Charnock's personal statement to the court. Why would a man defend himself against his wife's accusations of cruelty by telling a public forum that his wife's 'abuses', which 'would have provoked any person', included a questioning of his very manhood? Why did John risk further laughter and scorn by appearing to admit his own weaknesses, and providing such explicit detail of why his wife had become a whore and a scold? His credit hung in the balance and hinged on one very important element of his story. He told the court how he had visited the relatives of

53. Hodgkin, 'Thomas Whythorne', p. 33.

54. P. Stallybrass, 'Patriarchal territories: the body enclosed', in M.W. Ferguson, M. Quilligan, and N.J. Vickers, eds, *Rewriting the Renaissance: The Discourses of Sexual Difference in Early Modern Europe* (Chicago, 1987); E.A. Foyster, 'The concept of male honour in seventeenth century England' (University of Durham PhD thesis, 1996), pp. 44, 137.

55. CA, Case 1813, (1673), Ee4, ff. 118^{v}–129^{r}.

one of Ellen's previous husbands, and that they had told him that she had treated her former husband 'in the like manner', and that, in their opinion, Ellen was 'not to be satisfied with one man'.[56] By unearthing Ellen's previous reputation as somebody else's wife, John skilfully minimized his responsibility for her whoredom and scolding. Previous experience had shown that Ellen was a scold and a whore; John was not to blame, for no man could control her.

Any man who accused his wife of adultery in this period exposed himself as a cuckold and risked public ridicule and humiliation. But if a husband could redirect blame back onto his wife by constructing her in his court narratives as a whore who could be ruled by none, then his honour could remain intact. Just as John Charnock's testimony rested on his account of his wife's previous marriage, so Edward Northmore's accusations of adultery against his wife, widow of Leonard Lacke, in 1676 depended heavily on the statement of one witness, Thomas Carter, a journeyman in his household. Thomas Carter describes Edward's wife, Elizabeth, as lascivious and insatiable. She was visited in her house in Oxford almost daily by a Master Brice of Magdalene College or a Master Cade of Christchurch. She was, Thomas relates, 'more ready to entertain them than they were ready to embrace her'. Her favourite was Brice, whom she would 'wantonly' entertain in the kitchen of the house. One day Thomas, and an apprentice, John Wheting, walked into the kitchen and found Brice with his hands so high under her clothes that he could see Elizabeth's knees, but even though they saw Thomas, they 'were not abashed thereat'. On 19 April 1673, when Thomas was in the larder, Elizabeth and Brice came into the kitchen and started to make love in a chair, Elizabeth supposedly telling Brice not to 'stoop lower' as they did so. After sex, Thomas related how he saw Elizabeth take her lover's 'yard and rolled it on her knee and wiped it with her shift', and then, without pausing for breath, turned to Thomas and 'asked him whether he was going to supp and told him that if he had not there was some victuals in the Cupboard'. Thomas's portrayal of Elizabeth is one of a shameless whore; she was openly committing adultery in a public room in her husband's house, unconcerned that others might see and hear her, and, once satisfied, she was immediately able to turn her attentions to the feeding of her household.

A month later, Thomas again saw Elizabeth and Brice making love, this time in her chamber. In court, it was their conversation

56. Ibid., f. 122^{r}.

which Thomas thought most significant to recall. They had already made love once when Elizabeth took Brice 'by the Middle', and asked 'will you have again?' Brice replied, 'I will deny thee nothing which I can afford thee . . . [but] . . . I think I shall not be sufficient to supply thy wants', to which Elizabeth promised, 'if you could hold out I could afford you in my body every hour'. They lay down and started making love, and Elizabeth, making a direct comparison between her former husband, Leonard Lacke, and her lover, declared, 'I love thee so dearly for 'tis more than anyone ever did besides my husband Lacke'.[57]

Edward Northmore could not match up to the lovemaking skills of Elizabeth's former husband, Leonard Lacke, and John Charnock did not compare with Ellen's judgment of what made a man. The power of women who had been previously married and widowed to question the manhood of their new husbands was obviously a matter of deep concern. Of course, both these stories of adultery, by John Charnock and Thomas Carter, could be total fabrications of what really occurred in these two marriages. But what is significant is that each story rested on the narrator constructing a picture of a woman whose behaviour was a logical consequence of her previous status as somebody else's wife. It is fascinating that in these cases it is this reputation as a former wife, rather than as a widow, which is recalled. But unless Thomas Carter's story is put within the context of the popular culture of the remarrying widow, it loses its impact: Thomas is nothing but a leering sexual pervert, and his master a public cuckold. In Thomas's story Elizabeth Northmore as a scolding adulterous wife could be portrayed as the natural successor to the fictional stereotypical lusty and domineering widow. Thomas tells us that Brice, no doubt in rather exhausted tones, declared on one occasion after making love to Elizabeth, 'I have done thee three Times since this day'. Thomas can confidently conclude, after all he has heard of the talk between Elizabeth and her lover, that 'their Conversation was so Intimate as if she had a perfect command over him'.[58] In the world of the remarrying widow, even their extramarital lovers struggle to satisfy them, and no man can lay any claim to rule them.

Despite the frequency of remarriage in the early modern period, there was little helpful or positive advice for individuals who undertook relationships with those who had been married before. Whilst these matches may not have been particularly unstable or subject to

57. CA, Case 6692, (1677), Eee6, ff. 123^{r}–126^{r}. 58. Ibid., ff. 124^{v}–125^{r}.

breakdown, the records of those marriages which did fail suggest that they could be prone to particular tensions and problems. Again and again, the couples themselves and their witnesses attribute these problems to the former status which a woman had held, and the experience she had undergone before she had entered into the current relationship. Women complain that their new husbands do not treat them as their former husbands had done. A community of neighbours and friends could be called upon to recall their memories of a woman's previous marriages. But just as women referred back to their previous status and experience, so also their husbands could point to the past in their defence. What could be expected from a woman whom no previous husband could control, John Charnock argued? This is just the type of behaviour you could predict from a widow who remarried, Thomas Carter claimed. By continually looking to the past, these couples appear to have been unwilling or unable to make the adjustments necessary for their present and future relationships. Within marriage they cannot escape from, or even come to terms with, what a woman has already experienced, and move on. The sexual reputation a woman acquired remained with her as she passed through the different stages of her life and could be recalled at any juncture. Hence in 1619 when Katherine Harrison, a widow of East Brandon, Durham, found her chastity in question, a witness declared in her defence, 'that the said Katherine both in her single life and after her marriage as also during her widowhood hath carried and demeaned herself very honestly and uprightly'.[59] While most advice and fictional literature warned men against marrying widows, for those who took the risk, this same literature offered men an exit from these marriages by laying the blame for breakdown firmly at the feet of the women who had been widows.

59. Durham Consistory Court Deposition Book, DDR.V.10B, f. 339v.

PART THREE

Marital and Family Constraints

CHAPTER EIGHT

Lineage strategies and the control of widows in Renaissance Florence[1]

ISABELLE CHABOT

'God send her a hundred years of misery to repay her for her madness!'[2] This was how Francesco Davizzi cursed his sister, this 'beast', this 'ungracious female', when he came to know what sort of life she had chosen. After her husband's death, Lena 'decided to live in poverty with the nuns of Foligno'. Even when others tried to discourage her, arguing that 'she would have better served God taking care of her family', she still 'wanted to follow her own way'.[3]

The biography of this Florentine widow who, against the wishes of her family, decided to dedicate herself to God, has come to us through letters sent between London and Florence from June to November 1422. Lena's three brothers were Florentine bankers and merchants active in London. During the winter and spring of 1422, Simone Strozzi, a friend of the Davizzi family, wrote to the Davizzi brothers to announce the 'foolish' intentions of their recently widowed sister Lena. Pinaccio Strozzi, another Florentine living in London, had certainly had the opportunity to discuss these events with the Davizzi brothers. Pinaccio, in turn, wrote to his brother Simone in July and his letter indirectly echoes the Davizzis' London conversations.[4] Powerless to act, because of the distance from their sister, the brothers sought the only possible recourse – invective. The last letter of the correspondence, addressed from Francesco Davizzi in London to Simone Strozzi in Florence, ends this extraordinary documentation on a note of anger.[5] The exchange

1. This chapter anticipates some of the conclusions of my book: *La Dette des Familles: Femmes, Lignages et Patrimoine à Florence aux XIVe et XVe siècles* (forthcoming, École française de Rome).

2. Carte strozziane, III serie, 32, f. 66^r, 16 June 1422; all the documents quoted in this article come from the Archivio di Stato di Firenze.

3. Ibid. 4. Ibid., f. 67^r, 14 July 1422. 5. Ibid., f. 68^r, 5 November 1422.

of letters echoes with rare intensity the reaction of a patrician family when faced with a choice like Lena's and casts light on the way in which men of this time perceived the control and devolution of female property.

We know very little of Lena Davizzi's life as wife and mother. We know nothing of her husband except that she made a good marriage. Her brothers deeply regretted having spent so much for her dowry, valued at 700 florins, in order to give her a comfortable and honourable future. As Francesco Davizzi recalled, they had even gone into debt to raise this sum.[6] To follow her vocation and enter the convent, Lena 'abandoned' her young children, and for her brothers and her in-laws the fact that she was a mother made her decision even more reprehensible. As Pinaccio Strozzi wrote: 'They would have liked her to stay and govern her children who were young and needed her.'[7]

In spite of all the silences which shadow Lena's biography, her actions speak for themselves, and her very strong personality emerges from the stream of recriminations that Francesco Davizzi poured out in his letters. As a result of her determination to answer the call of God, she found herself up against both her family of origin and her husband's family, who tried every means possible to discourage her. In a certain way, she also found herself coming up against the church, which, even though it exalted the superiority of widowhood, did not really encourage mothers to forsake their children in the service of God. Lena Davizzi also showed great acumen because, while her religious vocation obliged her to strip herself of all her wealth, she did not renounce the rights over the patrimony she had recovered on her husband's death. Instead she enlisted the help of a notary and organized the dispersal of her property before she entered the convent. 'She has asked for her dowry and mainly distributed it to God', wrote a distressed Francesco Davizzi. In fact, Lena's directions were more complex than her brother's statement suggests, and her careful arrangements reveal how she acted with an almost subversive determination.

First of all, she left her young children 600 florins, the main part of her dowry. To prevent her in-laws from wasting this money before her children became old enough to inherit it, however, she arranged that the money should be immediately invested in a farm. She further stipulated that if her children died before reaching adulthood or before founding their own families, Lena's three

6. See below, n. 129. 7. Carte strozziane, III serie, 32, f. 67^{r}.

brothers would have the right to enjoy the farm until their deaths, after which the property would pass to the church.[8] Then, she divided the profits recoverable from her last hundred florins of capital between an old woman and Gherardo, one of her brothers, stipulating once again that after each of their deaths 'some monks' or more generally 'God' would inherit the original sum. Lena's testament therefore placed a man from her own patrician family and a poor woman on the same level. But worse was to come. In order to obtain what was little more than a pittance, Gherardo Davizzi would have to write to his sister and justify his needs. This humiliation was even more intolerable because, as luck would have it, Gherardo was currently serving time in a London jail for debts and his family was living off the generosity of Pinaccio Strozzi.[9] Gherardo saw this clause in the will as another sign of God's punishment, but his brother Francesco took a more cynical view, suggesting that it would be better for Gherardo to die of hunger than to demean himself by accepting these extraordinary conditions. 'Let Gherardo and Lena know', he wrote to Simone Strozzi, 'that I would like to melt down all this money and force it down some monk's throat'.[10]

Commenting on the Davizzi reaction to Lena's distribution of property, Pinaccio Strozzi wrote to his brother Simone to explain that for reasons strictly linked to the social strategies of her family, Lena Davizzi had received more for her dowry than was to be expected from her father's inheritance:

> [The Davizzi] are really upset about the way Lena has distributed her dowry, seeing how little she has remembered her brothers and how she has preferred friars and other strangers, by giving to them what she was obliged to leave her own family, even if she did not want to leave [the dowry] to her children. Because she should have known that what she had been given [as a dowry] was not what she ought to have received . . . and that her brothers had done everything they could, and even went into debt, to give her comfort and honour.[11]

Her brothers demanded the expression of her gratitude through unconditional adherence to automatic inheritance through the male line. According to Francesco Davizzi, if for some reason his sister's dowry did not pass down to her children, her legitimate and unquestionable heirs, it must revert to the estate from which it came. In no case should the dowry go to fulfilling the woman's personal

8. Ibid., f. 66^r. 9. Ibid. 10. Ibid., f. 68^r. 11. Ibid., f. 67^r.

aspirations. 'If she had left her goods to her children, I wouldn't have said anything', asserted Francesco, 'but she has preferred to give everything to some good-for-nothing monk instead of us'.[12] By willing that if her children were to die without legitimate heirs 'God should benefit from everything', Lena Davizzi organized the distribution of her property according to her own set of maternal and spiritual values rather than according to the implacable logic of patrilineal succession.

The experience of this widow is exemplary, but it remains an exception in Florentine society of the late Middle Ages. There is no doubt that Lena was free to act because her brothers were living far away and could not thwart any of her projects. A husband's death freed his widow's goods from all familial control and, theoretically, opened the way for her to exercise full freedom of disposition. Yet Florentine families did not easily accept this legal emancipation of female patrimonies, which gave the widow economic, and therefore social, autonomy. The widow could ask for the return of her dowry and give it either to a new husband if she remarried, or to a convent if she wished to become a nun. If she decided to remain a widow, she could do what she liked with her patrimony, whether investing it to secure a life annuity for herself or squandering it as she liked. Last but not least, she could bequeath it. It was of the utmost importance, therefore, to both the widow's paternal family and her husband's family to try to re-establish the widow's previous links of dependence within their respective family groups. By settling a widow into their own houses they could not only ensure her protection and the maintenance of family honour, but also gain control of her assets and absorb them into their patrimony.

Male wills regularly set out to establish the place of residence of future widows, daughters and wives. As Christiane Klapisch-Zuber aptly points out, women did not have a fixed position in houses made by and for male members of the lineage. As 'passing guests', they had to be *invited* to stay, or else to return to one of the houses where they had lived before becoming a widow.[13] This duty of hospitality fell upon the family of origin as well as the family of alliance, and theoretically allowed a widow to choose where to live. If a widow could not, or did not want to, find housing and protection with her husband's heirs, she would be welcomed at her father's

12. Ibid., f. 68ʳ.

13. Christiane Klapisch-Zuber, 'The "cruel mother": maternity, widowhood, and dowry in Florence in the fourteenth and fifteenth centuries', in Christiane Klapisch-Zuber, *Women, Family, and Ritual in Renaissance Italy* (Chicago, 1985), p. 118.

or brothers' home. Yet, when widowhood came too soon, Florentine widows who were still of marriageable age became the objects of contradictory claims by the two family groups to which they belonged. These young widows effectively lost the freedom to choose their family surroundings. The duty of hospitality shared by father and husband thus became a right of ownership of both the person and the assets of the young widow – a right which placed the widow's paternal family in conflict with her husband's family.

In the following pages, I want to consider the way the family representatives carried out their protective duties towards widows, and how the widow's family of birth clashed with her family by marriage, in the fight to exercise their rights over the person and property of these women. The deeply patrilineal nature of the Florentine inheritance system ensured that both of a widow's families had an interest in her welfare and in the control of her patrimony. And this shared set of goals almost inevitably led to conflict.

The power of fathers

The succession of Florentine wives and mothers who died *ab intestato*, that is without making a will, was governed by statute.[14] A series of laws enacted between 1325 and 1415 set out the following complicated pattern of inheritance and privileges favouring a widow's most recent husband and her male heirs. If a remarried widow died leaving no surviving children from her new match, then her widowed husband got to keep her dowry and a third of her non-dotal goods, even if she had children from a previous marriage.[15] If she did have children from this latest match, they did not have to divide their maternal inheritance with their half brothers and sisters. Finally, daughters could not inherit from their mother if brothers or even nephews were alive. Thus, the Florentine inheritance system contrasted sharply with most of the legislation of Italian communes because, in the first instance, the mother's inheritance was not divided between *all* her children but reserved instead for the sons

14. Isabelle Chabot, 'La loi du lignage: notes sur le système successoral florentin (XIVe/XVe–XVIIe siècles)', *Clio: Femmes, Histoire et Sociétés* 7 (1998), pp. 51–72. See also Thomas Kuehn, 'Some ambiguities on female inheritance ideology in the Renaissance', *Continuity and Change* 2 (1987), pp. 11–36; now available in Kuehn, *Law, Family and Women: Towards an Anthropology of Renaissance Italy* (Chicago, 1991), pp. 238–57.

15. Julius Kirshner, '*Maritus lucretur dotem uxoris sue premortue* in late medieval Florence', *Zeitschrift der Savigny-Stiftung für Rechtsgeschichte* 77 (1991), pp. 111–55.

born in her most recent marriage. Secondly, in Florence the blood relatives of a woman who died childless, but who was survived by her husband, lost all their rights of inheritance. Roman law, by contrast, allowed a father to recover the dowry in these circumstances.[16]

Whenever they could, Florentines attempted to evade these restrictions relating to widowed daughters or sisters by making alternative arrangements. During the summer of 1400, Mattea, widow of Matteo da Panzano, had taken refuge in San Gimignano with one of her brothers, Goro di Andrea del Benino, to escape the plague. In such troubled times, Goro decided to make his sister write her last will. Mattea had three young sons who, according to Florentine law, would inherit her large dowry, valued at 1200 florins; however, 'if they died without legitimate heirs', a testament would prove indispensable to make this money 'revert to Goro, Nanni, Bartolomeo and Niccolò, sons to Andrea del Benino, or to their heirs'. So the del Benino brothers applied the same logic of inheritance that Francesco Davizzi wished to impose on his sister Lena. In 1401 they actually gave Mattea away to a second husband. Six years later, Luca da Panzano mentioned in his diary a conversation with his mother about this will. He asserted that, 'according to the lawyers', her remarriage had rendered the will null and void. The da Panzano and the del Benino families could no longer inherit Mattea's dowry because it had been transferred into a new lineage through remarriage: 'the statutes say it clearly'.[17]

In Renaissance Florence, the fate of widows and their dowries was decided right after the church ceremony. 'Tradition' demanded that, on the evening of her husband's funeral, a widow should return immediately under the paternal roof, if that was what had been decided. The *tornata*, the 'return', was an important step in the ritual of mourning. Significantly, it was a reverse of the ceremony enacted by the newly married bride entering her husband's house. The widow left her husband's home with a procession of men and women from her own family and was followed by the trunk or *cassone* containing her trousseau.[18]

16. For a comparative overview of different inheritance systems in late medieval Italy, see F. Niccolai, *La Formazione del Diritto Successorio negli Statuti Comunali del Territorio Lombardo-Tosco* (Milan, 1940); Isabelle Chabot, 'Risorse e diritti patrimoniali', in A. Groppi, ed., *Storia delle Donne Italiane*, 4 vols (Rome/Bari, 1996), II, *Il Lavoro delle Donne. Parte I: L'Età Medievale*, pp. 47–70.

17. Carte strozziane, II serie, 9, f. 2^v.

18. Isabelle Chabot, '"La sposa in nero": la ritualizzazione del lutto delle vedove fiorentine (secoli XIV–XV)', *Quaderni Storici* 86 (1994), pp. 443–5.

The *tornata* was also a right of daughters, established by the city statutes, and usually confirmed in father's or brothers' wills.[19] In the male testaments I have analysed, 73 per cent of daughters, 40 per cent of sisters and 35 per cent of nieces were given shelter in the family house in the event of widowhood or extreme hardship.[20] This right was sometimes accompanied by maintenance or a right to enjoy movable or immovable assets. Some testators explicitly demanded that maintenance be granted to sisters or daughters if these women 'lost' their dowries.[21] Others expressed concern that sisters or daughters might not be able to meet the demands of their upkeep.[22] Obviously, the *tornata*, pensions and other life annuities, which constituted the majority of bequests to women, were designed as complementary measures, if not as compensations to women as a result of the rule of *exclusio propter dotem* (the exclusion of married daughters from patrilineal inheritance on account of their dowries). It was precisely because male heirs did not share the inheritance with their sisters or other close female relatives that male testators confirmed their responsibilities and legal duties to their female relatives in their wills. Even if these bequests provide ample evidence of the attention families paid to the material lot of daughters and sisters, the *tornata* also underlines how ephemeral a daughter's place in her *casa* (family of origin) really was.

Florentine practice, however, highlights the ambiguity of the *tornata*. For a widow who could not, or who did not wish to, go on living with her husband's heirs, especially in cases where these heirs were not her own children, the *tornata* represented an important right of asylum in her paternal house. In the fifteenth-century fiscal census, many household heads acknowledged the presence of a widowed daughter, a sister or an old aunt under their roof. Some testators made provisions granting generations of female relatives asylum in the family home. In his tax return to the *Catasto* in 1427, Giovanni Corbinelli recalled that his brother Antonio had

19. *Statuta populi et communis Florentiae . . . anno salutis MCCCCV*, 4 vols (Fribourg, 1778–81), I, p. 224.

20. My investigations dealt with 292 male and 158 female testaments written between 1350 and 1440.

21. See the testament of Priore di Mariotto Banchi, 21 June 1411, Notarile antecosimiano (hereafter NA), 10519, ff. 71^v–72^r.

22. Matteo Castellani wanted his heirs to give every year to one of his two sisters a certain amount of grain, pork and wood because without it 'she will not be able to live on the income from her dowry', as quoted in Gene Brucker, ed., *The Society of Renaissance Florence: A Documentary Study* (New York, 1969), pp. 53–4. For the Italian see Gene Brucker, *Firenze nel Rinascimento* (Florence, 1980), p. 267.

bequeathed the use of his house 'to all the widows descending in the male line from our father Tommaso', before listing the eight daughters and nieces already born who might, one day, claim this right.[23] To male heirs, however, such arrangements often represented an imposition and a drain on their inheritance. Having to share a house with a widow might be inconvenient, and make it difficult to rent or sell the property for profit. In order to free estates of these obligations, families negotiated settlements between the men who owned property and their female relatives who possessed rights in that property. Thus Giovanni and Lodovico di Adovardo de' Riccardi asked their sister Bionda to renounce the *tornata* her father had bequeathed her, apparently without offering any compensation in return.[24] In most cases, however, widows who relinquished their rights over particular property received financial compensation in return. In 1451, according to her father's will, Lena, daughter to Vanni di Stefano Castellani and widow of Guidetto Monaldi, claimed her right to settle in the family palace. However, Francesco di Matteo Castellani, who owned the palace, showed no intention of accommodating his cousin Lena and she was forced to turn to private arbitration. A few months later the case was resolved through a compromise which forced Francesco to pay Lena an annual rent of 20 florins for the rest of her life.[25] Thus, in some cases, instead of opening the family house to sisters or close relatives, male heirs paid them an annuity, more or less willingly, to live elsewhere. This way of bypassing the right of *tornata* was by no means common practice, but I believe it reveals a more general tendency to give women financial compensation in return for their temporary rights over property. As we shall see, this tendency to compensation was corroborated by statutory law.

The *tornata* also served as a means for a father to reassert his *patria potestas* or his control over his daughter and her dowry. Young widows were seldom free to 'return' spontaneously to their family, instead they were led back. The widow's age was the major criterion for this decision. A Florentine father usually welcomed his daughter to the paternal household only if the family believed they could reasonably remarry her to a new husband without too much delay. The story of Tancia Bandini, the eldest daughter of the notary

23. Catasto, 17, f. 750^r.

24. See the testament of Giovanni di Adovardo de' Riccardi, 6 October 1414, NA, 11877, f. 31^v.

25. Francesco di Matteo Castellani, *Ricordanze*, I, *Ricordanze A (1436–1459)*, G. Ciappelli, ed. (Florence, 1992), p. 143.

Giovanni Bandini, demonstrates how difficult it could be for young Florentine women to oppose paternal authority. In February 1448, two years after her wedding, Tancia's husband died, transforming her overnight into a 20-year-old childless widow. We know from her father's diary that he immediately took her back and hurried to claim her dowry – worth 300 florins – from the dead man's brothers because he wanted to remarry her as soon as possible.[26] As often happened, Tancia's in-laws delayed the payment of their debt. In the meantime, Tancia decided to enter a nunnery and showed great determination in her attempts to oppose her father's matrimonial projects. In July 1450, when her dowry was about to be recovered, she went to a notary and arranged to reserve a hundred florins for her monastic dowry, then she divested herself of all her other goods by giving them to her mother through a *donatio inter vivos* (a transfer of property or gift from one living person to another). Extremely upset by the fact that his daughter had acted against his will, Giovanni Bandini confided to his diary that he would be ready to give her another dowry worth the same amount of money if he could find a new husband in time.[27] And no more than a month later, Tancia married a silk merchant. In Florence, the widow's right of *tornata* was often a denial of rights.

For many young widows, the return to a life of dependence on their paternal family also meant a denial of their roles as mothers. In Florence, orphans did not follow their mother when she left the marital house because the children belonged to their father's lineage. The women's powerlessness in the face of the antagonistic rights of both lineages is clearly apparent in the case of a young and pregnant Florentine widow of the late fifteenth century. After the burial of her husband her family took her back to the paternal house, then gave her back to her husband's family until the birth of the child because the unborn child belonged to its father's lineage. After the birth, the young widow and mother was again returned to her blood relatives and soon remarried.[28] Separation from children meant that widows were quickly discharged of their legal responsibilities. When, in 1389, the Sassetti brothers took their sister Isabetta back, they forced her to renounce the tutorship of her three children granted to her by her husband's testament, because – as they said – 'we *had* to remarry M[adonn]a Isabetta'.[29]

26. Corporazioni religiose soppresse, 102, 82, ff. 13^{v}–14^{r}.
27. Ibid., f. 15^{r}.
28. Klapisch-Zuber, 'The "cruel mother"', p. 125 n. 33.
29. Ibid., p. 124. My emphasis.

A mother's remarriage also had serious patrimonial consequences because, as we have seen, her children lost almost all their rights over their future maternal inheritance. Yet in fourteenth-century Florence, it was rare to find a man willing to marry a woman who already had children, because if he died before his wife and without a direct descendant, his male heirs – brothers or nephews – would be forced to give the dowry to his widow's children born of the previous marriage. This was the only case in which, according to Florentine law, the children from the first marriage bed recovered their rights to the maternal inheritance. In 1415, however, a reform of the Florentine statutes definitively removed this weak successorial link between a remarried woman and her children of the first marriage bed. From this date a childless widower was entitled to the whole dowry of his deceased wife in addition to a third of her non-dotal assets even if children from her former marriage were still alive. According to one of the jurists involved, the reform of the law stemmed from popular demand because 'widows could not find a husband if they had children'.[30] Before this date, the father and the future husband of a widow could exploit a contractual loophole to circumvent the legal effects of the blood link between mother and children. Let us look at an example. When, in 1385, Valorino Ciurianni married the widow Caterina degli Alberti, he claimed his father-in-law should pay the dowry himself. Valorino asserted that he did not want 'to receive the dowry from the said Caterina because she had a daughter from her first husband Lippo Soldani'.[31] In so doing, Caterina, a widow and a mother, returned to her former status of daughter, dowried for the first time by her father. Valorino would consent to marry her only if she ceased to exist for her little daughter. The social practices and norms which ruled the remarriage and the inheritance of Florentine widows reveal the extent to which the negation of maternity *and* of maternal transmission of wealth was at the core of lineage strategies.

The Florentine husband who opposed the tradition of the *tornata*, which gave a father exclusive rights over his daughter's person and goods, and wished to keep a young widow near her children and retain her dowry within her in-laws' estates faced an uphill struggle. Persuasion, in the form of material advantages bequeathed in a last will, was the husband's only weapon. But practice shows that the testament was still a weak tool. In 1380, Valorino Ciurianni watched

30. Kirshner, '*Maritus*', p. 134.
31. Manoscritti, 77, f. 27^r. See also Chabot, 'La sposa in nero', pp. 451–3.

powerless as his stepmother, Lisa Frescobaldi, 'returned to her brother's house' after the burial of his father.[32] He remembered with anger how she had 'promised' her dying husband that she would not abandon their young son and had received, in exchange, numerous advantages in Barna's will.[33] What Valorino forgot was that this epilogue had actually been planned fifteen years before, at the time of his father's remarriage. Instead of a cash dowry, Lisa had brought into the marriage a farm situated in Valdelsa, and according to a settlement arbitrated and forced upon her before the arrangement of the dowry contract, her brother retained legal ownership of this farm. The severe financial hardships of the Frescobaldi family explain the very unusual presence of an *inaestimata* dowry (a dowry composed of immovable goods), and are reflected in the agreement which deprived Lisa of any rights as a widow over the farm she had brought to marriage. While the young woman had had to meet the demand of her brother, her husband Barna Ciurianni had actually agreed to a very unusual dowry contract which allowed Berto Frescobaldi to take his sister back, if widowed, in order to reclaim his property.[34]

Husbands' wishes

A husband's testament could hardly oppose such power. Of the married testators in my sample, 20 per cent immediately renounced their rights over dowry property and limited themselves to reminding their heirs of their obligation to return the dowry to their widow.[35] Even more than the absence of children, a widow's youth usually explains the sense of resignation on the part of these husbands who did not make provisions for their widows in their wills. In 80 per cent of cases the heads of household who bequeathed nothing to the surviving wife actually had under-age children. Thus, they probably considered it useless to give the management of the family and its patrimony to their widows, who, because of their youth, would almost certainly be obliged to renounce it to remarry.

Among those testators who attempted to ensure their widows some autonomy, the gifts they gave and the extent of the powers

32. Manoscritti, 77, f. xxii^{r}. 33. Ibid., f. xx^{r}. 34. Ibid., f. xiiii^{v}.

35. The following observations are based on 194 testaments of married men. Thirty-nine testators left nothing other than the dowry. The remaining 155 testators who made provisions for the surviving spouse have been divided into the following four groups: (1) childless, 42; (2) with under-age children, 41; (3) with under-age and of age children, 28; (4) with of age children, 44.

they granted varied considerably, according to the presence of children and especially the age of those children. All in all, roughly a third of the testators who had children named their wife '*domina et usufructuaria omnium bonorum*' (the widow had the right of usufruct over the entire estate or all the goods of her deceased husband during her life). However, a closer analysis clearly shows that this grant of management and usufruct of the estate occurred at particular moments in the family life cycle. Seventy per cent of the surviving wives granted status as *domina* were, in fact, young mothers who would have to take care of children who were under-age. It should be noted that they were mainly mothers to sons who stood to inherit both the paternal and maternal goods. Usually, the *domina* was also named tutor. There was no doubt that, if the mother agreed to stay with her young children, she had to be legally empowered to do so. Two-thirds of fathers did not hesitate to make their widows, together with other relatives, responsible for their young children, and a few fathers decided that their widows did not have to share this responsibility. To prevent their young widows from remarrying and taking their dowries into another lineage, Florentine husbands seemed to be ready to give them full powers over the family.

However, the power these widows held should not be overemphasized. Not only was the widow's position as a *domina* conditional on her 'chaste' and 'honest' lifestyle, but it was also subject to the late medieval legal interpretation of female usufruct or rights over an estate.[36] By the second half of the fourteenth century, in fact, statutory laws tended to convert the women's usufruct rights into simple alimony (*alimenta*)[37] so that, in practice, the widow should be '*domina et usufructuaria omnium bonorum*', but only '*pro sui victo et vestito*' (for her support, food and clothes).[38] In early modern Siena legislators interpreted the rights of a wife named *domina usufructuaria* in the husband's will according to his familial situation. If the deceased had male descendants, undowried daughters or male relatives

36. The *domina* must live 'chastely and honestly' and, above all, leave her dowry incorporated to the estate. These stipulations mark the great difference between this type of provision and the dower a widow in London could expect even if she remarried. See Barbara Hanawalt, 'The widow's mite: provisions for medieval London widows', in Louise Mirrer, ed., *Upon my Husband's Death: Widows in the Literature and Histories of Medieval Europe* (Ann Arbor, Mich., 1992), pp. 21–45.

37. See Niccolai, *Formazione*, pp. 186–7, 190; on the transformation of female usufructs into alimony in the Florentine statutes of 1415, see Kuehn, 'Some ambiguities', pp. 242–3.

38. This precision can be found in the testament of Antonio Schiattesi written in 1413, NA, 10519, f. 81^{r}.

in the collateral line with their own descendants, his widow could only demand alimony or maintenance. Childless widows, on the other hand, could enjoy real usufruct, as long as they obtained an inventory of the estate and provided appropriate guarantees.[39] This amounts to saying that a widow living with her father-in-law or brother-in-law did not wield any patrimonial power over the inheritance of her children.

The handing over of tutorship was seen as the best way to guarantee orphans both affective and patrimonial protection. They would be educated and cared for by their mother, who would lose her legal authority on remarrying; and the maternal goods would be kept within the father's estate which the orphans would inherit later. To be more secure, Iacopo di Zanobi Schiattesi entrusted his wife with the tutorship of their young son on the sole condition 'that she remained a widow and did not ask for her dowry'.[40] To the same end, Tommaso di Messer Uberto de' Gianfigliazzi had to be even more coercive. In his will, written 28 May 1411, he entrusted his son Andrea and his daughter Leonarda to his second wife Evangelista Bellandi and, if she should die, to the *Ufficiali dei Pupilli*.[41] But in a codicil he added later on the same day, Tommaso specified that she would be able to exercise her tutorship only if, within two months of his death, she would donate to her son Andrea the farm she had brought with her dowry, reserving the usufruct for herself. Only if she should survive her son would this *donatio* be nullified, and she could freely dispose of her goods. In practice, Tommaso wanted to secure for his son, and for him only, what most testators took for granted if their widow did not leave the house, that is the transmission of the whole maternal inheritance. But unlike the great majority of Florentine men who received money from their wives, Tommaso needed precise guarantees because Evangelista had given him lands which she could claim back at any time without special procedures. With this *donatio* Tommaso avoided two major risks: Evangelista would not be able either to alienate her farm during her life, or divide her inheritance between her son and her daughter.

39. M. Ascheri, ed., *L'Ultimo Statuto della Repubblica di Siena (1545)* (Siena, 1993), p. 258. See also G. Lumia, 'Mariti e mogli nei testamenti senesi di età moderna', in Giulia Calvi and Isabelle Chabot, eds, *Le Ricchezze delle Donne: Diritti Patrimoniali e Poteri Familiari (XIII–XIX sec.)* (Turin, 1998).

40. NA, 10519, ff. 30^r–31^v, 27.X.1410.

41. On these important communal magistrates who cared for orphans, see the chapter by Giulia Calvi in this book.

When time had strengthened the family, Florentines did not need to be so earnest about holding their widows back. Once a widow entered her thirties, her opportunities for remarrying diminished and it became more and more likely that she would remain in her late husband's home.[42] Significantly, the older that children became, the less likely it was that their mother would be deemed '*domina et usufructuaria omnium bonorum*'. Obviously, the husband established the right of his widow to live with her children based on the goods of the household, but he might also desire that the estate his sons would inherit should be free from legal encumbrances linked to a widow's rights. Nevertheless, some widows received rents from a farm[43] or the profits from capital lent in bonds,[44] although most wills granted them no more than the use of the house, or merely a bedroom, and the furniture; they also confirmed a woman's rights over her bridal gifts, clothes and jewels, a symbolic gesture which signalled the attachment of a widow to her husband's lineage.[45] Some testators foresaw that conflicts might arise from retired widows cohabiting with sons who now enjoyed the status of head of family. They arranged for a life annuity, some pieces of furniture, or the right to inhabit a house in town[46] or a farm in the country,[47] to be available to a widow should she wish to separate from her children or enter a convent; on condition, of course, that she would not take her dowry with her.[48]

Keeping the dowry within the family patrimony was a prerequisite for all the gifts, both great and small, that might come to a widow by will. At first sight, a husband's bequests would seem to be designed as compensation due to the surviving wife in return for giving up the management of her dowry property. Yet it seems that widows who chose to stay with their late husband's heirs and let them control their dowry rarely benefited from this reward. In 1427, three sons, Niccolaio, Francesco and Iacopo, acknowledged that they did not give their widowed mother the yearly instalment of 25 florins that her husband had bequeathed to her, although they claimed they would do so 'if she asked for it, that is to say if she left us'.[49]

The brothers' statement helps us to read between the lines of male wills. It appears that husbands did not establish gifts to

42. Klapisch-Zuber, 'The "cruel mother"', p. 120.
43. NA, 13948, ff. 11^{r}–13^{v}; NA, 205, f. 118^{r-v}; NA, 10519, ff. 190^{v}–192^{r}; 287^{r-v}.
44. NA, 2546, ff. 194^{r}–195^{v}; 289^{r}–291^{r}.
45. Chabot, 'La sposa in nero', pp. 438–40.
46. NA, 11877, ff. 42^{r}–45^{r}, 28 November 1416.
47. NA, 13948, ff. 89^{r}–90^{v}, 17 January 1395; see also NA, 11877, ff. 6^{r}–8^{r}.
48. NA, 205, ff. 107^{r}–108^{r}, 5 August 1383.
49. Catasto, 37, ff. 979^{r}–82^{r}.

grant their widows a modicum of financial autonomy. Rather, they intended them as a sort of insurance against the risks of a lonely old age. Hence, these bequests only became effective when a widow could no longer live with her children, either because she ceased to get along with them or because they died before she did. Thus, Francesco di Andrea Quaratesi bequeathed 400 florins to his widow if she kept on living with her children, but she would receive this money only if she survived both her sons or if they behaved badly towards her.[50] Indeed, as long as women lived within the family, the marital bequests, as well as the heirlooms they might acquire from other relatives, accrued not to themselves but to their dowries. The men who made these bequests seemed intent on protecting their sons' rights over the maternal inheritance, by preventing their widows from remarrying, and by maintaining the status quo. Consequently, the widow who settled with her children was precluded from the use of her dowry and lived off the goods of the household, effectively remaining in the same condition as when her husband was alive.

However, if a man's sons died before their mother, his will sometimes rewarded the faithfulness of his wife and, in a way, took charge of her future. When Giovanni di Filippo de' Carducci wrote his last will he had five sons, all of them old enough to inherit. It was very likely that his wife, Piera Biliotti, would go on living with them and be maintained at the expense of the family inheritance, but Giovanni nevertheless bequeathed her the income from a shop because he foresaw that 'her dowry was meagre' and was insufficient for her upkeep if for any reason she could not rely on the support of her children.[51]

Testamentary practice shows that Florentines who did not have direct male descendants granted their widows gifts of a very different nature. These men did not have to talk their wives out of demanding back their dowries: quite the contrary. They were the only testators who left their heirs precise instructions about how their widows' dowries should be recovered. Napoleone de' Franzesi even ordered his heirs to pay the dowry back within a year of his death or else they should grant his widow two hundred extra florins.[52] For the great majority of these men, however, the repayment of the dowry did not preclude a few extra gifts. Many of these husbands took care to secure a home for their widows, leaving them the

50. NA, 10518, ff. 242^{r}–247^{r}, 9 May 1423.
51. NA, 2546, ff. 17^{r}–19^{v}, 22 June 1427.
52. NA, 2546, ff. 169^{r}–172^{r}, 1 July 1430.

ownership[53] or, more often, the use of a house for life.[54] Some added to these provisions a small pension,[55] the income of an estate[56] or an *ultra dotem* gift of a few tens or hundreds of florins.[57] Among testators without children, about one in three left his widow the right to enjoy all of his goods, after which they would pass to his relatives or to some religious or charitable institution. Given their family situation, what we see here is a disinterested gesture of marital solidarity which secured the widow against material hardship and guaranteed her rights against heirs who were not related to her. In these cases there was no need to ensure that the dowry remained within the estate, because the testator's heirs could not claim it anyway. The widow of Bartolomeo di Giovanni de' Carducci, for example, was left '*dominam usufructuariam omnium bonorum . . . tam repetendo quam non repetendo dotes suas*' ('in control of all his estate whether or not she asked for the return of her dowry')[58] and only by remarrying could the widow lose this advantage.

We even encounter some husbands who not only did nothing to suppress their wives' control over property should they remarry, but who actually increased the dowry to enhance the widow's ability to remarry. Matteo di Morello Morelli thus left his wife the income of a farm '*donec vixerit in quocumque gradu vel statu*' ('for as long as she lives whatever her marital status') in case his only son and heir died, yet he excluded the potential second husband from taking advantage of this benefit.[59] Santi di Niccolaio left his wife, Bartolomea, the usufruct of all the estate that his nephews would inherit, but should she choose to remarry, he granted her a hundred florins to add to her dowry worth 70 florins.[60] The same 'paternalistic' care can be found among the rare testators with children who openly encouraged their future widows to leave the family house and even gave the widow a certain amount of money over and above

53. NA, 13948, ff. 107^{r}–108^{v}; NA, 6361, f. 129^{r-v}, 19 March 1417.

54. Diplomatico, Santa Maria Novella, 16.XII.1362; ibid., 16.V.1393.

55. The notary Piero di ser Lorenzo asked the hospital of the Innocents, which would inherit his estate, to pay every year a pension of twelve florins to his widow 'to convert to rent for a house or whatever pleases her': NA, 2546, ff. 2^{r}–14^{r}, 2 May 1427.

56. NA, 13948, f. 117^{r}, 27 March 1399; NA, 205, ff. 8^{r}–10^{v}; ff. 46^{r}–47^{v}; NA, 11877, ff. 39^{r}–40^{r}.

57. NA, 205, ff. 11^{r}–12^{r}, 6 June 1363; ff. 44^{r}–46^{r}; NA, 11877, f. 6^{r}; NA, 10519, ff. 88^{r}–90^{r}.

58. NA, 2546, f. 272^{r}, 4 March 1435. Andreolo di Niccolò di Franco de' Sacchetti left his 'beloved wife' free to ask for her dowry (1500 florins) 'when she would like'; yet she would still enjoy the usufruct of all his goods: ibid., f. 245^{v}, 13 August 1433.

59. NA, 2546, ff. 194^{r}–195^{v}, 7 September 1430.

60. NA, 6361, ff. 169^{r}–170^{r}, 25 July 1421.

her dowry '*pro ea nubenda*' or 'for her marriage'.[61] This apparently paradoxical behaviour confirms the very precise successorial calculations that underpinned the advantages granted to wives who outlived their husbands.

Writing their wills in the first decades of the fifteenth century, Stefano di Salvi di Filippo and Paliano di Falco presented to their wives a double offer. Both foresaw that their widows might want to stay with their children, and they arranged bequests that would shelter them from material cares. Niccolosa, the wife of Stefano, would get the usufruct of the house and the furniture and receive a suitable pension for her upkeep and the salary of a servant. As for Paliano, he left Gianna the usufruct of all his goods and put their children under her tutorship.[62] Yet both of these men recognized that their wives were still young and might prefer to remarry, or would be forced to do so by their families. In that case, Niccolosa would get 300 florins '*ultra suam dotem*' or 'in addition to her dowry',[63] while Paliano increased the dowry of Gianna, his 'beloved wife', by 50 per cent 'in order that she could remarry easily and with more honour'.[64] How can such exceptional and somewhat curious generosity be explained? Neither Stefano nor Paliano had *male* heirs who could inherit from their mother. So, if their wives remarried or left their dowries to their daughters in a will, these goods would, in any case, go out of the estate of the lineage.

In Renaissance Florence, the manipulation of women's patrimonial rights was at the core of the strategies used by both fathers and husbands in order to lay claim over young widows and their property. As we have seen, fathers could decide to separate their daughter from her children to make her remarry, male relatives could arrange the remarriage of a woman who was already a mother, and husbands, for their part, tried to discourage or, alternatively, encourage the remarriage of their wives. In all these cases, Florentine men were manipulating maternity – with all the affective ties and links of inheritance that it implied – according to their own social and patrimonial strategies. On the one hand, we see that maternal links were depreciated by physical separation and their legal effects

61. See the testament of Baruccino di Neri Barucci, who gave his only daughter, Bella, a dowry valued at 1000 lire '*pro ea nubenda*' (literally 'to marry her') and bequeathed a hundred lire '*ultra dotem*' ('in addition to the dowry') to his wife Mingardesca, also '*pro ea nubenda*': Diplomatico, Coperte di libri, 27.X.1295.

62. Carte strozziane, IV serie, 364, f. xvij^{r}, 118^{v}. This testament was written on 31 December 1406.

63. NA, 10518, ff. 386^{r}–387^{v}, 22 July 1425.

64. Carte strozziane, IV serie, 364, f. 117^{v}.

could be circumvented by means of contractual tricks. On the other hand, maternity was overvalued, in ways that were highly selective, according to a hierarchy of heirs dictated by the Florentine laws of patrilineage, which asserted the priority of sons over daughters, and of the offspring born from the second marriage over the first. To guarantee the superiority of patrilineal family ties and ensure the male monopoly over the transmission of wealth, Florentines of the Renaissance toyed with maternity.

CHAPTER NINE

Property and widowhood in England 1660–1840

AMY LOUISE ERICKSON

> *Mr Peachum*: And had not you the common views of a gentlewoman in your marriage, Polly?
> *Polly*: I don't know what you mean, sir.
> *Mr Peachum*: Of a jointure, and of being a widow.
> *Polly*: But I love him, sir: How then could I have thoughts of parting with him?
> *Peachum*: Parting with him! Why, that is the whole scheme and intention of all marriage articles. The comfortable estate of widow-hood, is the only hope that keeps up a wife's spirits. Where is the woman who would scruple to be a wife, if she had it in her power to be a widow whenever she pleas'd?
>
> John Gay, *The Beggar's Opera* (1728)

Newly wed to MacHeath, Polly Peachum has not yet acquired her father's hard-headed assessment of the benefits of widowhood. In Gay's time, as from the Middle Ages to the late nineteenth century, the laws of inheritance in Britain were relatively egalitarian by European standards, but the laws of marriage were not. The common law fiction of coverture, whereby a woman lost all personal property and control of all real property to her husband, meant that widowhood might be seen as a release by any woman with a less than ideal husband. As a widow, a woman owned her own earnings or income and controlled her own property. For men, marriage imposed no legal or financial costs – only benefits. Hence their lives as widowers bore no legal or financial implications.

Other writers of the late seventeenth and early eighteenth centuries were even less oblique than Gay in their criticism of marital property law. Daniel Defoe's Roxana learns only when her husband's desertion leaves her penniless that 'the very nature of the marriage-contract was, in short, nothing but giving up liberty, estate, authority, and every-thing, to the man'. Only in her middle years did Roxana acquire the breadth of experience which enabled her to discern the love from the marriage. She refused the offer of a suitor (whom she had already bedded) to make her, as he thought, an honest woman, saying, 'It is not you . . . that I suspect, but the laws of matrimony puts the power into your hands; bids you do it, commands you to command; and binds me, forsooth, to obey'.[1] Mary More's essay 'The woman's right', written and circulated in the 1670s, cautioned her teenage daughter that 'the laws of our country give a man after marriage a greater power of their estate than the wife unless the wife take care before hand to prevent it (which I advise thee to doe)'.[2]

The most comprehensive and scathing attack on marital property law appeared in 1735: *The Hardships of the English Laws. In Relation to Wives. With an Explanation of the Original Curse of Subjection Passed upon the Woman. In an Humble Address to the Legislature.* The anonymous author was Mrs Sarah Chapone, friend of George Ballard, Mary Delaney, Elizabeth Elstob, Samuel Richardson and John Wesley, wife of a Gloucestershire clergyman, and the mother-in-law of Hester Chapone.[3] Impassioned and eloquent, she opens with a quote from Job, protesting his oppression in a voice full of pain and incomprehension, then proceeds to excoriate the common law for going far beyond the biblical curse of subjection. At the same time she had clearly studied her case reports, referring to decisions and judges by name. She knew her civil or Roman law of community property as well, with which the English common law compared badly. The common lawyers' answer that the Court of Chancery would always defend married women (provided they had made a premarital property settlement) was also rejected by Chapone in terms that suggest she might have been thinking of Polly Peachum:

> if we reflect how extreamly ignorant all young women are as to points in law, and how their education and way of life, shuts them out from the knowledge of their true interest in almost all things, we shall find that their trust and confidence in the man they love . . . leave few in a condition to make use of that precaution.[4]

The uncongenial effects of coverture could be circumvented if a bride took preventive action prior to her marriage, in the form of a

1. Daniel Defoe, *Roxana* (1987; 1st edn 1724), pp. 187, 190.
2. Mary More, 'The woman's right', in Margaret J.M. Ezell, *The Patriarch's Wife: Literary Evidence and the History of the Family* (Chapel Hill, NC, 1987), p. 192.
3. Virginia Blain, Patricia Clements and Isobel Grundy, eds, *The Feminist Companion to Literature in English* (London, 1990), p. 196.
4. [Sarah Chapone], *Hardships of the English Laws* (1735), p. 33.

premarital property settlement or a marriage settlement. A settlement could specify many arrangements, including the bride's portion, the jointure to which she would be entitled upon widowhood, and any 'separate estate' or 'pin money' which she was to have during marriage. Separate estate developed primarily as a means to facilitate the preservation of family wealth through daughters, and to provide maintenance in the event of separation.[5] The standard manual *Precedents in Conveyancing* (1744) covered all types of property transfers, but devoted more than a third of its pages to examples of marriage settlements, most of which included separate estate as well as portions and jointures. However, any disputes over separate estate were enforced exclusively in the Court of Chancery by the eighteenth century. Chancery delays and bribes could be afforded only by the wealthy, and there is a widespread assumption that the use of separate estate was therefore limited to the wealthy.

But in the seventeenth century ordinary women made arrangements comparable to separate estate and jointure, without using those terms. Instead of a trust, they drew up a bond in which the groom promised to pay to a relation of the bride (slightly more often than not a male relative, but it could also be her mother or grandmother) a certain amount of money for the bride's benefit either during marriage or, more usually, upon her widowhood. This bond could be enforced in a local common law court by the third party, without resort to the expensive Court of Chancery. Such a bond could also secure payments for the benefit of the bride's children by a previous marriage: widows remarrying were twice as likely as first-time brides to make a property settlement.[6] Remarrying widows may have had a reputation for financial astuteness: the playwright and political satirist Delarivier Manley mentioned in 1707 a man in debt who had married in high hopes of cash, but whose 'lady, like a right widow, had secured the greatest part of her fortune to her own use'.[7]

First-time brides were perhaps, as Sarah Chapone suggested, too ignorant of the law and too confident in their husbands. By the early eighteenth century that combination was exacerbated by a romantic ideal of marriage which deemed financial considerations

5. Susan Staves, 'Pin-money', *Studies in Eighteenth-Century Culture* 14 (1985), pp. 47–77, or *Married Women's Separate Property in England, 1660–1833* (Cambridge, Mass., 1990), ch. 5.

6. A.L. Erickson, *Women and Property in Early Modern England* (London and New York, 1993), p. 149.

7. Delarivier Manley, *The Lady's Paguet of Letters* (1707), reprinted as *Court Intrigues* (1711), in Fidelis Morgan, ed., *A Woman of No Character: An Autobiography of Mrs. Marley* (London, 1986), pp. 122–3.

– at least on a wife's part – mercenary. According to Richard Steele in *The Tatler*, for example, arrangements to secure a wife's separate property would 'create a diffidence; and intimate to the young people, that they are very soon to be in a state of war with each other . . . Thus is tenderness thrown out of the question.'[8] Popular novels and periodicals like *The Spectator* (1711–14) scorned any discussion of property in marriage as unfeminine and disruptive of domestic peace.[9] The mid-century *Female Spectator* avoids the subject entirely. Through Roxana, an elderly Defoe in 1724 dismissed the new romantic ideal succinctly: 'the pretence of affection takes from a woman every thing that can be call'd herself; she is to have no interest; no aim; no view; but all is the interest, aim, and view, of the husband'.[10] *The Hardships of the English Laws* likewise commented acidly, 'A good husband would not desire the power of horsewhipping, confining, half-starving his wife, or squandering her estate; a bad husband should not be allowed it.'[11]

But by the later eighteenth century the romantic proposition that true love required a woman's legal and economic 'annihilation' within marriage precluded objection. This word was freely used by William Alexander in the 1770s, but he assured his readers that 'by this little mortification' a married woman 'is no loser'.[12] Contemporary feminist and reforming writers did not discuss property law at all. The so-called 'Bluestockings' (Elizabeth Montagu, Elizabeth Carter, Fanny Burney, Hester Thrale, Hannah More), and even the radicals of the 1790s (Mary Wollstonecraft, Mary Hays, Priscilla Wakefield, Mary Ann Radcliffe), put their faith entirely in the efficacy of educational and moral reform.[13] Wollstonecraft did note in *A Vindication of the Rights of Woman* (1792) that she meant to take up 'the laws respecting women', and particularly what she called the 'absurd unit of a man and his wife' in a future volume, but this never appeared.[14]

In striking contrast to Mary More's advice to her daughter in the 1670s is Sarah, Lady Pennington's oft-reprinted *Unfortunate Mother's*

8. As quoted in Katherine Rogers, 'The feminism of Daniel Defoe', in Paul Fritz and Richard Morton, eds, *Woman in the 18th Century and Other Essays* (Toronto, 1976), pp. 22–3.

9. See Staves, 'Pin-money', or *Married Women's Separate Property*, ch. 5.

10. *Roxana*, p. 189. 11. *Hardships*, p. 50.

12. William Alexander, *The History of Women, from the Earliest Antiquity to the Present Time*, 3rd edn (London, 1782), p. 486.

13. See further William Stafford, 'Narratives of women: English feminists of the 1790s', *History* 82 (1997), pp. 24–43.

14. Mary Wollstonecraft, *A Vindication of the Rights of Woman* (London, 1985), p. 159.

Advice to Her Absent Daughters (1761), giving moral instruction to the children her husband took with him when he left her. The background to this state of affairs, the author tells us, is that after fifteen years of marriage her husband became 'greatly incensed that my father's will gave to me an independent fortune [separate estate], which will [my husband] imagined I was accessary to, or at least could have prevented'. Lord Pennington thereupon accused her of infidelity and removed himself and her daughters.[15] Despite the economic basis of her personal tragedy, Sarah Pennington plunges immediately into religious devotion, the management of servants and household discipline, what a young girl ought to read, and what theatre is acceptable. She never mentions her father's will again, or her fortune, or the property hazards of marriage.

Individual aristocratic women continued to publicize their legal battles over marital property throughout the eighteenth and into the nineteenth century, but on an individual level. Caroline Norton's personal marital history, published in 1854 with the expansive title *English Laws for Women in the Nineteenth Century*, directly brought about the first sign of change in marital law, the Matrimonial Causes Act of 1857, which regularized legal procedures for obtaining separation or divorce.[16] However, these were women still married but separated. I am not aware of any prominent widows publishing pamphlets about the dire circumstances in which their husbands left them.

After *The Hardships of the English Laws* in 1735, no specifically legal protests were voiced again for over a century. Was this merely a shift of interest among the literate and well-to-do? Did the upper social levels generally protect women's property sufficiently with marriage settlements so that it was no longer a pressing concern? Certainly their use was virtually universal among the top 5 per cent of the population. It is difficult to tell what proportion of the rest of the population made use of settlements. The ordinary bond form of marriage settlement appears only in probate accounts, and even there it is only by inference: the widow deducts the amount for which she had contracted before marriage out of her husband's estate. In seventeenth-century England, 10 per cent of all probate

15. Lady Sarah Pennington, *Unfortunate Mother's Advice to Her Absent Daughters*, 4th edn (London, 1767), pp. 10, 13.

16. Clare Brant, 'Speaking of women: scandal and the law in the mid-eighteenth century', in Clare Brant and Diane Purkiss, eds, *Women, Texts and Histories 1575–1760* (London and New York, 1992); Mary Poovey, 'Covered but not bound: Caroline Norton and the 1857 Matrimonial Causes Act', *Feminist Studies* 14 (1988), pp. 467–85.

accounts mention a settlement on the wife's behalf, but this is a minimum figure since it was not required that such an arrangement be listed in the account. By contrast, in later eighteenth- and early nineteenth-century South Carolina and Virginia marriage settlements were publicly registered. But less than 2 per cent of all marriages made one.[17] It is possible that the English bond system also worked in the colonies without ever reaching a register book. In Massachusetts (1765–71), for example, over 10 per cent of men's wills referred to a prenuptial property agreement of some sort, although we do not know what type of provision was being made.[18] In England public registration of settlements was not required or even possible.

The probate accounts in which settlements appear (the final reckoning of the administrator to the court, filed one year after death and listing all expenses of an estate) drop sharply in number in the late seventeenth century and disappear altogether, except in contested cases, from the early eighteenth. Of the other probate documents, which form the bulk of evidence about ordinary people, inventories become too sketchy to be of use after 1740: instead of itemizing goods individually they start to summarize by room or by type of property.

Wills are the only source which survive in almost undiminished numbers over the whole period, to give some clue as to property practices 'on the ground'. Although we have no direct evidence on marriage settlements, they leave a documentary shadow in the number of wills made by married women, since one indication of separate property is the ability to bequeath it. The wills of Lancashire and Cheshire are suitable for long-term quantitative analysis because they are indexed chronologically, by decade or pair of decades, and the index generally lists occupation or marital status. Table 1 charts the marital status of women who made wills in Lancashire and Cheshire between 1660 and 1837. But Table 1 shows a decrease rather than an increase in the number of wives making wills from the late seventeenth to the mid-eighteenth century, not rising to more than 2 per cent of all women's wills until the 1820s. The practice of married women making wills, normally indicating separate

17. Marylynn Salmon, 'The legal status of women in early America', *Law and History Review* 1 (1983), p. 149, or *Women and the Law of Property in Early America* (Chapel Hill, NC, 1986), ch. 1; Suzanne Lebsock, *Free Women of Petersburg: Status and Culture in a Southern Town 1784–1860* (New York and London, 1984), p. 72.

18. Gloria Main, 'Widows in rural Massachusetts on the eve of the Revolution', in R. Hoffman and P.J. Albert, eds, *Women in the Age of the American Revolution* (Charlottesville, Va., 1989), p. 74 n. 15.

TABLE 1 *Status of women will-makers in Lancashire and Cheshire, 1660–1837*

Dates	*Total**	*% Spinsters*	*% Wives*	*% Widows*	*% Occupations*
1660–1680	*526*	18.8	0.4	80.2	0.6
1681–1700	*676*	15.7	1.5	82.5	0.3
1701–1720	*390*	18.5	0.3	80.5	0.8
1721–1740	*193*	20.2	–	79.2	0.5
1741–1760	*343*	24.1	–	75.2	0.6
1761–1780	*367*	29.7	1.9	67.8	0.5
1781–1790	*572*	28.3	1.6	69.2	0.9
1791–1800	*335*	28.1	1.2	69.0	1.8
1801–1810	*432*	31.7	1.2	64.1	2.8
1811–1820	*513*	30.4	1.8	65.7	1.9
1826–1830	*314*	31.5	3.8	60.5	4.1
1834–1837	*445*	33.5	5.6	57.8	3.1

Source: *Wills at Chester*, Lancashire and Cheshire Record Society Series 15 (1887), 18 (1888), 20 (1889), 22 (1890), 25 (1892), 37 (1898), 44 (1902), 49 (1902), 62 (1911), 78 (1928), 113 (1972) and 120 (1980), sampled for the years indicated.
* This is the total number of women's wills for which a status was specified in the index, over three-quarters of the total. The numbers in Tables 2 and 3 are larger because they include those women's wills for which no status was given.

estate, may have varied considerably in different areas. In Norwich, in a sample of 250 women's wills indexed between 1687 and 1750, 9 per cent were those of married women. In the sixteenth and seventeenth centuries, family tradition appears to have influenced a married woman's chance of making a will,[19] and it seems likely that other forms of separate estate or jointure practices also depended on personal knowledge of the experience of mothers and aunts. But without more detailed studies of the wills themselves we know nothing about chronological shifts or the possible reasons for such a high level of wives' wills.

It is still possible that the use of marriage settlements in Lancashire and Cheshire increased in the eighteenth century but that they are not reflected in the number of wives making wills, either because the separate estate did not include the power to make a will, or because settlements were made for payments upon widowhood rather than for separate estate during marriage. Another possible indication of marriage settlements may be an increase in men

19. Mary Prior, 'Wives and wills 1558–1700', in John Chartres and David Hey, eds, *English Rural Society, 1500–1800: Essays in Honour of Joan Thirsk* (Cambridge, 1990).

specifying in their wills the return to a widow of the goods or cash which she brought with her to marriage. This appears to happen more frequently over the century, but it also happens more frequently where the widow is not made executrix and she is increasingly not made executrix over the century (see below). It might even be expected that the frequency of premarital property settlements at all social levels would actually *increase* during the eighteenth century, if women were attempting to compensate for statutory reductions in their entitlement to their husbands' estates upon widowhood.

From the late seventeenth century Parliament and the judiciary steadily eliminated widows' property rights, after a long period (two or three hundred years) of relative stasis. It was in probate law that some of the most important changes affecting ordinary people occurred. Probate and the distribution of personal property (everything movable plus leases of land) came under the jurisdiction of the ecclesiastical courts until the nineteenth century. And the majority of most people's wealth throughout this period was in personal, not real property.

Most people (approximately 70 per cent) died without having made a will: that is, intestate. According to the ecclesiastical law of intestate inheritance, the personal property of a married man was divided into thirds: one-third to his widow and two-thirds to all his children equally. In the absence of children the entire estate went to the widow, and vice versa. But in 1670 Parliament intervened with the Act for the Better Settling of Intestates' Estates (22 & 23 Car. II *c.* 10). This Act primarily only restated in statute form the existing ecclesiastical division of intestates' goods into thirds, one to the widow and two to the children. Records unfortunately do not survive from this period to give some clue about what Parliament thought it was doing. Ecclesiastical powers of enforcement were curtailed fourteen years later by the Statute of Distributions (1 Jac. II *c.* 17) to cover only estates for which an interested party had specifically requested an account of the distribution. (Such a request could come from the next-of-kin or a creditor of the deceased, or on behalf of a minor.) The only fragment of debate which survives on the 1670 bill and on two earlier similar but unsuccessful bills suggests that their intent was to extend the jurisdiction – and income – of the secular courts by allowing widows and children to sue for their thirds there, rather than in ecclesiastical courts.[20]

20. See further Erickson, *Women and Property*, pp. 37–8.

There was only one actual change in the law of intestate distribution as restated by Parliament: a childless widow's allocation was reduced from the whole, to one-half of her husband's personal estate; the other half henceforth went to his next-of-kin. Motherless children continued to receive the entire estate. Although potentially devastating for poorer widows, we have no way of tracing the effects of halving a childless widow's entitlement. The infringement is nowhere explained. In addition to this overt circumscription the Act of 1670 had another malign, and possibly unintended, consequence for widows with children. Prior to the Act it is clear from probate accounts that the ecclesiastical courts consistently awarded the widows of intestate men *two*-thirds of the residual personal estate: that is, twice their legal entitlement. After the Act this practice was abandoned and, on the evidence of probate accounts, the widow's award was kept strictly to one-third.[21]

Changes were also made in the law of inheritance of personal property in the 30 per cent of cases where a married man made a will. In the seventeenth century, a married man living in the City of London (and possibly other cities too) or in the Northern Province (that is, north of a line between the River Humber and the River Dee) could only dispose of one-third of his personal property by will. That man's widow was entitled to one-third of his estate, and his children to one-third. This law of 'reasonable parts' (called *legitim* in the Middle Ages) also obtained in Wales and Scotland. It had at one time prevailed in southern England too, but vanished there sometime before 1500.

The widow's and children's right to reasonable parts was abolished in the rest of England and Wales by four statutes between 1692 and 1725.[22] The parliamentary record surrounding these bills is again lost, although from the text of the 1704 Act it appears that the freemen of the City of York, who had been excepted from a previous Act affecting the Northern Province, actually asked for – and were granted – relief from the onerous duty of providing their widows and children with reasonable parts. (The City of Chester appears to be the only place in England where the right to reasonable parts was never abolished.)

Eighteenth-century legal writers regard this series of statutes as procedural: the anonymous author of *The Laws Respecting Women*

21. Ibid., p. 179.

22. 4 Wm. & Mary *c.* 2 (1692), Northern Province except freemen of York and Chester. 7&8 Wm. III *c.* 38 (1696), Wales. 2&3 Anne *c.* 5 (1704), City of York. 11 Geo. I *c.* 18 (1725), City of London.

(1777) explained soothingly that their purpose was 'to favour the power of bequeathing, and to reduce the whole kingdom to the same standard'.[23] Two hundred years later, it is still seen this way: the various regions 'came to permit complete freedom of testation',[24] implying a progressive evolution of individual rights to private property. However, in the process of establishing a man's absolute right to his private property in testamentary disposition, the abolition of reasonable parts necessarily obliterated his wife's right to private property from the date of her marriage.

More work on eighteenth-century wills has been done for colonial America. There, changes in property distribution and even restrictions on separate estate are traced to regional demographic or economic adjustments, and the general trend is seen as progress towards equality and ultimately reform, assisted by a decline of patriarchal marriage over the century and its replacement by what is usually called 'companionate marriage'.[25]

In England the more acerbic description of 'gentle tyranny' is more appropriate.[26] In Lancashire and Cheshire the proportion of *all* women who made wills, not just wives, declined (erratically) from 27 per cent of the total number surviving just before 1700 to 13 per cent in the decade prior to 1800 (Table 2). Thereafter the proportions rise again, but by 1837 they have still not reached late seventeenth-century levels. It is unlikely that all women found will-making less necessary to their financial autonomy. The only comparative figures available for other parts of the country are not differentiated chronologically: over the entire eighteenth century, women left 23 per cent of the 2620 wills in Birmingham and 18 per cent of the 1818 wills in Sheffield;[27] between 1687 and 1750, 25 per cent of a sample of 1000 Norwich wills were made by women. There are no long-term studies available for the American colonies.

And furthermore, if women were voluntarily renouncing testation as a result of new spousal affection and egalitarianism, we would expect the phenomenon to occur more markedly among the upper classes. The only means of distinguishing will-makers by wealth

23. *The Laws Respecting Women* (London, 1777), p. 223.

24. John Baker, *Introduction to English Legal History*, 2nd edn (London, 1979), p. 321. The statutes do not appear at all in Alan Harding's *Social History of English Law* (Harmondsworth, 1966).

25. For example, Salmon, *Women and the Law of Property*, pp. xvi, 84–7.

26. Ruth Perry, 'Radical doubt and the liberation of women', *Eighteenth-Century Studies* 18 (1985), p. 475.

27. Maxine Berg, 'Women's property and the industrial revolution', *Journal of Interdisciplinary History* 24 (1993), p. 237.

TABLE 2 *Proportion of wills made by women in Lancashire and Cheshire, 1660–1837*

Dates	*Total extant*	*% made by women*	*No. made by women*
1660–1680	*3593*	24.2	*868*
1681–1700	*3551*	27.3	*970*
1701–1720	*2152*	21.0	*452*
1721–1740	*2539*	20.3	*516*
1741–1760	*2176*	22.0	*478*
1761–1780	*2412*	17.5	*422*
1781–1790	*3931*	16.6	*653*
1791–1800	*3033*	13.3	*404*
1801–1810	*3069*	17.7	*542*
1811–1820	*2860*	20.0	*573*
1826–1830	*1676*	21.1	*354*
1834–1837	*2038*	23.3	*475*

Source: as for Table 1. The editors of the indices cannot explain the considerable variation in the total number of wills surviving per decade. It would appear that they do not represent the total ever proved and that certain years may be lost.

– short of analysing individual wills – is the ecclesiastical court's separate classification of those who had inventories valued at less than £40. The £40 figure is arbitrary, set by statute in 1529 (21 Hen. VIII *c.* 5), and means something quite different in 1700 than it does in 1800. It should also be remembered that the goods valued in an inventory are only personal estate, not real estate: the inventory of one John Jones, a 'stonegetter' of Chester, in 1730 was valued at a mere £8, but his will refers to seven houses, two butts (ridges of a field), one addition and two and a half quarries.[28] This might have made him reasonably well off in Chester terms, but it is interesting to note for comparison that the lowest rung of the London middle class in the early eighteenth century is considered to be those with 'less than £500' of domestic goods *alone* in their inventories.[29] So the £40 demarcation is certainly not one of upper and lower classes but, in the absence of painstaking analysis of individual wills, it is the only demarcation available.

Table 3 separates the wills of those with less than £40 from those with more than £40. The proportion of women among those with

28. Chester Record Office WI 1730. For further discussion of inventories' silences and the reasons for them, see Erickson, *Women and Property*, pp. 33–4.

29. Peter Earle, *The Making of the English Middle Class: Business, Society and Family Life in London 1660–1730* (London, 1989), p. 291.

TABLE 3 *Wealth variations in women's wills in Lancashire and Cheshire, 1660–1837*

Dates	*Estates>£40*	*% by women*	*Estates<£40*	*% by women*
1660–1680	*2083*	19.2	*1510*	31.2
1681–1700	*2029*	22.3	*1522*	34.0
1701–1720	*1552*	19.0	*600*	26.2
1721–1740	*1376*	17.8	*1163*	23.3
1741–1760	*1151*	21.5	*1025*	22.4
1761–1780	*1777*	17.9	*250*	14.0
1781–1790	*2989*	18.4	*942*	11.0
1791–1800	*1291*	17.9	*1742*	9.9
1801–1810	*1993*	19.3	*1076*	14.6
1811–1820	*2305*	19.7	*555*	21.3
1826–1830	*1321*	21.1	*355*	21.1
1834–1837	*382*	23.4	*403*	23.1

Source: as for Table 1. The sample includes all those indexed with less than £40 inventories and letters A–C of those with more than £40 inventories.

more than £40 who make wills remains relatively consistent, between approximately 18 and 22 per cent, until 1830. But the poorer women, those with estates of less than £40, are the ones ceasing to make wills, dropping dramatically from 34 per cent of all wills in 1700 to 10 per cent in 1800, at which point the rate rises quickly to the same level as wealthier women, although still considerably below the late-seventeenth-century levels of under-£40-women. I cannot explain these peculiar patterns. More work on the regional distribution of the wills within the two counties and local economic information may shed some light on them. What is quite clear is that increased spousal affection and trust is not a factor.

In fact, *decreasing* spousal affection and trust is suggested by a closer look at the contents of eighteenth-century wills, where we find that fewer women were given responsibility in their husbands' wills. In late seventeenth-century England approximately 80 to 90 per cent of married men appointed their widow executrix and most (three-quarters) of those were sole executrix.[30] However, in a

30. Erickson, *Women and Property*, p. 158. The same was true in Maryland and New Hampshire until the first decades of the eighteenth century. Lois Green Carr and Lorena S. Walsh, 'The planter's wife: the experience of white women in seventeenth-century Maryland', *William and Mary Quarterly* 34 (1977), pp. 555–6; L.T. Ulrich, *Good Wives: Image and Reality in the Lives of Women in Northern New England* (New York, 1982), p. 38 n. 6.

sample of fifty married men's wills from Cheshire in the 1720s, the proportion of widows named executrix was down to 57 per cent, of which about half were sole and half were joint. By the 1780s (in another sample of fifty), the proportion was only 41 per cent, of which two-thirds were joint and one-third were sole.

A similar decline is evident in colonial America. In Massachusetts it has been explained in terms of demographic changes: widows became older, and so had more adult sons to take over the responsibility of taking care of the family property.[31] While plausible for Massachusetts, the demographic argument does not explain the changes in England. Cheshire testators of the 1720s and of the 1780s had almost exactly the same likelihood of having an adult child. In fact, in both decades those men who made their wives joint executrix *and* had an adult son tended *not* to make that son joint executor. Men who relieved their wives of responsibility altogether were still almost as likely *not* to name their adult son to the post. Finally, the most common family situation of those women who were named sole executrix was that they had an adult son. In England at least, the executrix question was a problem in changing ideas about power, not a pragmatic response to demographic or economic circumstance. A widow – in Lancashire and Cheshire and elsewhere – was still normally her husband's principal beneficiary, at least for life, but she exercised control over that property less and less.

Maxine Berg observes that 'expectations concerning the role of executors differed over time, place, and social class, and numbers of female executors alone cannot indicate a direction of change in women's property rights'.[32] Certainly part of the disappearance of the widow-executrix may be attributed to increasing legal professionalization over the century. A closer analysis of wills might determine how often men appointed their lawyers executor, over time, place and social class. But even if it were lawyers who were displacing widows, the removal of a married woman from the management of household financial affairs would not bode well for her widowhood. In conjunction with legal changes, the decline in the numbers of widows named executrix is suspicious.

It would appear from crude numbers of wills that, especially at lower social levels, neither brides nor their families took any steps to compensate for increasing legal disadvantages in widowhood.

31. Main, 'Widows in rural Massachusetts', p. 74, Table 1, and p. 89. See also D.E. Narrett, 'Men's wills and women's property rights in colonial New York', in Hoffman and Albert, *Women in the Age of the American Revolution*, p. 119, Table 4.
32. 'Women's property', p. 239.

Certainly there is no evidence of public outcry. Most manuals on the law affecting women, available throughout this long eighteenth century, did not discuss the statutory changes to either intestate distribution or reasonable parts.[33] Even the most outspoken, *The Lady's Law* (1732), which advertised that 'the fair sex are here inform'd, how to preserve their lands, goods, and most valuable effects, from the incroachments of anyone',[34] did not suggest there had ever been a time that women had enjoyed rights to personal property upon widowhood without the necessity for a premarital contract. Only *The Laws Respecting Women* (1777) suggested that some of its readers might object to 'the right which is now vested in the husband, to bequeath his substance at his own free will, to the exclusion of his wife, if he should be so inclined'. But the anonymous author was conciliatory: 'a court of Chancery is ever disposed to exert its authority in relief of women who have been injuriously treated, and in cases of extreme hardship would cause equity to supply the defects of natural affection'.[35]

The Court of Chancery, of course, was busily doing everything it could to minimize the benefits of separate estate to women. The extraordinary late-eighteenth-century device called the 'restraint on anticipation', to limit married women's access to their separate property, has been exposed by Susan Staves. The eighteenth century also looms large in Eileen Spring's depiction of a long-term decline in women's access to property.[36] Both of these historians deal exclusively with the upper classes, hence they address changes in settlement structure and practice, but neither mentions the ecclesiastical courts. A less well-known change in separate estate, and one with more immediate ramifications for a much broader range of people, was Chancery's preoccupation with the exact terminology used to establish separate estate. In the seventeenth and through the mid-eighteenth century, if an estate was given to the husband for the wife's use, then 'technical words are not necessary to make it a separate trust'.[37] But by 1800 all of the following phrases had become *in*sufficient to create a separate estate: 'for her own use and benefit', 'under her sole control', 'her absolute use', or 'into her own proper

33. *Baron and Feme* (London, 1700, expanded edn 1738); *A Treatise of Feme Coverts: Or The Lady's Law* (London, 1732, 2nd edn 1737); Peregrine Bingham, *The Law of Infancy and Coverture* (1816).

34. *The Lady's Law*, p. vii.

35. *The Laws Respecting Women*, pp. xi–xii.

36. Eileen Spring, *Law, Land and Family: Aristocratic Inheritance in England 1300–1800* (Chapel Hill, NC, 1993).

37. *Darley* v. *Darley*, 3 Atk. 399 (6 Dec. 1746).

hands, to and for her own use and benefit'.[38] This raising of the terminological standards must have filtered down to people in the provinces who would never themselves see the Court of Chancery. What else explains why men's wills at the end of the eighteenth century, but not those written earlier, go to great lengths to circumscribe their daughters' bequests? For example, a Cheshire blacksmith in 1790, giving his married daughter two dwelling houses in Etchells, stated that they were 'for her own proper use and behoof . . . independent of her . . . husband, and wherewith he shall not intermeddle nor have any control nor authority over'.[39] Wills of the late seventeenth and early eighteenth centuries are apt to use only one of these phrases or, even more simply, 'for her sole use' to invoke separate estate, so that the property remained the daughter's, whether married, widowed or remarried.

It is striking that the mid-nineteenth-century campaigners for reform of the married women's property law showed no awareness of the constriction of separate estate over the preceding century.[40] Perhaps less surprisingly, given the affluence of the campaigners, there was no awareness either of the disadvantages imposed on widows by statutory changes in the late seventeenth and early eighteenth centuries. The total lack of opposition contrasts markedly with recent discussions about the significance of popular defence of other types of much less formalized custom and the growing strength of radicalism from the mid-eighteenth century.[41]

Why were late eighteenth- and early nineteenth-century women not up in arms? Perhaps, as Mary Wollstonecraft observed in a slightly different context, their 'understanding . . . [was] so bubbled by this specious homage' of sentimental men.[42] In legal thought, however, the stripping of women's property rights coincides curiously with a vigorous defence of the rights of the 'individual' to private property. This paradox may only be resolved by the proposition that women were not at any point considered to be 'individuals'

38. Thomas Barrett-Lennard, *The Position in Law of Women* (Littleton, Colorado, 1983; reprint of original 1883 edn), pp. 82–4; E.H.T. Snell, *The Principles of Equity* (London, 1868), p. 282.

39. Cheshire Record Office, Chester, WS 1790 (John Bancroft).

40. See for example William Thompson, *An Appeal to One Half the Human Race* (1825), Marion Reid, *Plea for Woman* (1843) or Barbara Leigh Smith, *A Brief Summary, in Plain Language, of the Most Important Laws Concerning Women* (1854).

41. Andy Wood, 'The place of custom in plebeian political culture: England, 1550–1800', *Social History* 22 (1997), pp. 46–60; John Rule, 'Against innovation? Custom and resistance in the workplace, 1700–1850', in Tim Harris, ed., *Popular Culture in England, c. 1500–1850* (Basingstoke, 1995).

42. Introduction to *Vindication*, p. 3.

and therefore had no 'rights'.[43] G.R. Rubin and David Sugarman contend that the eighteenth-century ideal of absolute rights to private property was qualified in practice by emphasis on the concomitant obligations connected to that property. But while citing the family in particular as an example, they do not mention women once.[44] And the statutes and case law discussed above suggest that familial obligations connected with the head of household's property were merely moral, and had lost all legal weight by the eighteenth century. It seems that the supposed increase in spousal affection and the undoubted increase in sentiment/sensibility over the eighteenth century were in direct contradiction to the economic evidence: men loved their wives more but no longer allowed them to control property while married or trusted them to take care of family estates as widows.

The statutory limitations of widows' rights to their husbands' property in the late seventeenth and early eighteenth centuries have been attributed to procedural regularization and secularization. The manipulation of separate estates in the later eighteenth century has been attributed to the extraordinary thoughtfulness of the Court in specially protecting women from potential abuse by their husbands. Whatever the intent, the effect of the legal changes looks like judicial selfishness on a scale which we would deplore in small children. In the eighteenth century the economic brutality was masked, to both parties, by a seductive formula: 'the generosity of our females will not allow them to wish to keep their property from those to whom they have not refused their person'.[45] The test of spiritual love became total material surrender. The psychologically destructive effects of this duplicitousness should not be underestimated. Janelle Greenberg has suggested that any legal action by a woman in the eighteenth century required 'a degree of awareness that a wrong had been done her', the likelihood of which was limited, 'given the prevailing view of a wife's proper relation to her husband'.[46] Perhaps, but Sarah Chapone's comment in 1735 suggests an intense awareness of wrong: 'The disdain and confusion of mind, which

43. Carole Pateman, *The Sexual Contract* (Oxford, 1988); Susan Moller Okin, *Women in Western Political Thought* (Princeton, 1979).

44. 'Towards a new history of law and material society in England 1750–1914', introduction to G.R. Rubin and David Sugarman, eds, *Law, Economy and Society 1750–1914* (Abingdon, 1984), pp. 1–23.

45. Paraphrasing an eighteenth-century Connecticut attorney quoted in Salmon, 'Legal status', p. 150.

46. Janelle Greenberg, 'The legal status of women in early eighteenth-century common law and equity', *Studies in Eighteenth-Century Culture* 4 (1975), p. 178.

naturally rises upon ill treatment, from those whom we have greatly trusted or loved, might make a woman in such circumstances destroy herself.'[47]

On a popular level, widows' immediate material well-being – in terms of their inheritance from husbands anyway – may not have changed. Long-term social changes also combined to deter any popular resistance to the constriction of women's property rights. High mobility and rapid urbanization through the eighteenth century, and perhaps especially in Lancashire and Cheshire, may have meant that older family members were less likely to be available to advise – perhaps, as brides saw it, to interfere – in new marriages. The median age at which women first married dropped steadily between the late seventeenth and the mid-nineteenth centuries, from 27 to 23.[48] So they spent a shorter period independent before marriage. They may have had less authority within the household, since although men's median age at first marriage also fell, far more widowers than widows remarried, so older men were marrying younger women. And of course they bore more children. As if that were insufficient to tie a woman firmly to immediate domestic concerns, the explosion of consumer goods – whatever value was attached to them, and whatever satisfaction might be derived from them – necessarily required more maintenance in the home, washing, polishing, and mending.

There is a growing literature on the significance of goods as a means of personal representation by women in the eighteenth century, based in considerable part on wills written by widows.[49] The study of this aspect of property ownership is partly due to the focus on consumption in the eighteenth century, and the personal significance of goods may have been equally gendered in earlier centuries. But we need to know if female self-definition through material objects is a distinctive feature of this period, and if so why it appears to accompany a decline in property ownership among women.

Linguistic changes suggest that the pressure to marry increased markedly during the eighteenth century. The term 'old maid' appears and the word 'spinster' becomes pejorative about 1700. Over the course of the century marital status was distinguished in

47. *Hardships*, p. 13.

48. E.A. Wrigley and R.S. Schofield, *The Population History of England 1541–1871: A Reconstruction* (Cambridge, 1981), p. 255, Table 7.26.

49. Berg, 'Women's property', pp. 246–7; Marcia Pointon, *Strategies for Showing: Women, Possession, and Representation in English Visual Culture 1665–1800* (Oxford, 1997), introduction and appendix; Joanne Lafler, 'The will of Katherine Maynwaring: an autobiographical reading' *Biography* 20 (1997), pp. 156–80.

honorifics for the first time, with the invention of 'Miss' and the shift of 'Mrs' from a designation of social status to one of marital status. However, among this sample of wills from Lancashire and Cheshire the proportion of single women making wills increases from less than one-fifth to over one-third of all women (Table 1). This may be due to the local economy attracting women for work in the textile and associated trades, and in coal mining.[50] Further research could ascertain more closely in what parts of Lancashire and Cheshire the wills originated, and what the ages and occupations of the single women were. At the same time, the proportion of widows' wills declines from over 80 per cent to less than 60 per cent of all women's wills: are there fewer widows in the population? or are they making wills less and less?

The drop in age at first marriage may also be connected with an overall decline in women's economic opportunities. While it is commonly supposed that rising wages mean people can marry earlier, this correlation has been made only with male wages. Lancashire and Cheshire have high marriage and birth rates throughout this period.[51] If the constriction of legal entitlement to property occurs concomitantly with the reduction of women's occupational choices and economic resources, it would help explain why there was virtually no objection to the changes. The expectation and the culture of ownership were evaporating.

While an ideology of romantic love, popularized at lower social levels to an extent not previously possible, may help to explain the lack of response to legal infringements upon property rights, it cannot explain the infringements themselves. Why did the freemen of the City of York in 1704 ask to be relieved of the onerous duty to leave their widows at least one-third of the personal marital estate? The legal changes were the result of changing ideas about power. The overall drop in the proportion of women making wills, especially among poorer women, until 1800, and the lack of any change in wives' wills to suggest an initiative toward separate estate, suggest a popular acceptance of the idea that women as wives ought to be 'at one' with their husbands physically, emotionally and financially and had to be 'protected against themselves'. The rapidly declining number of widows named executrix following the statutory limitations of the late seventeenth and early eighteenth century reflects

50. C.B. Phillips and J.H. Smith, *Lancashire and Cheshire from AD 1540* (London and New York, 1994), esp. pp. 88–105, 132–7.

51. Ibid., p. 137.

the limitation of widows' power intended by those statutes, adopted by ordinary men.

The next problem is to explain why a culture of ownership revived, at least insofar as will-making is concerned. In the first four decades of the nineteenth century the trend is reversed: the proportion of all wills made by women rises from 17.7 per cent to 23.3 per cent (Table 2), and the number of wives making wills – reflecting separate estate – rises to an all-time high (Table 1). These women were the wives of farmers, cordwainers and plasterers, as well as of merchants, manufacturers and gentlemen. Is the reason local wages or sources of income? Is it local tradition? Do other areas show the same pre-reform groundswell of changing habits? We have much to find out.

CHAPTER TEN

Religious difference and the experience of widowhood in seventeenth- and eighteenth-century Germany[1]

DAGMAR FREIST

A powerful image of the mourning widow has survived in the unique portrait of Katharina von Bora entitled *D. Martini Luthers nachgelassene Witfrawn/in ihrer Traurung* – 'The widow of Martin Luther in mourning' (see Figure 2, p. 178). The coloured woodcut is dominated by the figure of Katharina wrapped in a black fur coat with a prayer book in her hands. The command for silence is symbolized by a long ribbon, which falls from her hat and ties her mouth.[2] Both the Catholic and Protestant faiths expected a widow to mourn her husband's death, and to live a life of chastity withdrawn from the world in prayer to God. Widows were allowed by law to remarry only after a period of mourning, usually one year, but in the sixteenth century the legal requirement gradually changed into a moral expectation.

The German term *Witwe* (widow), which derived either from the old Saxon *witgen* or the lower Saxon *wedeweh*, signifies, in fact, the idea of mourning, *witgen* meaning to lament, to moan, to cry, and *wedeweh* describing a pitiful state in a life of poverty and sorrow.[3] The Bible conveys strong images of the suffering widow who deserves the protection of God and mankind. Yet, at the same time, Holy Scripture also warns of the lusty young widow who threatens

1. I am highly indebted to Heide Wunder who read an earlier version of this chapter and gave, as always, helpful comments. I owe many thanks to my former colleague Angela Davies from the German Historical Institute in London who proofread this chapter and greatly improved my English, which is not my native tongue.

2. The woodcut by Lucas Cranach the Elder dates from 1546, the year of Martin Luther's death.

3. Johann Heinrich Zedler, *Grosses vollständiges Universal-Lexikon aller Wissenschaften und Künste*, 64 vols (Halle, Leipzig, 1962; 1st edn 1732–54), LVII, pp. 1938–9.

to seduce faithful men. Since widows had sexual knowledge but were no longer under male authority they were seen to pose a danger to the social and moral order. These conflicting images of the suffering and the dangerous widow influenced both church and secular legislation as well as popular literature and custom.[4] Before the Reformation the Catholic church only half-heartedly accepted the idea of remarriage. The preferred option for widows was to enter a nunnery. The reformer Martin Luther idealized the ultimate role of a woman as wife and mother. In Protestant thought marriage became the primary goal for women. The Christian household provided a place of authority for the wife in co-operation with and in obedience to her husband. Under the impact of the Reformation and the Council of Trent (1563), the patriarchal conception of household and marriage became the organizing principle of the early modern state.[5] Single women, unmarried or widowed, did not fit into this pattern and, being outside male control, were easily suspected of unchaste and unruly behaviour. It is difficult to know the extent to which these images and norms influenced the experience of widowed women in everyday life. In 1568, after the death of Hans Jäger, his widow wrote that 'the evil talk, which I sometimes have to endure in my widowhood', had led her to consider remarriage.[6]

In order to understand the condition of widowhood in the early modern period we need to look at demographic data, social status, economic situation, age, number and age of children, family ties, legal rights and community networks. However, if we wish to reconstruct women's subjective experience of widowhood new questions need to be asked and new sources explored. This chapter provides a general overview of the situation of widows in early modern Germany,[7] and examines in detail the fate of the Mennonite widow Barbara Maurerin, who lived in the Palatinate in the late eighteenth century. Her story reveals how the religious differences between

4. Irmgard C. Taylor, *Das Bild der Witwe in der deutschen Literatur* (Darmstadt, 1980).

5. Heide Wunder, 'Herrschaft und öffentliches Handeln von Frauen in der Gesellschaft der Frühen Neuzeit', in Ute Gerhard, ed., *Frauen in der Geschichte des Rechts. Von der Frühen Neuzeit bis zur Gegenwart* (Munich, 1997), p. 36; Lyndal Roper, *The Holy Household: Women and Morals in Reformation Augsburg* (Oxford, 1989).

6. Roper, *Holy Household*, p. 53.

7. There is still no comprehensive study of widows in early modern Germany. For an overview see the chapter on widows in Heide Wunder, *He is the Sun, She is the Moon: Women in Early Modern Germany* (Cambridge, Mass., 1998), pp. 128–42. See also the chapter on widowhood in Lyndal Roper, *Holy Household*, pp. 49–55. There are a few articles which deal with specific aspects of widowhood which will be cited below.

Catholicism and the varieties of Protestantism might affect the experience of widowhood. The tragedy of her case unfolds as a struggle to retain the custody, and right of religious instruction, of her children against the deathbed wishes of her estranged Catholic husband. This Protestant widow's situation allows us to examine the question of state intervention in the family and in matters of religious faith. But let us first consider some general aspects of widowhood.

Widows far outnumbered widowers in early modern Germany. However, the common arguments that there was a surplus of women and that women had a longer life expectancy are not adequate explanations. Surely, the Thirty Years War had a devastating impact on ordinary people. Widows were hit especially hard. The acute surplus of unmarried women in some areas meant that it was very difficult to find a partner. At the end of the war the percentage of female households in Augsburg had risen from 20.2 per cent in 1618 to 26.9 per cent in 1646.[8] However, research has shown that remarriage patterns were gender-specific; widowers remarried more often and more quickly than widows. Between 1600 and 1779 in the small reformed village of Hesel near Bremen 30.3 per cent of women and 53.6 per cent of men under 55 remarried. The discrepancies between the remarriage patterns of men and women were even more extreme in Philippsburg, a Catholic fortress town near Karlsruhe which had suffered badly during the Thirty Years War and the French war at the end of the seventeenth century. Among those under 55, only 14.5 per cent of widows had remarried after 39.4 months, in contrast to 81.1 per cent of men who had married a second time after only 15.3 months. In the Protestant region of Schwalm near Kassel remarriage patterns for men were similar to those in Hesel whereas only 14.1 per cent of widows under 55 remarried. As in other parts of Europe, a widow's tendency to remarry decreased with age.[9] While widowers remarried more quickly and with greater frequency than widows, urban widows in particular had to compete with young and single female servants on the marriage market. Remarriage also influenced the

8. Bernd Roeck, *Eine Stadt in Krieg und Frieden*, 2 vols (Göttingen, 1989), II, p. 882.

9. All figures taken from Arthur E. Imhof, 'Wiederverheiratung in Deutschland zwischen dem 16. und dem 20. Jahrhunderts', in Rudolf Lenz, ed., *Studien zur deutschsprachigen Leichenpredigt der frühen Neuzeit* (Marburg/Lahn, 1981), pp. 185–222. See also Arthur E. Imhof, 'Remarriage in rural populations and in urban middle and upper strata in Germany from the sixteenth to the twentieth century', in Jacques Dupâquier *et al.*, eds, *Marriage and Remarriage in Populations of the Past* (London, 1981), pp. 335–45.

economic situation of men and women, as shown in a case study of Neckarhausen, a small village on the upper Neckar River in Swabia, where, for both sexes, remarriage involved the accumulation of wealth. Since here, too, widowers married more often than widows, original equality in marital funds tipped toward hypergamy, with men accumulating larger amounts of wealth.[10]

If remarriage was not an option the material circumstances and the number of dependent offspring influenced the experience of widowhood. The husband's will could make a decisive difference to the widow's fortune. Generally, a widow had the right to her dowry, the right to live in the conjugal home and whatever her husband had settled upon her. However, in practice considerable complications could arise, especially in the event of remarriage. Disputes about property and the repossession of a widow's assets have not been adequately studied for early modern Germany. Furthermore, questions of regional and religious difference have not been addressed. In some *Landjudenschaften* (Jewish corporations), for instance, Jewish widows received their inheritance only after they had paid off any debts their family owed to the Jewish *Landtag* (parliament).[11]

With few exceptions, a widow had to earn her livelihood, or at least supplement what was bestowed upon her in her husband's will. Throughout the Middle Ages so-called *Witwenprivilegien* (widows' privileges) gave a widow entry to a guild in place of her husband and allowed her to continue his trade or craft. From the sixteenth century the guilds made it increasingly difficult for masters' widows to continue the workshop on their own, and as a result of these restrictions these widows were often obliged to marry a younger journeyman or else give up the craft. Farmers' widows needed male help to continue running their farms and were under a similar pressure to remarry. Trading women were more independent and often quite successful. Among the merchant classes, widows often managed to maintain a successful business. Anna Bierling (1605–75), for example, continued her husband's trade in Leipzig for 35 years after his death, and Helene Amalie Ascherfeld (1732–1810), the

10. David Warren Sabean, *Property, Production and Family in Neckarhausen, 1700–1780* (Cambridge, 1990).

11. Daniel Cohen, 'Die Landjudenschaften in Hessen-Darmstadt bis zur Emanzipation als Organe jüdischer Selbstverwaltung', in *Neunhundert Jahre Geschichte der Juden in Hessen: Beiträge zum politischen, wirtschaftlichen und kulturellen Leben, Kommission für die Geschichte der Juden in Hessen* (Wiesbaden, 1983), pp. 164–5. On *Landjudenschaften* in Southern Germany see Rolf Kießling, ed., *Judengemeinden in Schwaben im Kontext des Alten Reiches* (Berlin, 1995).

second wife of Friedrich Jodocus Krupp, expanded his business in Essen after his death and purchased mines.[12] One of the most famous examples of a successful widow trader is the Jewish widow Glückel von Hameln (1646–1724).[13]

We still know little about the experience of widows among the urban middle and upper classes. A case study of the period 1510 to 1719 based on funeral sermons has shown that widows of the new *Bildungsbürgertum* (educated middle classes) waited on average for 43.3 months after their first, and 48.9 months after their second, marriage before they remarried.[14] If these figures were to be supported by further research, the question of how widows of officeholders, doctors and lawyers were provided for becomes a central issue. In contrast to crafts or trade, these rising professions of the early modern state left little room for a woman to participate in her husband's professional life or to continue his occupation after his death. For example, the ideal set before the wife of a Protestant pastor was to fulfil her roles as mother and wife. Obeying her husband and setting a good example to others, she was in charge of the household and the education of their children.[15] Thus, as early as the sixteenth century the problem of the poor pastor's widow was met by the foundation of a church widows' fund, followed by charities for widows of state or civic officeholders.[16] Many less fortunate widows earned a small living in typically female occupations such as the retail trade, food production or textile industries. Most widows lived with their children or with other women. Only a few lived on their own. Tax lists and poor lists demonstrate that widows and children were among the poorest of society. Among the 1400 people in receipt of poor relief in late sixteenth-century Augsburg there were 200 widows, 700 children, 150 orphans, and 70 sick people in hospital.[17]

12. Wunder, *He is the Sun*, pp. 90–1.

13. Natalie Zemon Davis, 'Glikl bas Judah Leib: arguing with God', in *Women on the Margins: Three Seventeenth-Century Lives* (Cambridge, Mass., 1995), pp. 5–62.

14. Imhof, 'Wiederverheiratung', pp. 213, 219.

15. Luise Schorn-Schütte, '"Gefährtin" und "Mitregentin": zur Sozialgeschichte der evangelischen Pfarrfrau in der Frühen Neuzeit', in Heide Wunder and Christina Vanja, eds, *Wandel der Geschlechterbeziehungen zu Beginn der Neuzeit* (Frankfurt, 1991), pp. 109–53.

16. Bernd Wunder, 'Pfarrwitwenkassen und Beamtenwitwen-Anstalten vom 16.–19. Jahrhundert: die Entstehung der staatlichen Hinterbliebenenversorgung in Deutschland', in *Zeitschrift für Historische Forschung* 12 (1985), pp. 429–98.

17. Roeck, *Eine Stadt*, I, p. 164. There are also some references to widows and poverty in Robert Jütte, *Obrigkeitliche Armenfürsorge in Deutschen Reichsstädten der Frühen Neuzeit: Städtisches Armenwesen in Frankfurt am Main und Köln* (Vienna, 1984).

It was not unusual for wealthy widows to found religious charities or monasteries, as did the Countess Sybilla Lodron. After the death of her husband, Count Maximilian Lodron, in 1635, Sybilla, daughter of the wealthy Augsburg Fugger family, decided to devote the rest of her life to God. In 1642 she joined the monastery she had founded in the same year.[18] The widows of princes and counts of small territories often ruled their dead husbands' territories, some of them as guardians until their sons came of age, others in their own right.[19] That this was not uncommon in the eyes of contemporaries is shown by the advice which Veit Ludwig von Seckendorff offered for the education of young princesses in preparation for possible rulership in his *Teutschen Fürstenstaat* (1656).[20]

It is difficult to make any generalizations about the legal status of widows because this varied from territory to territory. The emancipation process of the late Middle Ages which had brought women increasing freedom in private and civil law came to a halt in many parts of early modern Germany. Widows were spared the reintroduction of gender tutelage which existed in many German territories late into the nineteenth century – the ruling that married (*cura maritalis*) and unmarried (*cura sexus*) young women who had not yet come of age could never sell or alter property without the permission of their fathers, husbands or guardians. In court they needed a court-appointed legal guardian, who was, however, almost always a close relative.[21] Widows could defend their rights before ecclesiastical and secular courts including the highest court, the Imperial Court. They were free to run their own businesses and make financial transactions. While widows could be listed as heads of households, they did not enjoy the right to hold office. Theories of the inferiority of women dictated that a widow be given custody of her children only with specially appointed male guardians from her deceased husband's family. Here again there was a great deal of variation from territory to territory and town to town. However, in the seventeenth and eighteenth centuries widows tried to gain the right of

18. Martha Schad, *Die Frauen des Hauses Fugger von der Lilie (15.–17. Jahrhundert)* (Augsburg, 1989), pp. 151–3.

19. Uta Löwenstein, '"Daß sie sich uf iren Withumbssitz begeben und sich sonsten anderer der Herrschafften Sachen und Handlungen nicht undernemen . . .": Hofhaltungen fürstlicher Frauen und Witwen in der frühen Neuzeit', in Jörg Jochen Berns and Detlef Ignasiak, eds, *Frühneuzeitliche Hofkultur in Hessen und Thüringen* (Erlangen, 1993), I, pp. 115–41.

20. As quoted in Wunder, 'Herrschaft', pp. 49–50.

21. For a general survey of guardianship see Ernst Holthöfer, 'Die Geschlechtsvormundschaft: ein Überblick von der Antike bis ins 19. Jahrhundert', in Gerhard, *Frauen*, pp. 390–451.

sole guardianship. A *Beistands-Verordnung* in the Palatinate in 1747, which reiterates that widows should have co-guardians, suggests that even in territories with more restrictive legislation, in practice widows had the custody of their children and managed the heirs' property alone.[22]

In order to explore the experience of widows further we need to take into account regional variations which influenced peoples' lives. The second part of this chapter focuses on the case of the widow Barbara Maurerin and her fight for the custody of her children. Although her case is not representative of the experience of widowhood in general, her fate was not uncommon for a widow living in the conditions of seventeenth- and eighteenth-century German territorial and confessional particularism.

Early modern Germany was a patchwork of territories operating within the relatively weak framework of the Holy Roman Empire. The Empire consisted of seven electoral estates (eight at the end of the Thirty Years War), numerous ecclesiastical and secular states of varying size headed by abbots, abbesses and bishops, princes, counts and lords, and approximately eighty-three imperial towns, each with its own set of rules and, in theory, confessional identity.[23] Thus, different authorities, laws, administrations and religious majorities were in place within a short distance of each other, and 'crossing borders' involved much more than simply moving from one region to another. Social control, for instance, could be evaded by crossing borders, as the Mennonite widow Barbara Maurerin née Ullmännin did in the late eighteenth-century Palatinate in order to defend her own and her children's religion after the death of her Catholic husband. As a punishment for religious deviance her daughters were eventually banned from their home territory and had to sit out their sentence in a neighbouring territory.

The religious parity throughout the Empire, granted by the Peace of Westphalia in 1648, was unique in Europe. The peace treaty prohibited discrimination for religious reasons. However, it did not always lead to peaceful religious coexistence at a local level. Secular and ecclesiastical authorities continued to interfere in religious disputes throughout the seventeenth and eighteenth centuries. Ordinary people experienced religious difference on a daily basis. Churches were used alternatively by Catholics and Protestants.

22. General Landesarchiv Karlsruhe (GLA) Zc 1002, No. 41.

23. For an introduction to the religious, territorial and constitutional history of Germany, see Mary Fulbrook, *A Concise History of Germany* (Cambridge, 1990), ch. 3, pp. 33–69.

Catholic priests needed special permits to attend to dying Catholics in a neighbouring Protestant territory. Church officials tried to keep Protestant servants out of Catholic households and vice versa. Catholic processions provoked Protestants in bi-confessional towns such as Augsburg or Oppenheim.[24] The accession of a Catholic prince to a mainly Reformed territory, as happened, for instance, in the Palatinate in 1685, and the subsequent political re-Catholicization influenced the religious climate of the state. In the case of Augsburg, which was re-Catholicized in the seventeenth century, more Protestant than Catholic widows remained unmarried, probably as a result of the resettlement of the city at the end of the Thirty Years War, which brought mainly Catholics to the area.

Wherever people of different confessions lived in close proximity mixed marriages occurred.[25] Some women, such as the Palatinate widow Barbara Maurerin née Ullmännin, unexpectedly found themselves in a mixed marriage at the end of their married lives as a result of the deathbed conversions of their husbands.[26] The miller Peter Maurer of Trippstatt in the Oberamt (district) of Germersheim had been a Mennonite like his wife; however, he converted to the Catholic faith shortly before he died in 1766.[27] Barbara Maurerin had separated from Peter Maurer three years earlier and had been living with their children in the region of Weissenburg. On his deathbed Peter Maurer 'reclaimed' his children and ordered that they should be brought up as Catholics. His wife refused to comply with his wishes, and when the magistrates of the Oberamt Germersheim

24. Etienne Francois, *Die unsichtbare Grenze: Protestanten und Katholiken in Augsburg 1648–1806* (Sigmaringen, 1991); Peter Zschunke, *Konfession und Alltag in Oppenheim: Beiträge zur Geschichte von Bevölkerung und Gesellschaft einer gemischtkonfessionellen Kleinstadt in der frühen Neuzeit* (Wiesbaden, 1984); Paul Warmbrunn, *Zwei Konfessionen in einer Stadt: Das Zusammenleben von Katholiken und Protestanten in den paritätischen Reichsstädten Augsburg, Biberach, Ravensburg und Dinkelsbühl von 1548 bis 1648* (Wiesbaden, 1983).

25. My current work on mixed marriages and religious identity in early modern Germany, with cross references to Great Britain, intends to throw light on this under-researched subject.

26. Documents relating to this case are held at the Generallandesarchiv Karlsruhe (GLA, 1766–83).

27. In the sixteenth century the former Catholic priest Menno Simons (*c.* 1496–1561) emerged as a new leader of the German Anabaptists and founded new communities in the northern parts of the Habsburg Empire. He rejected the Anabaptists' original apocalyptic world view and instead preached that the Mennonites enjoyed God's grace already before the Last Judgment. His followers are still known as Mennonites. They shared his belief in adult baptism, in living in the image of Christ and in the practice of religious ban (excommunication). After the Thirty Years War, Mennonites who had been persecuted by both Catholic and Protestant princes found refuge, among other places, in the Palatinate, and in the eighteenth century many emigrated to North America.

arrived in Weissenburg to make his orders known, the widow had already secretly taken her children across the border to the Oberamt Lautern. Somehow she had been informed about her husband's intentions and hoped to escape them by moving to a different district. In the meantime, Peter Maurer died. The officers of the Oberamt Germersheim now asked the council of the Prince Elector for advice, who decreed in 1767 that the children should be taken away from their mother, put in a Catholic orphanage in Mannheim and baptized as Catholics. The mother was hardly allowed any access to them. Her complaints about the miserable conditions in the orphanage and her worries about the children's health, especially the poor state of her youngest child, a five-year-old son, went unheard. He subsequently died. The widow even promised that the children would receive religious education from the Catholic priest of Dörenbach, a village near her new home, if only they could be returned to her. In his report to the Prince Elector in 1780 the Catholic deacon of Mannheim, Adam Tolles, summarized the case as follows:

> One of these children, named Joseph, died here. The second, Maria Josepha, after she had been released from the orphanage, worshipped here for a while and practised as a Catholic. But then she went to her mother and rejoined the Mennonite sect. The third, Maria Theresia, worshipped here and practised as a Catholic after she had been released from the orphanage but later she followed her sister, returned to her mother and rejoined the sect.

The girls, by now seven and eleven, were returned to the orphanage, but refused to remain Catholic and at subsequent hearings defended their Mennonite beliefs. State and church officials filled numerous pages with legal and theological opinions about what to do in such a case. Even a *Rechtsgutachten* or legal reference from the theological faculty of the University of Heidelberg was sought. In November 1780, as a punishment for abandoning the Catholic faith, the girls were sent to an asylum for one year and were eventually banished from their home territory. With the help of a lawyer, the widow sent numerous petitions to the Prince Elector pleading for the return of her daughters, whose support she desperately needed, 'especially now with the approach of winter'.

Barbara Maurerin was not alone in her fate, although she was especially vulnerable as a member of a religious sect. The Palatinate was infamous for violent re-Catholicizing throughout the eighteenth century. Lutheran and Reformed widows who had lived in mixed marriages were also forced to have their children baptized by the Catholic church. The wife of the Lutheran Johann Georg Hammel in Oppenheim fled with her six-year-old daughter when her husband converted to Catholicism on his deathbed: 'because of his Reformed wife's bad example and disturbingly poor child-rearing . . . he explicitly demanded that his child, a girl of six years, and the one with which his wife was pregnant, should be brought up in the Catholic faith and other good practices'.[28] With the help of a Reformed pastor, Hammel's wife and daughter found their way to the wife's mother in Heidelberg, where the pair were eventually found by officials from the Oberamt Oppenheim. The case was reported to the Prince Elector in 1740. Even if a Lutheran widow remarried a non-Catholic and wished to bring up her daughter in her own religion, she was forced by the government to bring up her child in the Catholic faith of her deceased former husband or forfeit her inheritance.[29] Did these widows have any rights regarding the religious education of their children? In theory the male head of a household had the right to determine the religious education of children and the wife had to supervise the religious life of the household including servants and apprentices. These arrangements, however, were challenged by the circumstances of mixed religious marriages.

In 1705, the Palatinate issued a *Religionsdeklaration* (Declaration of Religion) which ruled that the parents in mixed marriages were free to decide the religious faith of their children. If no marriage contract existed, all children had to be educated in the religion of the father, and if one spouse died, the surviving parent had the right to determine the children's religion.[30] According to this declaration a woman had the right to negotiate the religious education of her children with her future spouse, and a widow was free to bring up her children in her own religion even if it differed from that of her dead husband. In the case of Barbara Maurerin it was argued that although Mennonites enjoyed the privilege of residence they were excluded from rules laid down in the Declaration of Religion. Despite the tolerant legislation of the Palatinate and the directives of the Westphalian Peace to allow freedom of conscience and confessional parity, during the eighteenth century the Prince Electors in the territory often gave biased support to members of their own

28. Zschunke, *Konfession*, p. 103. 29. GLA (1759).

30. Alfred Hans, *Die Kurpfälzische Religionsdeklaration von 1705: Ihre Entstehung und Bedeutung für das Zusammenleben der drei im Reich tolerierten Konfessionen* (Mainz, 1973), p. 202.

Catholic religion. In the Oberamt Germersheim, in particular, widows were regularly forced to bring up their children in the Catholic faith. It could be argued that, in the case of the Palatinate, the rigorous re-Catholicizing and the installation of Catholics as local officeholders created the circumstances which allowed the tolerant Declaration of Religion to be largely ignored.

Given the irreconcilability of Catholic and Protestant doctrine and the obligation of spouses of all confessions to bring up children in their own religion and to try to convert their partner, secular legislation in the various German territories was often unable to come up with any satisfactory solution. Catholics described the widespread rule that sons be brought up in the religion of the father and daughters in that of the mother as a 'godless pact'. In seventeenth-century Germany laws on mixed marriage favoured which ever religion or religious confession the prince belonged to. In the Reformed Palatinate until 1685, for example, all children of mixed marriages had to be baptized and brought up in the Reformed church. In the eighteenth century legislation was to some extent marked by religious tolerance, which manifested itself in unrestricted permission to enter into private marriage contracts. However, if we compare the laws in various German territories of the eighteenth century no uniform picture emerges and there is still evidence of a tendency to increase the confessional homogeneity of a territory by means of the religious education of children and through a marriage policy such as the prohibition of mixed marriage. Thus in theory a widow could determine her children's religion and was sure to enjoy the support of the local clergy of her own confession. In practice, however, the prince could overrule the father's right to determine the religion of his children if he belonged to a religious minority. In mixed marriages the whole concept of *patria potestas* (parental, usually paternal, authority) came under challenge and the question of religious upbringing according to the preference of the parent arose – placing under scrutiny the gender roles of parents and undermining the patriarchal hierarchy. To what extent was a mother able to put her religious ideas into practice against the will of her husband? The influence of father and mother on the religious socialization of the children, regardless of the law, can be seen in the children's conduct once they reached the age of religious majority and were allowed to convert. In the case of the widow Barbara Maurerin, her children followed their mother's faith in spite of severe punishments and attempts at their religious re-education. Yet they paid a high price.

The case of Barbara Maurerin and her children allows us to look beyond statistics and generalizations in order to grasp the experience and realities of widowhood in the past. If we wish to learn more about what widowhood could mean in the early modern period we need to look closely at the historical context and to supplement statistics and normative sources with court records and so called ego-documents or autobiographies such as the famous memoirs of the Jewish widow Glückel of Hameln (1646–1724) or the *Lebensbeschreibung* of the twice-widowed Catholic Maria Cordula Freifrau von Pranck (b. 1634), who travelled across half of Europe following her first husband's army. From the sixteenth century, women increasingly participated in writing their family histories and in passing on memoirs from one generation to the next, often dedicating their work to their children. These memoirs not only provide a woman's perspective on the course taken by her life: in the case of widows they can also convey the emotions and feelings of loss experienced and expressed on the deaths of their husbands.[31]

Funeral sermons, a source not yet adequately studied by gender historians, offer another type of life history.[32] Between about 1550 and 1750, funeral sermons were printed in honour of deceased Protestant men and women of the middle and upper classes, among them a high proportion of widows. Although these sermons followed a fixed pattern, with a theological part and a 'personalia' or 'curriculum vitae' of the deceased accompanying the main body of the sermon, they provide insights into the life and death of a 'good Christian' woman. The widow Katharina Zell (1497/98–1562), the wife of the Strasbourg reformer Matthäus Zell, published the funeral sermon given for her husband after his death in 1548. During her widowhood Katharina also delivered the 1562 funeral sermon for Elisabeth Hecker, a well-known member of the Schwenkfelder sect.[33] We have only just started to analyse this early modern German material and to place it in the context of politics and social and gender relations.

31. Wunder, *He is the Sun*, pp. 1–15; Bertha Pappenheim, *Die Memoiren der Glückel von Hameln* (Vienna, 1910; 2nd edn, Weinheim, 1994); Marvin Lowenthal, *The Memoirs of Glückel of Hameln* (New York, 1932; 2nd edn, 1977).

32. For an introduction see Rudolf Lenz, ed., *Leichenpredigten als Quelle historischer Wissenschaften*, 3 vols (Marburg a.d. Lahn, 1984). See also Rudolf Lenz, *De mortuis nil nisi bene? Leichenpredigten als multidisziplinäre Quelle* (Sigmaringen, 1990). For the relevance of funeral sermons for gender history see Heide Wunder, 'Frauen in den Leichenpredigten des 16. und 17. Jahrhunderts', in Lenz, *Leichenpredigten*, III, pp. 57–68.

33. Wunder, 'Frauen in den Leichenpredigten', p. 66.

Did widowhood mean sorrow and poverty, as the German term suggests, and as some images of widowhood, such as that of Katharina von Bora, would have us believe? The 'comfort books' printed for widows are another source of German representations of the experience of widowhood. One of the earliest known 'comfort books' written by a woman is the *Witwentrostbuch* of the Herzogin Elisabeth von Calenberg-Göttingen (1510–58). She devoted her comfort book to the widowed countesses Katharina (1509–67) and Elisabeth von Schwarzburg as well as to all honourable and modest widows of high and low standing.[34] Although Elisabeth emphasized that trust in God and the willingness to suffer were central to a widow's life, she also pointed to the vulnerable situation of widows deserving of society's pity, protection and support.

Especially after the Reformation, when Protestants saw the highest ideal a woman could aspire to as lying in her role as a wife and mother, widows often felt a social and moral pressure, if not economic necessity, to remarry. However, the large proportion of unmarried or widowed single women in the early modern period raises the question of whether women were happy to remain without a spouse, thus enjoying greater freedom and independence. As we have seen, widows were officially accepted as heads of households and enjoyed the rights and duties of citizens. Especially in smaller territories it was quite common for princely widows to rule as guardians until their offspring came of age. A number of well-off widows ran their own businesses and enjoyed more rights than married women. During the Thirty Years War, in particular, many women successfully pursued the trade of their dead or absent husbands. The reasons why successful tradeswomen, for instance, remarried are illustrated by the circumstances under which a widow from Danzig consented to a third remarriage. Still young after several marriages and funerals, she felt tired of the world. Having lost most of her children, she dreaded the loss of her last little daughter

34. *Der Widwen Handbüchlein: Durch eine Hocherleuchte Fürstliche Widwe vor vielen Jahren selbst beschrieben und verfasset. Jetzt abero wiederumb auffs newe gedruckt. Allen Christlichen Widwen hohes und nieder Standes zu besonderm Trost* (Leipzig, 1598). For a detailed discussion see Inge Mager, '"Wegert euch des lieben heiligen Creutzes nicht": das Witwentrostbuch der Herzogin Elisabeth von Calenberg-Göttingen', in Hartmut Boockmann, ed., *Kirche und Gesellschaft im Heiligen Römischen Reich des 15. und 16. Jahrhunderts* (Göttingen, 1994), pp. 207–24, and Barbara Becker-Cantarino, 'Die schriftstellerische Tätigkeit der Elisabeth von Braunschweig-Lüneburg (1510–1558)', in Joseph P. Strelka and Jörg Jungmayr, eds, *Virtus et Fortuna: Festschrift für Hans-Gert Roloff* (Berne, 1983), pp. 237–58. Mager and Becker-Cantarino discuss the same Elisabeth although they refer to her by different names and titles due to the different territories covered by her reign.

Hedwig and contemplated entering a monastery should Hedwig die. When she made her worries known, the local priest called her a sinful woman for anticipating someone's death. She was further admonished for deliberately exposing herself to danger by running a large workshop on her own. She was pressed to marry again. 'After a long talk she was prevailed upon to agree to this [remarriage], and they mentioned Jakob Lubbe. She knew him quite well, and he was agreeable to her because he was advanced in years and their businesses in merchant goods fit together well.'[35]

Barbara Maurerin did not marry again. The last we hear of the widow in the surviving documents is her renewed plea to end her daughters' expulsion from their home territory: 'Expulsion is even harder if it affects the female sex, but I, the mother who carried these my children under my heart, suffer most, knowing them in foreign parts, and seeing myself deprived of their support in old age.'

35. Wunder, *He is the Sun*, p. 136.

FIG. 2 *D. Martini Luthers nachgelassene Witfrawn/in ihrer Traurung*, 'The widow of Martin Luther [Katharina von Bora, 1499–1552] in mourning', by Lucas Cranach the Elder (1546). Schloßmuseum Gotha, Xylographica I, No. 241.

PART FOUR

Narratives and Constructions of Widowhood

CHAPTER ELEVEN

Elite widows and religious expression in early modern Spain: the view from Avila[1]

JODI BILINKOFF

In her autobiography the future Saint Teresa of Avila recalled a pivotal moment around 1560, when 'the Lord was pleased that I become friendly with a widow of high nobility'. This 'servant of God', Guiomar de Ulloa, was a 'very intelligent and trustworthy person to whom the Lord ha[d] granted much favour in prayer' and 'desired to enlighten . . . in matters about which [even some] learned men were ignorant'.[2] The deepening friendship between nun and pious widow would prove crucial, not only in the personal lives of these two Spanish women, but also in the history of Teresa's efforts to reform the Carmelite order. Doña Guiomar was one of the earliest and staunchest supporters of Teresa's new convent of San José, founded in 1562 and, according to some accounts, would have taken the veil there herself had she not been prevented by poor health.[3]

By Teresa's time wealthy widows serving as founders and patrons of religious houses and even entering them as nuns was a well-established phenomenon in Avila, the breathtaking walled city in central Castile. The last decades of the fifteenth century and first of the sixteenth witnessed a boom in new religious institutions, nearly

1. I treat some of this material in a somewhat different context in Jodi Bilinkoff, *The Avila of Saint Teresa: Religious Reform in a Sixteenth-Century City* (Ithaca, NY, 1989), pp. 35–52. My thanks to the following colleagues for their helpful advice and for making available to me their unpublished work-in-progress: Kathryn Burns, Elizabeth Lehfeldt, Nancy van Deusen, David Vassberg and Alison Weber.

2. *The Collected Works of St. Teresa of Avila*, trans. Kieran Kavanaugh and Otilio Rodríguez, 3 vols (Washington, DC, 1976), I, pp. 160, 195. See also pp. 216–17, 234, 241.

3. Bilinkoff, *The Avila of Saint Teresa*, pp. 125–6, 165–6.

all of them established by five widows: Catalina Guiera, Elvira González de Medina, María Dávila, Mencía López and María de Herrera. In this chapter I examine the foundational efforts of these widows, and attempt to look at class, family strategies and religious expression in a traditional Catholic society.

From the outset it is important to clarify that I am not treating average widows, but rather an elite group. These women belonged to Avila's privileged classes, ranging from the upper bourgeoisie to the titled nobility. Two of them, Catalina Guiera and María Dávila, were heiresses who inherited considerable wealth from parents as well as from husbands. Three of the five, Catalina Guiera, Mária Dávila and María de Herrera, had no surviving children and were thus the main beneficiaries of their husbands' estates. All five must be considered among the ranks of those upper-class medieval and early modern widows whose control of economic resources, relative autonomy, and assertion of power and prerogatives drew the intense interest of suitors in their own day, and of historians in recent times.[4] They are unusual as historical subjects for another reason as well: four of the five left wills and/or foundation charters. These documents, with their articulations of privilege and spiritual goals as well as economic concerns, have much to say about the intersection of family and religious history that David Herlihy urged scholars to explore over ten years ago.[5]

Between 1463 and 1512 the five widows from Avila listed above decided to spend at least part of their inherited wealth in a specific way: by founding a religious house of some sort, usually for other women. In making this choice they were hardly alone: a quick survey of recent research on early modern Italy, Spain and Spanish America reveals that female founders and patrons of religious

4. For an overview of literature on the subject see Louise Mirrer, ed., *Upon My Husband's Death: Widows in the Literature and Histories of Medieval Europe* (Ann Arbor, Mich., 1992), pp. 1–17; Robert J. Kalas, 'The noble widow's place in the patriarchal household: the life and career of Jeanne de Gontault', *Sixteenth Century Journal* 24 (1993), p. 521. For more 'average' Iberian widows, that is, of the peasant or urban artisanal classes, see David E. Vassberg, 'The status of widows in sixteenth-century rural Castile', in John Henderson and Richard Wall, eds, *Poor Women and Children in the European Past* (London, 1994), pp. 180–95; Equip Broida, 'La viudez: triste o feliz estado? (Las últimas voluntades de los barceloneses en torno al 1400)', in Cristina Segura Graiño, ed., *Las Mujeres en las Ciudades Medievales* (Madrid, 1984), pp. 27–41.

5. David Herlihy, 'The family and religious ideologies in medieval Europe', in Tamara Hareven and Andrejs Plakans, eds, *Family History at the Crossroads* (Princeton, 1987), p. 3 (first published in *Journal of Family History*, 1986).

institutions were virtually always widows.[6] This strong correlation suggests that religious patronage represented a socially and culturally acceptable way for widows to invest their resources, as well as one that proved meaningful to them as individuals. Why should this have been so?

One answer lies with the socio-religious system in which elites in early modern Avila, as in other parts of Catholic Europe, had heavy investment. Here a profound spiritual concern, the state of souls after death, was linked to an important secular concern, the perpetuation of the name, status and position of one's lineage. Widows, often the only surviving representatives of their generation, seem to have regarded this task of family commemoration and continuity with particular seriousness. All five widows under study made financial arrangements ensuring burial in their new foundations and prayers recited in perpetuity for their souls and for the souls of their ancestors and heirs.

For example, in her will of 16 June 1502 María Dávila, twice married and twice widowed to wealthy and powerful men, founded a community of Poor Clares (Franciscans) dedicated to Santa María de Jesús. One of Doña María's first stipulations was a basic one, that 'at whatever hour I might die [the abbess and nuns] hold at least an hour-long mass and that during it my body be buried [in the convent]'. She went on to specify exactly where in the nuns' choir she wished to be buried ('by the wall in front of the altar of the Corpus Christi'), and the religious image she wished to be displayed

6. P. Renée Baernstein, 'In widow's habit: women between convent and family in sixteenth-century Milan', *Sixteenth Century Journal* 24 (1994), pp. 787–807; Kathryn J. Burns, 'Convents, culture, and society in Cuzco, Peru, 1550–1865', Harvard University PhD thesis, 1993, ch. 3, see also Burns, *Colonial Habits: Convents and the Spiritual Economy of Cuzco, Peru* (Durham, NC: forthcoming 1999); Marilyn R. Dunn, 'Spiritual philanthropists: women as convent patrons in seicento Rome', in Cynthia Lawrence, ed., *Women and Art in Early Modern Europe: Patrons, Collectors, and Connoisseurs* (University Park, Pa., 1997), pp. 154–88; Asunción Lavrin, 'Female religious', in Louisa Schell Hoberman and Susan Midgden Socolow, eds, *Cities and Society in Colonial Latin America* (Albuquerque, 1986), pp. 170–1; Elizabeth Lehfeldt, 'Sacred and secular spaces: religious women in Golden-Age Valladolid', Indiana University PhD thesis, 1996, ch. 1; Carolyn Valone, 'Roman matrons as patrons: various views of the cloister wall', in Craig A. Monson, ed., *The Crannied Wall: Women, Religion, and the Arts in Early Modern Europe* (Ann Arbor, Mich., 1992), pp. 49–72; Valone, 'Piety and patronage: women and the early Jesuits', in E. Ann Matter and John Coakley, eds, *Creative Women in Medieval and Early Modern Italy: A Religious and Artistic Renaissance* (Philadelphia, 1994), pp. 157–84; Nancy E. van Deusen, 'Defining the sacred and the worldly: *beatas* and *recogidas* in late seventeenth-century Lima', *Colonial Latin American Review* 6 (1997), pp. 441–77; Alison P. Weber, 'Teresa's problematic patrons', *Journal of Medieval and Early Modern Studies* (forthcoming).

there ('Our Lady with Our Redeemer in her arms'). She also requested a daily mass during the year following her death.[7]

After arranging burial and commemorative prayers for herself, Doña María took pains to provide for members of her family, including both her parents and her two husbands, mandating that:

> the convent of Santa María de Jesús and its abbess and nuns be obligated to have said in the church of the said convent . . . every day in perpetuity for ever and ever four masses one for the souls of Gil Dávila and Doña Inés de Zabarcos, my lords and parents . . . And the other for the soul of the [royal] treasurer Hernando Núñez Arnalte, my lord . . . And the other for . . . Hernando de Acuña, my lord . . . And the other for my soul, with a collect *pro defunctis* for each one of the souls of those who inherited before me the said goods that I leave to the said convent.[8]

Catalina Guiera, who in 1463 founded the small community that would eventually become the Dominican convent of Santa Catalina, stated more simply, but as pressingly, that the women religious should 'live well and beg God for the soul[s]' of her and her deceased husband Hernando de Belmonte. And María de Herrera, in establishing the Hospital and Chapel of Nuestra Señora de la Anunciación in 1512, likewise ordered prayers for her soul, that of her late husband, and of all their departed family members ('nuestros difuntos').[9]

These ostensibly private matters – provision for burial, special prayers, devotional images and the like – had very public manifestations as well. Avila's elite widows guaranteed the identification of religious houses with themselves and their families through the use of iconography. This visual reinforcement of dynastic pride and status usually came in the form of coats of arms, also used to adorn the many *palacios* constructed in the city in roughly the same period. María Dávila ordered the shield (*escudo*) of her father's branch of the Dávila family as well as the shields of her two husbands to be

7. Manuel de Castro, *Fundacion de 'Las Gordillas' (Convento de clarisas de Santa María de Jesús de Avila)* (Avila, 1976), pp. 56–8. This book's appendix, pp. 56–93, consists of a facsimile reproduction of Doña María's will, with facing transcription. For a fascinating and exhaustive study of Spanish wills in this period see Carlos M.N. Eire, *From Madrid to Purgatory: The Art and Craft of Dying in Sixteenth-Century Spain* (New York, 1995), bk I.

8. Castro, *Fundacion*, p. 74.

9. Will of Catalina Guiera, 18 February 1463, Archivo Histórico Nacional, Madrid (AHN) Sección Clero, legajo 449 n.p. Manuel de Foronda published a transcription of María de Herrera's foundation charter, 'Mosén Rubín: Su capilla en Avila y su escritura de fundación', *Boletín de la Real Academia de Historia* 63 (1913), p. 342.

displayed over the main entrance of the convent of Santa Mária de Jésus and other conspicuous places. She also commissioned from the well-known sculptor Vasco de la Zarza an impressive alabaster sepulchre, complete with life-sized tomb sculpture and, again, the three sets of shields.[10] María de Herrera not only made extensive use of *escudos* and tomb sculpture at her chapel (and insisted that they be 'very well made'), but required the poor men and women who would reside at her new hospital to wear a sort of 'uniform', outer garments decorated with emblems of Nuestra Señora de la Anunciación.[11] Visitors coming to hear mass at a convent chapel, or even passing a poor hospital inmate on the street, would have no difficulty making the connection between these religious institutions, their founders, and the lineages from which they descended.

Avila's pious and privileged widows took care to provide for living and future family members as well as deceased ones. They used wills and foundation charters to grant kinsmen and kinswomen positions within their new religious institutions, perpetuating relationships of patronage and clientage developed during their lifetimes. María Dávila, for example, named her personal chaplain and relative ('mi pariente') Alvaro de Castro as chaplain to her new convent of Santa María de Jesús. She entrusted the post of patron, the convent's lay administrator, to the current head of the House of Villafranca y las Navas 'from whose line I succeed'. Doña Mária charged her kinsman with faithfully carrying out the terms of her will, a responsibility he would surely undertake as 'an affair of his lineage' ('una cosa de su linaje'). Finally, she extended an offer of acceptance to any of her cousins' daughters who might want to become nuns, waiving for them the entry fees customary for religious houses at the time.[12]

The efforts of founders to involve family members in their religious establishments could lead to the formation of veritable 'empires' or 'dynasties' that dominated institutions over several

10. Castro, *Fundacion*, pp. 58, 78, 88 and pp. 47–8 for photographs of tomb sculpture and shields. Also reproduced in Eduardo Ruiz Ayúcar, *Sepulcros artísticos de Avila* (Avila, 1985), pp. 155–6.

11. Foronda, 'Mosén Rubín', pp. 339–42, 349. Ruiz Ayúcar, *Sepulcros*, p. 171 for photograph.

12. Castro, *Fundacion*, pp. 62, 76, 86. Alison Weber notes that Teresa of Avila clashed on more than one occasion with female patrons who presumed that 'having endowed the convent, their relatives or protégés were entitled to places in it': see 'Teresa's problematic patrons', forthcoming. Catalina Guiera and María de Herrera also made provision for their domestic servants in their wills, as did María Dávila, who in addition ordered that all her male and female slaves serve her new convent for ten years, after which time they were to be freed.

generations. A fascinating and somewhat special case was that of Elvira González de Medina. For analytical purposes I include her among the other widows from Avila, but she actually never married. Doña Elvira maintained a relationship of many years' standing with Nuño González del Aguila, a scion of a family entrenched in local urban politics and the lord of an extensive estate in the countryside. He was also a member of the clergy, an archdeacon and canon of Avila's cathedral. They had four children together.[13] Before his death in 1467 Don Nuño provided for his companion by selling to her all or part of his property, although due to protracted lawsuits with her oldest son Diego del Aguila she was unable to gain complete control of these resources until 1478. The following year Doña Elvira began a small community for religious women in her home that would eventually evolve into the very large Carmelite convent of la Encarnación where the future Saint Teresa would spend her first twenty-five years as a nun.

The documents surrounding Doña Elvira's religious foundation reveal her desire to include family members, especially her own children, perhaps in part to somehow 'legitimate' the offspring of her irregular liaison. She named her younger son Pedro del Aguila as lay patron; he was to be followed by a grandson. After Doña Elvira's death in 1486 she was succeeded as the community's 'mother and president for life' ('madre e presydente, por toda su vida') by her widowed daughter Catalina del Aguila.[14] María de Herrera too appointed as 'patron, governor and principal administrator' of her chapel and hospital her closest living relative, Diego de Bracamonte. She specified in her will that he be succeeded 'after his days [by] Mosén Rubín de Bracamonte, his legitimate son . . . and after him, his legitimate male descendants, one after the other'.[15] In this case, the identification between dynasty and religious foundation became so strong that to this day residents of Avila refer to the house, located directly across from the Bracamonte family palace, as the

13. Bilinkoff, *The Avila of Saint Teresa*, pp. 41–2. David Vassberg has also argued recently for treating certain categories of abandoned wives as 'near-widows' or 'virtual widows': David E. Vassberg, 'Widows and their children in early modern rural Castile', paper presented at Symposium 'Widowhood: Conditions and Constructions', University of Exeter, 16–17 May 1996, p. 2.

14. Nicolás González y González, *El Monasterio de la Encarnación de Avila*, 2 vols (Avila, 1976), I, pp. 45–6, 65, where he coins the expression 'el imperio de los Aguila'. Eventually the community of Carmelites elected abbesses for three-year terms. For other cases of family 'dynasties' within religious houses see works by Burns, Lehfeldt and Baernstein listed above in n. 6.

15. Foronda, 'Mosén Rubín', p. 346.

Chapel of Mosén Rubín rather than by its official name, Nuestra Señora de la Anunciación. Similarly, the convent of Santa María de Jesús is nearly always called las Gordillas, for the country estate where the community was originally housed. The association here is with the family and property of the house's founder, María Dávila, rather than with a saint or religious order. In early modern Avila, as elsewhere in Catholic Europe, elites succeeded in linking liturgy with lineage, a process in which widows played a crucial role.

For widows of modest means the death of a husband often signalled the break-up of a household.[16] But for Avila's well-to-do widows establishing a religious community offered a way of preserving a household, or rather, of fashioning a new kind of household, one that did not fall under the authority of fathers, husbands or sons. Nearly all the communities under study began life in their widowed founders' own homes. The case of Mencía López is rather poorly documented but we do know that by 1507 Doña Mencía, who had been widowed in 1504, two of her daughters and a female friend had resolved to live together in her home observing the rule of St Augustine. This group became the kernel for the Augustinian convent of Nuestra Señora de Gracia.[17] We have seen that Elvira González de Medina also started a community in her house in Avila, as did Catalina Guiera, and that María Dávila bequeathed part of her country estate of las Gordillas, about 20 kilometres from the city, for this purpose. Their situation as wealthy widows enabled these women to transform family residences headed by males into exclusively female communities of prayer.[18]

The documents relating to the four houses in Avila that eventually became convents are replete with the language of family, as had been the case in Christian monasticism since its earliest origins. Catalina Guiera, Mencía López, Elvira González de Medina and María Dávila all became the first abbesses of the religious communities they founded. They were now to be addressed, and respected, as 'Mother'. For the childless widows Catalina Guiera and María Dávila, might not the opportunity to serve as spiritual 'mothers' to

16. Vassberg, 'Status of widows', pp. 184–5.

17. Bilinkoff, *The Avila of Saint Teresa*, pp. 42–3.

18. Many of the authors of studies listed above in n. 6 make similar observations. This point is particularly well developed by Baernstein, who comments that the 'convent, too, was a household, whose residents shared a collective past and collective future', 'In widow's habit', pp. 806–7. See also Mary Martin McLaughlin, 'Creating and recreating communities of women: the case of Corpus Domini, Ferrara, 1406–1452', in Judith M. Bennett *et al.*, eds, *Sisters and Workers in the Middle Ages* (Chicago, 1989), pp. 261–88.

spiritual 'daughters' have helped to console and compensate them for the lack of biological children? María Dávila clearly designated her convent of Santa María de Jesús as the chief beneficiary of her estate, as did María de Herrera with regard to the hospital and chapel of Nuestra Señora de la Anunciación. In this sense as well, religious foundations could take the place of children.[19]

It is equally fascinating to speculate about the cases of widows with surviving children. What were the interpersonal dynamics within Nuestra Señora de Gracia, where the daughters of Mencía López were now bound to her by both the ties of blood and the monastic vows of obedience? Founding a religious house gave Elvira González de Medina, the reformed 'concubine' locked for years in legal battles with her oldest son, the opportunity to reconstitute an 'ideal family'. In an extraordinary statement she not only set herself up as the community's 'lady mother and spiritual patron and administrator and governor and superior' ('señora madre y patrona espiritual y administradora y gobernadora y superiora') but requested that the other women accept her 'with grateful and humble honour, giving and exhibiting to her deserved and devout obedience and reverence, receiving humbly her wholesome corrections and orders and carrying them out efficiently, in such manner that the said lady patron and administrator rejoices to have found in the said *beatas* [such] daughters of devotion, and they rejoice to have found in her [such] a spiritual and benevolent mother'.[20] Given the circumstances of Doña Elvira's life, her fervent desire to spend her last years surrounded by humble, obedient and respectful yet happy 'children' seems somehow more poignant than tyrannical.

In any case, for Avila's elite widows religious patronage could function as an extension of certain biological and cultural roles traditionally associated with women of their station, the perpetuation of

19. Castro, *Fundacion*, pp. 62, 66, 78; Foronda, 'Mosén Rubín', p. 340. See studies by Valone, Baernstein and Weber for the role of religious houses in perpetuating lineages. For an earlier period of Spanish history see Miriam Shadis, 'Piety, politics, and power: the patronage of Leonor of England and her daughters Berenguela of León and Blanche of Castile', in June Hall McCash, ed., *The Cultural Patronage of Medieval Women* (Athens, Ga., 1996), p. 217. Kathryn Burns has noted the predominance not only of widows but of childless widows as founders of female religious houses in colonial Cuzco and examined the ways in which 'a convent could compensate for a child, and the extension of one's lineage', 'Convents', pp. 104, 106, 111, 119, 122–3.

20. González, *El Monasterio*, I, pp. 48–50. He too muses on Doña Elvira's transformation from 'biological mother, aged by years and disputes with her children, to spiritual mother of devotional daughters' ('de madre corporal, envejecida por los años y los disgustos de sus hijos, en madre espiritual de unas hijas de devoción').

lineages and the formation and preservation of households. But as crucial as were the manifold connections between religious institutions and families, it is also important to recognize that for women in early modern Avila, as in the rest of Catholic Europe, widowhood carried with it a profound spiritual significance. A widow's decision to endow, and enter, a religious house was highly respected as a sign of special grace.

A long legacy dating back to the early centuries of Christianity afforded considerable prestige to widows who, rather than remarrying, dedicated themselves to Christ through ascetic denial and pious works. According to some early Christian sources, widows, especially older women, could join a consecrated 'order', similar in many respects to that of nuns.[21] Throughout the Middle Ages moralists celebrated the ideal of 'chaste widowhood' in hagiographical texts and sermons. After all, these women, unlike virgins, had actually tasted the joys of marital sex and had still heroically overcome their bodily appetites to spend the remainder of their lives in abstinence and prayer.[22] It seems likely that Avila's elite widows, as well as their contemporaries, would have understood that by embracing the religious life they were situating themselves within a time-honoured tradition.

An important aspect of this model of Christian widowhood was the distribution of charity, and here too Avila's widows conformed to expectations. As mentioned above, María de Herrera willed her considerable fortune to the Hospital of Nuestra Señora de la Anunciación for poor men and women. This institution, as was commonly the case for late medieval and early modern 'hospitals', operated more as a hospice for the indigent than as a place to receive medical treatment.[23] The aristocratic María Dávila may have been the single largest benefactor in late fifteenth-century Avila. In

21. Bonnie Bowman Thurston, *The Widows: A Women's Ministry in the Early Church* (Minneapolis, 1989).

22. See for example: André Vauchez, *The Laity in the Middle Ages: Religious Beliefs and Devotional Practices* (Notre Dame, Ind., 1993), pt III; Anna Benvenuti Papi, 'Mendicant friars and female Pinzochere in Tuscany: from social marginality to models of sanctity', in Daniel Bornstein and Roberto Rusconi, eds, *Women and Religion in Medieval and Renaissance Italy* (Chicago, 1996), pp. 88–9; Angela Muñoz Fernández, *Mujer y Experiencia Religiosa en el Marco de la Santidad Medieval* (Madrid, 1988), for the important Iberian cult of St Isabel of Portugal.

23. In fact María de Herrera specified that persons suffering from incurable or contagious diseases should not be admitted to her hospital. She also worried lest these people return to begging in the streets after leaving the hospital, which may indicate her concern for both their welfare and her own honour and reputation. Foronda, 'Mosén Rubín', pp. 348–9.

addition to Santa María de Jesús, Doña María founded the magnificent Dominican monastery of Santo Tomás in 1482, following the wishes of her first husband. She made generous donations to the popular shrine (*ermita*) of Nuestra Señora de Sonsoles, which, due to its location along a major north–south road, often served as a waystation for travellers and pilgrims. And in her 1502 will establishing her community of Poor Clares Doña María also established a chapel. Here, 'in order that God be served and the poor aided', an annual distribution of grain to the poor ('personas neçesitadas y menesterosas') would take place on the feast of the Annunciation.[24]

Founding religious houses also gave Avila's elite widows a way of providing for needy women. The communities established by Catalina Guiera, Elvira González de Medina, María Dávila and Mencía López all began as houses of *beatas*, or *beaterios*. *Beatas* were laywomen who resolved to follow a religious vocation, either alone or in groups. They were sometimes affiliated with religious orders, but made simple (non-binding) vows, as opposed to nuns, whose formal vows were legally binding. Because *beatas* did not have to pay the dowries or entrance fees required at most convents they usually derived from much more modest socio-economic origins than did nuns.[25] In her will Catalina Guiera expressed both a proprietary interest in and charitable solicitude for what she called 'her women' ('mis mujeres'). She granted them a large annual endowment 'in order to help with their maintenance' and two female servants, which suggests that they were not the sort of women who had domestic servants of their own. Elvira González de Medina likewise donated funds for the 'food and sustenance' of the *beatas* living in her house.[26] Later in the sixteenth century all four of these communities evolved into full-fledged convents and accordingly imposed the customary entrance requirements based upon wealth, status and ethnic purity. But in this early stage they represent the efforts of wealthy widows to provide for pious but less fortunate women,

24. Castro, *Fundacion*, pp. 13–15, 56, 80–6. Maureen Flynn notes the 'European-wide practice' of dowering poor girls on the Feast of the Annunciation. Perhaps this devotion eventually became associated with acts of charity more generally. As we have seen, María de Herrera's hospital was dedicated to Our Lady of the Annunciation and grain was to be distributed at María Dávila's chapel on this feast day. Maureen Flynn, *Sacred Charity: Confraternities and Social Welfare in Spain, 1400–1700* (Ithaca, NY, 1989), pp. 61–2, 79.

25. Bilinkoff, *The Avila of Saint Teresa*, pp. 39–40, 96–106; Bilinkoff, 'A saint for a city: Mariana de Jesús and Madrid, 1565–1624', *Archive for Reformation History* 88 (1997), pp. 322–37.

26. AHN Clero leg. 449 n.p. Doña Catalina stated that she was bequeathing funds 'para servicio de Dios y amparo de buenas mujeres', González, *El Monasterio*, I, p. 48.

a trend that has been noted throughout Catholic Europe and its colonies.[27]

Finally, in using their inherited resources to establish religious houses Avila's widows found what Asunción Lavrin has termed 'a channel for personal expression'.[28] Sometimes this took visual, artistic forms. María Dávila commissioned two sculpted images of the Virgin holding the infant Jesus, one to be hung above her sepulchre, and the other placed over the doorway to the charitable chapel she founded. Given that this woman named María also dedicated her new religious community to St Mary of Jesus it seems reasonable to assume that she was particularly devoted to this Mother and Child.[29] María de Herrera also made a Marian foundation. She ordered that in the chapel a 'very good' altarpiece (*retablo*) be painted with 'the story of the Annunciation of Our Lady the Virgin Mary', as well as saints Jerome and Anthony of Padua 'for whom I . . . have much devotion'.[30] Today only a part of the original façade of the convent of Santa Catalina remains, but plainly visible is a bas-relief of St Catherine of Alexandria, holding the wheel of her martyrdom. One can only speculate whether it was Catalina de Guiera herself who ordered that image for a house dedicated to her namesake and patron saint.

On other occasions Avila's elite widows specified the recitation of prayers and the celebration of feast days that held special significance for them or persons close to them. María de Herrera directed that the Feast of the Annunciation be celebrated at her chapel 'very solemnly', complete with vespers, mass and a sermon preached by either a Dominican or Franciscan friar. She mandated similar pomp for the feast day of 'the glorious Doctor of the Church, my lord St Jerome'.[31] María Dávila made an interesting stipulation in her will. After requesting certain prayers chanted for her soul and those of her two deceased husbands, Doña María, noting how she had received many favours from 'the most illustrious queen' [Isabel I of Castile], ordered a daily mass at Santa María de Jesús to offer prayers for the monarch and her successors. In addition, every

27. Sandra Cavallo notes that in early modern Turin an 'important feature of women's charitable activity . . . [was] the fact that it [was] aimed at women', *Charity and Power in Early Modern Italy: Benefactors and their Motives in Turin, 1541–1789* (Cambridge, 1995), ch. 4. This observation is borne out by research by Lehfeldt, Lavrin and Burns, listed above in n. 6.

28. Lavrin, 'Female religious', p. 191.

29. Castro, *Fundacion*, pp. 58, 80. For widows and artistic patronage and expression see essays by Dunn and Valone cited above in n. 5.

30. Foronda, 'Mosén Rubín', p. 339. 31. Ibid., p. 349.

year during the Octave of the Kings the convent's chaplains were to celebrate a solemn mass on the Feast of St John before the Latin Gate 'to which Her Majesty is very devoted'.[32] Surely Doña María's ability to determine the liturgical programme inside Santa María de Jesús gave her a deep sense of satisfaction, personal and spiritual. But in a world in which religious belief, politics and social relationships were inextricably linked, her public expression of private devotions and obligations also served to remind a larger community of her status as pious Christian widow and her rank within a privileged class and lineage.

In the final analysis, founding and patronizing religious houses enabled elite widows in early modern Avila to address several of their most pressing concerns. By investing their wealth and energies in this enterprise women such as Catalina Guiera, Elvira González de Medina, María Dávila, María de Herrera and Mencía López provided for the secular and spiritual needs of family members, past, present and future, and helped to socially reproduce their class. They created new, all-female households with themselves as 'mothers' to 'daughters' in Christ. They successfully placed themselves within a time-honoured tradition of chaste and charitable Christian widowhood. And they found ways of expressing publicly and creatively their own religious vocations and devotions. The foundational efforts of a group of pious and privileged widows had a profound impact on the urban landscape of sixteenth-century Avila, the results of which can still be seen and pondered today.

32. Castro, *Fundacion*, pp. 74, 80.

CHAPTER TWELVE

Widows at law in Tudor and Stuart England[1]

TIM STRETTON

On the day a Tudor or Stuart woman lost her husband, she shed the restrictive bonds imposed by coverture and regained her independent legal status.[2] Now she could own property, enter into contracts, make a will, buy and sell goods, collect rents, accept gifts and bring legal actions. Widowers experienced no such transformation of status at the death of their wives, which helps to explain the scant attention commentators have paid them, but widows saw their fortunes change dramatically. Historians have rightly recognized widowhood as the period of greatest legal independence for women. But what exactly did this mean for widows in sixteenth- and seventeenth-century England? What levels of legal independence did women from different backgrounds actually achieve?

Historians' impressions of widows' relationship with the law in the sixteenth and seventeenth centuries, based on analyses of conduct books, statutes, legal commentaries, private papers and diaries, have fluctuated over the past hundred years, shifting between positions of relative optimism and unconstrained pessimism. Writing at the end of the nineteenth century, Frederick Pollock and F.W. Maitland believed that although widows could not vote, hold public office or serve on juries, in general legal terms they were 'on the same level as men'.[3] Twentieth-century feminist historians have tended to

1. I would like to thank Cambridge University Press for allowing me to reproduce in this chapter material taken from my monograph *Women Waging Law in Elizabethan England* (Cambridge, 1998).

2. Under the doctrine of 'unity of person' the common law regarded husband and wife as one person for most legal and some criminal purposes. Therefore, according to the legal idea of coverture single women and widows were 'femes sole', with fairly full legal rights, but wives were 'femes covert' and lived under the restrictive legal 'cover' of their husbands.

3. Frederick Pollock and F.W. Maitland, *The History of English Law Before the Time of Edward I*, ed. S.F.C. Milsom, 2nd edn, 2 vols (Cambridge, 1968), I, p. 485.

be more circumspect, suggesting that widows were legally independent only in comparison with other women. Widows, in other words, had marginally more rights and opportunities than married women, who were subject to their husbands, and unmarried women, who might be subject to their fathers or to other male kin, but they were never on a par with men.[4] Ongoing research based on wills, probate documents and the records of litigation points towards a third view, one that combines elements of both optimism and pessimism. It is this picture that I intend to sketch and expand upon in this chapter, making use of the records of the Court of Requests, a central equity court much frequented by women which flourished from the mid-sixteenth century until its demise in the 1640s. An analysis of pleadings, depositions and decisions in Requests confirms that widows enjoyed substantial legal entitlements, and that many individuals went to law in pursuit of them. However, those widows who set out to assert their rights or to protect their property interests under any of the major forms of English law, whether equity, common law, ecclesiastical law or custom, had to negotiate a whole series of obstacles that widowers simply did not have to face.

Levels of litigation

Widows participated in legal actions, either as plaintiffs or defendants, in every major court for which records survive. During the sixteenth and seventeenth centuries, levels of civil, or non-criminal, litigation rose dramatically, with business in individual equity, common law and church courts doubling, trebling, or in some instances quadrupling between the 1550s and the 1620s.[5] Women were party to this growth, and in the largest English courts in the later sixteenth century female litigants were named (alone or with others) in around a tenth of cases in Star Chamber, a quarter of all cases in Chancery and Queen's Bench and just under a third of all cases in Common Pleas and the Court of Requests.[6] In the seventeenth century the proportion of cases involving female litigants fell slightly

4. See for example Eileen Spring, *Law, Land and Family: Aristocratic Inheritance in England 1300 to 1800* (Chapel Hill, NC and London, 1993), pp. 47–65.

5. C.W. Brooks, *Pettyfoggers and Vipers of the Commonwealth: The 'Lower Branch' of the Legal Profession in Early Modern England* (Cambridge, 1986), p. 51.

6. In a sample of Star Chamber suits initiated by individuals, women were involved in 36 out of 346 suits (10.4%); unpublished PRO calendar 'Star Chamber Proceedings Elizabeth', Vol. 4; Amy Louise Erickson, 'Common law versus common practice: the use of marriage settlements in early modern England', *Economic History Review* 43 (1990), pp. 21–39, p. 28; and see Stretton, *Women Waging Law*, ch. 2.

in the common law courts of Common Pleas and King's Bench, but it rose to above a third in the equity courts of Chancery and Requests.[7] In terms of total numbers of litigants, women made up only between around 5 and 20 per cent of litigant populations in these civil and criminal courts, a far cry from 50 per cent, but judges in the highest courts in the land heard cases brought by, or against, women every day their courts were in session.[8] In the church courts the percentages were even higher. Laura Gowing has calculated that women brought 31 per cent of all actions in London's consistory courts in 1590, rising to 54 per cent by 1633, and Amy Louise Erickson estimates that perhaps three-quarters of all those who appeared before ecclesiastical probate courts were women.[9] Despite the legal and social restrictions under which they laboured, women were no strangers to courts of law.

How many of these female litigants were widows? Widows dominated the lists of executors and administrators of deceased persons' estates who approached the ecclesiastical probate courts to prove wills, exhibit inventories and file accounts. In other courts, however, they did not always constitute the majority of female litigants, an honour that regularly went to married women.[10] In most instances procedural rules prevented wives from participating in court actions without their husbands, but this did not stop thousands suing, or being sued, with their husbands.[11] Proportionally, however, widows were easily the most prominent group of female litigants. According to Peter Laslett's averages for 61 English communities during the period 1574–1821, widows made up just under 9 per cent of women in the population, compared with just under 60 per cent who were single and about 32 per cent who were married.[12] Widows

7. In Hilary term 22 James I, women were involved in 83 out of 220 Requests actions (37.7%); PRO Req 1/32, pp. 399–428, 449–506; W.R. Prest, 'Law and women's rights in early modern England', *The Seventeenth Century* 6 (1991), p. 182.

8. In a sample of Star Chamber suits initiated by individuals, only 66 out of at least 1377 litigants were women (less than 5%); unpublished PRO calendar 'Star Chamber Proceedings Elizabeth', Vol. 4; in Hilary term 22 James I, 96 out of 531 Requests litigants were female (18.1%); PRO Req 1/32, pp. 399–428, 449–506.

9. Laura Gowing, *Domestic Dangers: Women, Words, and Sex in Early Modern London* (Oxford, 1996), Table 2, p. 35, and see Table 3, p. 37; Amy Louise Erickson, *Women and Property in Early Modern England* (London and New York, 1993), p. 223.

10. In Common Pleas, for example, a sample of 150 cases taken from the roll of warrants of attorneys for Easter term 2 Elizabeth I (1560) includes the names of six spinsters, 29 wives and 23 widows (out of a total of 431 litigants); PRO CP40/1187.

11. Married women were able to bring suits without their husbands in the church courts, and very occasionally in courts of equity and common law.

12. Peter Laslett, 'Mean household size in England since the sixteenth century', in Peter Laslett and Richard Wall, eds, *Household and Family in Past Times* (Cambridge, 1972), Table 4.7, p. 145.

may have represented closer to 15 or 20 per cent of women over the age of eighteen, yet they made up between 40 and 50 per cent of the female litigant populations in Queen's Bench, Common Pleas and Requests, and in late Elizabethan England they made up around 5 or 6 per cent of total litigant populations in these major courts.[13] Widows, in other words, were the only group of women whose share of litigation came near to matching the level of their presence in society.

With levels of litigation on the rise, the numbers of widows involved in lawsuits increased steadily and the image of the widow at law grew in the popular consciousness. In 1593, for example, Thomas Nashe described in his satire of London life, *Christs Teares over Jerusalem,* how bawdy-house keepers explained the presence under their roofs of a woman 'of middle years' by saying that 'she is a widow that hath suits in law here at the Term, and hath been a long Council table petitioner'.[14] Seventeenth-century dramatists, including John Webster, John Ford, Thomas Middleton, Francis Beaumont and John Fletcher, regularly depicted widow characters in legal situations in their plays. Some, like Valeria in Middleton's *The Widow,* appear as plaintiffs who use the law, while others, such as the Duchess in Webster's *The Duchess of Malfi,* appear as defendants who fall victim to it. William Wycherley created the consummate example of the active widowed plaintiff in his Restoration comedy *The Plain Dealer,* in which the comic Widow Blackacre is described as 'a petulant litigious Widow always in Law' and a 'Litigious She-Pettyfogger, who is at Law and difference with all the World'. When threatened with an enforced remarriage she utters the memorable lines, 'Matrimony, to a Woman, [is] worse than Excommunication, in depriving her of the benefit of the Law: and I wo'd rather be depriv'd of life'.[15]

The contrast between the feisty temperament of Widow Blackacre and the demure behaviour that authors of conduct literature recommended for widows could hardly be sharper. As Barbara Todd points out in chapter 5, the moral commentator Juan Luis Vives

13. Barbara Todd, 'Widowhood in a market town: Abingdon 1540–1720' (University of Oxford D.Phil. thesis, 1983), p. 1; in Requests in 1603, 6% of litigants named in decree and order books were widows; PRO Req 1/21; in Chancery, and at times in Common Pleas and King's Bench, widows made up only about 2–3% of litigants; Brooks, *Pettyfoggers,* pp. 281–3; Erickson, *Women and Property,* Tables 7.1, 7.2, p. 115.

14. Thomas Nashe, *Christs Teares over Jerusalem* (London, 1593), f. 79^{v}; spelling and punctuation in this and in subsequent quotes have been modernized.

15. William Wycherley, *The Plain-Dealer,* I. i. 393–4; V. ii. 459–61; in Arthur Friedman, ed., *The Plays of William Wycherley* (Oxford, 1979), pp. 376, 390, 501.

was adamant that wherever possible widows should avoid going to court, for in court they risked exposing their honour to danger. If they had to pursue legal claims he recommended they seek out 'feeble attorneys', or none at all, 'for then shall the judges take on them the room of attorneys, when they withstand often times mighty defenders and advocates'. Having approached a 'feeble' attorney, her cause 'shall be so much more recommended unto them the less that she recommendeth it. And her cause shall be more like to be good whom men think so good and vertuous that she will neither ask nor hold that is not her own', for 'she that is babbling and busy and troublous must needs weary men and make them to loathe her and hindreth her of the succour that I spake of'.[16]

These quotes from Vives suggest a certain uneasiness in the minds of advice givers that questions of justice could raise. On one level, writers regarded widows as especially deserving of justice. As repeated illustrations in the Bible made clear, widows, like orphans, could be potent symbols of weakness and innocence, in need of protection from the powerful and the unscrupulous. According to Richard Brathwait, widows who had legal business should ground their faith in the promises of Christ, for 'Your Lord maketh intercession for you, rendering right judgement to the Orphan, and righteousness unto the widow'.[17] However, law courts were confrontational arenas where litigants spoke their minds in public, either personally or through their lawyers, and the belief that innocent widows deserved justice was matched by a general dislike of widows, or indeed any other women, speaking out or exercising independence in front of an audience. The tension between these two images was considerable, for in the mind of a moral observer such as Vives it did not take much for a shamefaced, 'deserving' widow to transmute into a boisterous, 'undeserving' widow merely by speaking her mind. Hence the common stress in advice literature on the need for widows to safeguard their modesty by avoiding going to court, by relying on others to protect their interests and to represent them, and above all by refraining from speaking in public.

Writers who voiced concerns about widows speaking obviously did not confine their observations to the law. But legal venues regularly exposed a potential contradiction between the desire that widows remain silent and the realization that their complaints needed to

16. Juan Luis Vives, *A Very Fruteful and Pleasant Boke Callyd the Instruction of a Christen Woman*, trans. Richard Hyrde (London, 1541), ff. 137^{r-v}, 140^{r-v} [*sic* 138^{r-v}].
17. Richard Brathwait, *The English Gentlewoman* (London, 1631), p. 111; see also Vives, *Instruction of a Christen Woman*, ff. 137^{v}–140^{r} [*sic* 138^{r}].

be heard. The ambivalence surrounding this subject can be seen in the use writers made of the parable of the importunate widow (Luke 18: 1–8), a woman who begged and begged a judge to hear her cause until finally he gave in, 'because of her importunateness', so that he might have some peace. In the mid-sixteenth century, bishop Hugh Latimer offered the story as comfort for any individuals denied justice in this life, encouraging them with the reassurance that the Lord would be their judge in the next life: 'You widows, you Orphans, you poor people, here is a comfortable place for you. Though these judges of the world will not hear you, there is one will be content with your importunity, he will remedy you.'[18] God would listen to the cries of widows, orphans and the poor, but many judges regarded pleas from importunate widows as a nuisance, and criticisms can be found in legal pleadings and judgments of the 'clamorousness' of widows who pursued their legal causes too vigorously or who spoke too loudly on their own behalf.[19] Yet silence was not a practical option for most women, unless they relied entirely on their lawyers, especially when judges, juries and legal observers all regarded silence from plaintiffs, defendants and suspects in criminal trials as a sign of guilt.[20]

In the ideal universe envisaged by the authors of conduct books and sermons widows clearly deserved protection, but only if they played the part of the 'good' widow. Those who strayed from the ideal risked finding themselves aligned with the image of the 'bad' widow, for conduct book writers, in common with the authors of ballads, satires and pamphlets, tended to deal in extremes when they characterized widows, producing portraits that are among the most two-dimensional imaginable.[21] These portraits bore little relation to the way widows actually lived their lives, but that does not mean that widows were unaffected by them. As we shall see, these stereotypical images, and the impulses authors drew on to create them, influenced the shape and character of pleadings prepared for and against widows and may have led some individuals to think twice about going to law.

18. Hugh Latimer, *Twenty Seven Sermons Preached* (London, 1562), f. 45^{v}.

19. See for example John Hawarde, *Les Reportes del Cases in Camera Stellata 1593 to 1609*, William Baildon, ed. (privately printed, 1894), p. 161; PRO Req 1/19, pp. 618–19, 827.

20. This last point is Heather Kerr's: see Heather Kerr, 'Thomas Garter's Susanna: "pollicie" and "true report"', *Journal of the Australasian Universities and Literature Association* 72 (1989), pp. 183–202.

21. See Charles Carlton, 'The widow's tale: male myths and female reality in 16th and 17th century England', *Albion* 10 (1978), pp. 118–29.

The subject of disputes

Research into the lives of English widows prior to the eighteenth century has revealed their active participation in a whole range of employments and economic activities. Independent widows ran estates and controlled manors, they established businesses or continued to operate their late husbands' businesses, they employed apprentices, they worked as midwives and healers, they acted as moneylenders. And when transactions failed or disagreements arose, many took their complaints to court. The subject matter of individual disputes varied considerably, but certain patterns are discernible in the litigating habits of widows in Requests. The first is the high proportion of widows who came to court within weeks or months of their husbands' deaths. The concentration of legal activity associated with the onset of widowhood is unmistakable, and it highlights the impact that the linking of legal and marital status could have on women. It also serves as a reminder that restored independence, symbolically so important from a modern perspective, was not always a welcome acquisition for widows.

It is not altogether surprising that widowhood acted as a catalyst for litigation, given the various rights that might accrue to widows on the deaths of their husbands. Common law, customary and equity court archives all contain claims for the traditional widows' rights of dower (a life interest in one-third of a husband's freehold lands), jointure (a life interest in land, or a money equivalent in the form of an annuity, pre-arranged at the time of marriage) and freebench or widow's estate (customary rights to between one-third and the whole of the interests a husband held by customary tenure, for life or for widowhood). Many widows found themselves competing for these entitlements with their husbands' heirs, especially if they were second or third wives and faced opposition from step-children. However, dower, jointure and freebench actions by no means dominated lists of widow litigation and a great many widows brought actions that were inspired by other matters connected with, or coinciding with, the death of their husbands. Widows fought to secure or maintain control of the houses in which they lived. They contested wills and claimed legacies owing to them. Others inherited unresolved legal actions brought by, or with, their husbands which they chose to continue in their own names by entering a 'bill of revivor'. In January 1625, Jane Fellowes revived an action her late husband Thomas had brought against two men who were suing him at common law for failing to make deliveries of malt. She argued that these men had tricked her husband into signing unfair and unreasonable agreements by 'procuring the said Thomas Fellowes to be drunk with several drugs and intoxicating ingredients'.[22]

As we have already seen, in many cases widows held responsibilities as executors or administrators, charged with overseeing the settling of their late husbands' estates and the division of assets among kin. In these capacities they routinely inherited, or otherwise had to make sense of, whole closets, cabinets or chests filled with deeds, leases, promissory notes, bills of sale, indentures and other papers and documents. Understanding and resolving the matters contained in this paperwork could produce an avalanche of litigation as widows attempted (on behalf of themselves or other beneficiaries) to collect money from debtors, satisfy creditors, and to claim from landholders, trustees and other parties the myriad interests that had belonged to their late husbands. Widows were expected to take on responsibilities, to be aware of legal rights and duties and to be supremely competent immediately upon the death of their husbands. Many of those who found uncancelled bonds among their 'writings', as Widow Blackacre called them, chased up these unpaid debts by bringing actions at common law to recover the penalties on bonds (usually twice the amount of the initial debt).

For a number of widows the sudden assumption of responsibility could be traumatic and leave little time for grieving. Rival claimants who alleged they owned title in property violently evicted widows from their marital homes or used force to carry away their movable goods.[23] Martin Billingsley, the author of *The Pens Excellencie*, suggested that no woman who survived her husband and inherited an estate ought to be without the ability to write: 'for thereby she comes to a certainty of her estate, without trusting to the reports of such as are usually employed to look into the same: whereas otherwise for want of it she is subject to the manifold deceits now used in the world, and by that means plungeth herself into a multitude of inconveniences'.[24] Marie Sutton found herself subject to some of the 'manifold deceits now used in the world' after her husband Robert, 'a seafaring man', died on board his ship called *The Husband* while on a voyage to Brazil. She decided not to take on the administration of his estate herself, because she lived 140 miles from London, but trusted an acquaintance to take on the responsibility in

22. *Jane Fellowes* v. *Nicholas Dixon et al.*, PRO Req 1/32, pp. 456–7.
23. *Johan Lewis* v. *Thobye Pleydell*, PRO Req 2/164/103.
24. Martin Billingsley, *The Pens Excellencie* [London, 1618], sigs Biv^{v}–C.

her stead. However, according to her bill in Requests this man had colluded with an accomplice and used fraudulent means to prevent her from recovering her husband's personal belongings, worth £10, plus 'his dividend share of goods gotten by the adventure of the said voyage which in truth was worth twenty pounds more'.[25]

In their capacity as executors or administrators, widows also found themselves on the receiving end of litigation, fending off or settling the claims of disgruntled creditors, heirs and other beneficiaries. Furthermore, when widows put bonds in suit at common law, their intended targets often counter-sued them in courts of equity. The expectation that widows be competent managers of property, money and other interests, when prior to achieving their new status they had (at least in theory) been excluded from this world, placed many widows at a significant disadvantage compared with widowers or other men when it came to legal dealings. However, while the resumption of legal status may have caused headaches for a number of widows, for others it represented a welcome liberation from the legal strictures imposed by marriage, and a significant proportion of widows went to law not because their situation demanded it, but because their new status allowed them to litigate.

Agnes Nowell, for example, sued Thomas Hall in Requests in 1591 immediately after her husband's death. The subject of her suit was a payment to Hall she had made fifteen or sixteen years earlier when she and her husband had agreed a temporary separation. Her husband had given her £20 for her maintenance and she had given the money to Hall to keep for her use. Now, all these years later, she wanted it back. Hall admitted receiving the money (although he alleged the separation had occurred 27 or 28 years ago), but said he had repaid it when the couple became reunited. Agnes was confused, he implied, because he had returned the money not to her, but directly to her husband, for 'being a feme covert . . . all things which she possessed was her said husbands'. Here we see a widow who brought an action as soon as she regained her legal status, relating to a time when she had enjoyed legal status (or quasi-legal status) in the past, even though between fifteen and 28 years had elapsed since the cause supposedly arose.[26]

Cases like Agnes Nowell's were not uncommon in Requests and similar examples can be found in Chancery of widows bringing actions relating to causes that were fourteen, 20 or even 30 years

25. *Marie Sutton* v. *John Smyth*, PRO Req 2/424/157.
26. *Agnes Nowell* v. *Thomas Hall*, PRO Req 2/166/134.

old.[27] It is interesting that judges were willing to hear these cases, when on other occasions they refused to hear actions delayed for more than a couple of years. It appears that they recognized the constraints wives endured under coverture, when a husband's refusal to co-operate in his wife's lawsuits effectively amounted to a veto, and wished to prevent widows from being unduly prejudiced by their changeable legal status. However, the Nowell case also illustrates the problems widows and wives might face as a result of their fluctuating legal status, which left them open to a series of allegations rarely levelled at men. It was quite plausible for opponents to argue, as Thomas Hall argued, that widows were unaware of the arrangement and repayment of loans because they had been 'femes covert' and had not been present to witness these transactions. Alternatively they argued that widows suing at common law were fully aware and were attempting to use their status as widows to commit fraud. In 1630 Thomas Warren complained that Dorothy Godley, widow and executor of Godfrey Godley, was suing him at common law over an old bond belonging to her late husband for which he had acted as surety. She was seeking to recover the penalty of £200 for the non-payment of £100, but Warren argued that the debt had long since been repaid, as Dorothy well knew, 'yet now finding the said Bond amongst the waste papers of her said deceased husband uncancelled, and conceiving some causeless displeasure against the said complainant although she well knoweth the said debt to be truly and fully satisfied, yet doth she put the same in suit at the common law thinking to recover the whole penalty thereof'.[28]

Opponents contended that widows were either ignorant dupes who did not realize that pieces of paper their husbands had left behind represented long-settled transactions, or alternatively that they were scheming manipulators who knew full well that they were 'double-charging' innocent parties.[29] John Leak complained that the administrator Elizabeth Hargrave 'giveth it out that she will sue and implead your said subject' upon several obligations 'albeit she well knoweth as well by view of the daybook . . . as by such notes as your subject hath showed unto her' that the debts were long settled.[30] Widows, in turn, often claimed that they were well-acquainted with their late husbands' affairs, and that it was their opponents who

27. See Maria Cioni, *Women and Law in Elizabethan England with Particular Reference to the Court of Chancery* (New York and London, 1985), pp. 81–2, 111–12.

28. *Thomas Warren* v. *Dorothy Godley*, PRO Req 1/34, p. 539.

29. *Maudlen Hollande* v. *Thomas Wilford & Robert Holland*, PRO Req 2/47/25.

30. *John Leake* v. *Elizabeth Hargrave*, PRO Req 2/165/135, B.

were trying to take advantage of them at their most vulnerable. Or else they responded to opponents' accusations by asking for proof. If these people had performed their promises, why had they allowed bonds to remain uncancelled? If they had settled their debts, where were the acquittances? Some widows who used these tactics appear to have been calling an adversary's bluff. Others seemed genuinely concerned to discover the truth about their late husbands' activities. When a defendant answered Dame Margaret Stanhope's bill of complaint by saying that her husband had granted him a lease of contested lands, she responded by offering to settle if he could produce the lease. As her counsel explained to the Masters, 'if it shall upon sight thereof fall out and appear that the same lease was so made by the said Sir Thomas Stanhop . . . she will permit & suffer the said defendant quietly to enjoy the same for & under the rents . . . therein expressed'.[31]

Opponents of widows were often well placed, thanks to the workings of coverture, to deny claims made against them. But by the same token, some widows found themselves in a position where they could attempt to double-charge their enemies if they so wished, and while many honest women suffered because they were unable to prove their knowledge of transactions, some dishonest women, or women who were genuinely unsure of their entitlements, may well have benefited from these uncertainties.

Widowhood, like marriage, was a major spur to litigation where women were concerned.[32] However, widows did not retreat from the courts once they had tied up the loose ends of their husbands' estates and negotiated the transformation from wife to widow. Widows can be found litigating at every stage of widowhood. Widow moneylenders sued for debts when debts went unpaid, while other individuals brought or answered legal actions connected with their property and trades. Dame Candy, who controlled a mill in Norfolk, successfully sued John Bateman in the 1620s after he threatened to 'break down the dams & sluices' which had directed the local stream to the mill 'for the time whereof the memory of man is not to the contrary'.[33] Elizabeth Reynolds came to court to counter demands for six years' worth of tithes arguing that she had already paid them. Her extensive farming interests included 40 dozen pigeons worth six shillings a dozen, 30 chickens 'hatched and brought up'

31. *Margaret Stanhop* v. *Thomas Roe*, PRO Req 1/21, p. 26.
32. On marriage as a catalyst for litigation, see Stretton, *Women Waging Law*, ch. 6.
33. *Mary Candy* v. *John Bateman*, PRO Req 1/32, pp. 458–9.

worth sixteen pence each, 'Plumbs, pears, Apples, damsons and such like fruit' worth 40 shillings per annum, and twelve cows. She could not produce written proof of tithe payments on these products from her lands and orchards, but she convinced the Masters of Requests and they found in her favour.[34]

Examples can be found of widows litigating almost every subject imaginable. Ann Hopkins, for example, sued James Heywood, the father of her sixteen-year-old illegitimate son, demanding retrospective maintenance payments to cover the cost of the boy's upbringing. What makes this case extraordinary is the willingness of a widow openly to admit fornication, an offence punishable in the church courts, for the sake of her son's livelihood. According to Ann she met James when she was a servant and 'a maiden and of good Credit and reputation' and after a period of courtship he had 'faithfully promised privately' that he would marry her. Subsequently Ann, 'giving Credit to his protestations and vows, was unhappily seduced' and had a son. Three months later she asked James to keep his word and marry her, but he refused, saying that if she had approached him before she had been 'brought a bed with the said son, he would have saved both their credits'. He left the country and she eventually married another man who later died. James rose to become a wealthy merchant, and on his return to England Ann sued him in Requests to recoup what she regarded as his share of their son's maintenance costs.[35]

In many respects the diverse range of lawsuits widows initiated in Requests and elsewhere are indistinguishable from those brought by other classes of litigant. Again and again, however, widows experienced problems linked directly to shifts in their legal and marital status, especially if they married more than once. As executor of the estate of her late husband, John Marshall, Elianor Marshall was responsible for the payment of his debts. She later married another man, but before it came time to settle a particular debt her new husband died without leaving a will. Even though she had contributed £100 in money and goods and a rent charge worth £10 per annum to this second marriage, and despite the fact that her husband's estate was worth over £600, a disputed agreement over the administration of his estate left her with no money to repay the outstanding loan and no means of defending herself against a debt action at common law. Her experience of being twice a wife and

34. *Elizabeth Reynolds* v. *Daniell Collins & Roberte Smith*, PRO Req 1/34, pp. 77–9.
35. *Ann Hopkins* v. *James Heywood*, PRO Req 2/420/82.

twice a widow saw her move in and out of the legal shadows once too often. A victim of unfortunate timing linked to her indeterminate status, she eventually achieved a just settlement after a hard-fought appeal in Requests (under the name Elianor Adgore).[36]

Representations of widowhood

The cases discussed in this chapter reveal the active nature of many widows' dealings with the law, as well as the practical difficulties different widows faced when they went to court. In addition, they show particular accusations opponents directed at widows, concentrating on their status and competence, their knowledge of transactions, their general demeanour and the motivations behind their actions. Counsel for both plaintiffs and defendants drew upon stereotypical images to bolster their arguments, suggesting, for example, that widow opponents were loud, immodest and sexually incontinent, or that they were bad mothers guilty of shaming the memories of their late husbands (accusations of a type rarely levelled at widowers).[37] Widows and their lawyers refuted these allegations and did their best to distance themselves from these damaging stereotypes of the 'bad' widow. However, they also made active attempts to align themselves with universal images of 'good' widowhood, good not just in the sense of admirable or ideal, but in the sense of deserving – deserving of sympathy and therefore of legal protection or remedy.

To make their clients appear deserving, lawyers emphasized widows' poverty, attempting to harness the sense of purity and innocence that in advice literature and the Bible so often attached to the figure of the defenceless widow. The framers of pleadings defined poverty in its widest sense, centring on widows' blighted circumstances or their lack of support as much as on their lack of material resources, with the result that widow defendants as well as plaintiffs stressed any aspect of their condition that might place them at a disadvantage in legal dealings. As well as their lack of adequate funds they stressed their age, if they were unusually young or very old, the number of children they had to bring up, the burden of debts and responsibilities they had to shoulder, the distance they lived from the court, and in some cases their lack of male

36. *Elianor Adgore* v. *Thomas Adgore et al.*, PRO Req 1/32, pp. 857–60.

37. See for example *Elizabeth Shipper* v. *Thomas Good & William Taylor*, PRO Req 2/39/60, m. 16; *Mary Cheeke* v. *Christopher Symcocks*, PRO Req 2/47/36.

support. Agnes Greenland described herself as an 'old woman' and 'sole', by which she meant 'feme sole', or no longer married. Her pleadings went on to describe her as 'a very poor & impotent creature without friends or ability to sue or defend her right', to whom failure at law would result in 'the utter impoverishing of your said subject, her children and family'.[38] Other widows accused their opponents of trying to 'abuse the simplicity of your poor subject', or of taking advantage of 'the unpower poverty and indigence' of a 'poor' widow, or of employing violence against a defenceless adversary.[39] Widows might have a hard time defending themselves against accusations that they were unworldly and ignorant, but in other contexts they proved capable of employing such claims to their own advantage.

The Court of Requests was known as the 'Poor Man's Court', and widows were not alone in pleading poverty in an attempt to qualify for its special brand of equitable relief. However, while almost every plaintiff in Requests made reference to their poor state, no grouping of litigants (except perhaps for orphans) concentrated on their poverty with the same intensity as widows. Even quite wealthy women complained that failure to recover debts or redeem bonds worth hundreds or thousands of pounds would be to their undoing, 'unless your highness's accustomed Justice to such poor widows be herein extended'.[40] Many phrases in widows' pleadings border on the formulaic, but the frequency with which individuals placed poverty at the core of their complaints or defences suggests that these descriptions were more than simply empty words. Most male litigants were reluctant to stress their own poverty and weakness more than was strictly necessary. As I have argued elsewhere, men tended to concentrate attention on the power of their opponents rather than on their own incapacity, but widows were unashamed in their declarations of impotence.[41] Clearly widows and their lawyers believed that such tactics were effective, and it seems likely that on occasion they were proved right. One commentator writing at the end of the sixteenth century believed that Requests had been established specifically 'to hear poor miserable persons causes, as Widows and Orphans, and other distressed people, whose cases

38. *Agnes Greneland* v. *Elianor Seward & John Stocker*, PRO Req 2/210/101.

39. *Agnes Chicke* v. *Elizabeth Clifton*, PRO Req 2/190/27, B; *Elizabeth Shipper* v. *Thomas Good & William Taylor*, PRO Req 2/39/60, B.

40. *Elianor Nanez & Fardinando Alveres* v. *Andrew Browne*, PRO Req 2/245/67, B.

41. See Stretton, *Women Waging Law*, ch. 8.

wholly rely on piety and conscience'.[42] Furthermore, Masters and scribes regularly attached the epithet 'poor' to widows' names, using it in the court's decision books to mean blameless and deserving of relief as well as lacking in property or income.[43]

Of course, one reason why widows complained of poverty more intensely than other classes of litigants was because they were more often poor. However, widows' actual lack of resources cannot by itself account for the rhetoric that even wealthy widows employed. The vehement challenges that so often met widows' cries of poverty suggest that these pleas were not always 100 per cent genuine. When a woman from Bath claimed she was a poor widow with no experience of the law, her accusers countered saying she was a woman of substance who could better serve God by relieving them.[44] Another litigant challenged the length of a woman's bill of complaint, for 'being drawn into a needless length with vain protestations of poverty and other idle suggestions'.[45]

It is difficult in any one case to discern from the whirl of claims and counter-claims about a widow's substance who was telling the truth, but the regularity with which all sides evoked images of the 'weakness' of widows adds weight to Linda Pollock's contention that 'both men and women manipulated the ideology of women to achieve particular objectives'.[46] Nevertheless, the odds here, as elsewhere, were stacked against widows engaged in legal battles. For those women who sought to manipulate their positions and shape their pleas to best advantage, the image of the defenceless, deserving widow might prove useful. But such appeals underline the absence of power or real independence in most widows' lives, for in many contexts, including evaluations of people's status and reputation or their credibility as witnesses in legal proceedings, poverty was not a universally respected attribute. Furthermore, while the common association of poverty with widowhood might lead to positive results for some women, most stereotypes connected with widows were negative both in their spirit and their effect, even if a few restored to widows a modicum of autonomy, as in Thomas Overbury's jest

42. Thomas Ridley, *A View of the Civile and Ecclesiasticall Law* (London, 1607), p. 228.

43. See for example PRO Req 1/19, p. 493.

44. *Michael & Friswithe Keynton & Johanne Ayle* v. *Alice Walley*, PRO Req 2/231/24, A and R.

45. *Thomas Good* v. *Elizabeth Shipper*, PRO Req 2/123/53, A.

46. Linda Pollock, '"Teach her to live under obedience": the making of women in the upper ranks of early modern England', *Continuity and Change* 4 (1989), p. 251.

that should a widow live to be thrice married, 'she seldom fails to cozen her second Husband's Creditors'.[47]

Over the course of the Tudor and Stuart period hundreds of thousands of widows went to law to assert or defend their rights in an array of different courts. For some this was a profitable and liberating experience. For others it was an unwelcome responsibility that came at a difficult time in their lives. Not only did they have to enter an environment that might be unfamiliar to them, but they had to overcome a whole raft of obstacles of the kind described in this chapter. The law alone was not to blame for the difficulties widows faced in exercising their rights – these often resulted from social, cultural or economic rather than exclusively legal causes, as the sheer numbers of widows who went to court attests – but it played a significant part, particularly through the doctrine of coverture. Confident and resourceful widows such as Elizabeth Russell ignored the barriers before them and confronted the law head on.[48] For others, however, the impediments ranged against them inhibited their behaviour. They either stayed away from the courts, through lack of resources or out of ignorance of their entitlements, or else they evaded the difficulties confronting them by delegating their legal and property affairs to others. Not to brothers, uncles and male advisers for modesty's sake, as conduct book writers recommended, but more often to trustees, lawyers and agents who could manage property and other interests on their behalf, regardless of their current or future status. What remains to be discovered is how active a part different widows played in their affairs after delegating them. For while calculations of widows' rates of participation in court actions provide an interesting guide to their legal fortunes, only by understanding the dynamics of different women's legal and professional relationships will it be possible to discover the actual levels of independence widows achieved and how these levels changed over time.

47. Thomas Overbury, *His Wife* (London, 1627), p. 205.

48. For an example of Elizabeth Russell's dealings with the law, see Hawarde, *Les Reportes*, p. 275.

CHAPTER THIRTEEN

Widows, the state and the guardianship of children in early modern Tuscany

GIULIA CALVI

Two legal cases involving a complex set of conflicts and negotiations in the lives of two widows were brought to the court of the *Magistrato dei Pupilli* in Florence. The two stories are set 150 years apart from one another, the first taking place in 1589 and the second in 1739. Among hundreds, they stand out as two exemplary narratives of the manifold ways in which widows confronted and used legal procedures and discourse vis-à-vis public institutions. Aimed at protecting widows and orphans in early modern Tuscany, the court of the *Magistrato dei Pupilli* functioned indeed as the legal scenario where women's empowerment strategies were played out.[1]

The first case introduces us to a violent dispute where the status and rights of a widow ultimately resulted from the interaction between state officials, family networks and the strategies widows employed to counterbalance patrilinear control over their lives. The second case, on the other hand, is an interesting example of how a lengthy practical experience in the workings of the law tended to empower widows to the point of turning them into conscious and possibly ambivalent manipulators of rules concerning family property and child custody.

The first story took place in Monte S. Savino, a hilltop village near Arezzo. On 30 November 1589 Count Nicola Orsino wrote an

1. Florence, Archivio di Stato (hereafter ASF), Magistrato dei pupilli et adulti avanti il Principato, F. 248, 'Statuti et ordini della corte et magistrato delli offitiali de' pupilli et adulti della città di Firenze riformati il XX Agosto 1565'. For an edition of the medieval statutes, see F. Morandini, 'Statuti et ordinamenti dell 'Ufficio dei Pupilli et Adulti nel periodo della Repubblica fiorentina (1388–1534)', in *Archivio Storico Italiano* CXIII (1955), pp. 522–51; CXIV (1956), pp. 92–117; and CXV (1957), pp. 87–104.

alarmed letter to the *Ufficiali dei Pupilli* (Officials of the Wards), in Florence. His daughter Settimia, a young widowed mother of four small children, had been granted guardianship according to her late husband's will. Count Orsino however was worried because he had planned and arranged a new marriage for his daughter and this had unleashed the violent reaction of her brother-in-law. Without refunding Settimia her dowry, the latter had appealed to the local officials in Monte S. Savino by producing a false certificate, which stated that the widow had already remarried. Since a remarried mother automatically lost tutorship, without enquiring any further, the *podestà* (the highest urban authority with civil judicial powers) had swiftly entrusted Giovan Battista Simoncelli with tutorship over his nephews. Soon after this locally settled change of guardianship had taken place, the brother-in-law had appeared in Settimia's home, carrying an arquebus and accompanied by six armed servants. The men had forced their entry into the house, where, after having rummaged and searched everywhere, they had taken all they could, writing an arbitrary inventory of the dead Simoncelli's belongings. No notary was present and the whole procedure was totally illegal. That was why Count Orsino, Settimia's father, had finally decided to appeal directly to the officials in Florence: local authorities were steadfastly backing up Giovan Battista's violence. Was Settimia going to be deprived of all her rights to guardianship and dowry as a mother and a widow? A few days later, the officials started their proceedings, writing to the lower and higher local authorities, who were ordered to offer an official justification of the whole matter. The *podestà* argued that Simoncelli had appealed, producing the required papers; having acknowledged Settimia's second wedding, the *podestà* entrusted Giovan Battista Simoncelli with tutorship over the wards, as the law prescribed. How could he have detected Simoncelli's plotting? Two months later, having gathered the necessary evidence, the officials gave judgment: Settimia was again entrusted with guardianship of her children and given back the 'wheat, wine, millet and chestnuts' that had been stolen from her house by her brother-in-law and his armed men.[2]

This is one of the earliest episodes I have come across in my research. Settimia, the widowed mother, never spoke for herself, acting as a sort of absent protagonist. The two men, her father

2. ASF, Magistrato dei pupilli et adulti del Principato (hereafter MPAP), Suppliche con informazione, F. 2282, ff. 274, 286.

Count Orsino and her brother-in-law, Giovan Battista Simoncelli, fought against each other and tried to manipulate her position and life. The father arranged for a new marriage to which she might not agree; the brother-in-law deprived her of guardianship and property. Never in the whole proceedings did Settimia express her will: she acted as a token, a pledge between two groups whose alliance she embodied.[3] The conflict between the two powerful local families and the way they used local political and juridical authority were the focal elements. The *podestà* was indeed just a meek mediator of Simoncelli's arrogance; in spite of his public function, he had no power to alter what were essentially face-to-face and typically medieval family relationships. Only the Florentine officials, acting in the name of the Grand Duke, could impose their solution as neutral adjudicators.

Count Orsino had appealed to the law of the state's magistracy as he was confronted by a biased and manipulated local arbitrator. Thus we have a combined conflict where a centre v. local dispute arose from one concerning lineage. It is significant that while the marital side appealed to the local structure of power, the woman's side resorted to the centre: this also implied an appeal to a larger external group and to a set of values not defined by predominant local face-to-face relationships but rather to the impersonal, distant, professionally administered power of the law.[4]

The *Ufficiali dei Pupilli*, originally created by the Florentine *Signoria* in 1393, were entrusted with the task of administering wards' patrimonies – which had to amount to at least 200 *scudi* – acting as testamentary executors and taking charge of all matters concerning the custody and guardianship of minors and handicapped adults in Florence and its territory. Undergoing a series of reforms aimed at increasing its sphere of action,[5] from the fourteenth to the

3. This case has some points in common with C. Klapisch-Zuber, 'The "cruel mother": maternity, widowhood, and dowry in Florence in the fourteenth and fifteenth centuries', in Christiane Klapisch-Zuber, *Women, Family, and Ritual in Renaissance Italy* (Chicago, 1985), pp. 117–31.

4. For an anthropological approach to social conflict, see S. Roberts, 'The study of dispute: anthropological perspectives', in John Bossy, ed., *Disputes and Settlements: Law and Human Relations in the West* (Cambridge, 1983); Thomas Kuehn, *Law, Family and Women: Towards a Legal Anthropology of Renaissance Italy* (Chicago, 1991).

5. For appointment procedures, jurisdiction and salaries, see ASF, Miscellanea medicea, 413, Niccolò Arrighi, 'Teatro di grazia e di giustizia ovvero formulario de'rescritti a tutte le cariche che conferisce il Ser. Granduca di Toscana per via dell'Uffizio delle Tratte e dedicato al Ser. Cosimo III' (1695); on how church courts administered guardianship in early modern England, see W. Coster, '"To bring them up in the fear of God": guardianship in the Diocese of York, 1550–1668', *Continuity and Change* 10 (1995), pp. 9–32.

nineteenth century the magistracy took care of boys under eighteen and girls up to 25 (but generally until the age of marriage or religious profession): children whose father had died intestate or who had not named guardians in his will. Aside from these basic conditions, further situations required the intervention of the magistrates, as testamentary guardians died, renounced the charge or began to dispute against one another, and widows who had been entrusted with guardianship remarried. In all these recurrent cases, the officials took over, taking the wards under their tutorship, or naming new guardians among surviving relatives who offered to undertake such charge. Therefore, throughout the years, widows and their children lived under close supervision: not only did paternal kin constantly try to interfere with widows' decisions concerning lifestyle, consumption and education, but the officials also kept a watchful eye over households governed by women, who were compelled to submit yearly statements of their administration to the magistrate's accountant.

Guardianship was rooted in paternal authority (*patria potestas*) so guardians could be appointed only by fathers or grandfathers. Mothers could not name guardians, but instead could be entrusted with the legal confirmation of the magistracy. Mothers entrusted with guardianship of their children had to name a guarantor on a yearly basis whose name had to be approved. Should they not keep to this procedure and not respect the prescribed deadlines, mothers would lose their prerogatives and the officials would assume guardianship. The naming of guardians spelled out a precise hierarchy of kin. Statutes listed, on the father's side, the grandfather and grandmother, the widow, the brother and cousin. Thus widows were lined up with their in-laws while their own kin went unmentioned, only taken into consideration if all the ward's paternal relatives were dead. However, in this patrilinear structure of protection, one condition was absolutely necessary in order to entrust someone: no guardian could expect to inherit from his or her ward. What the magistrates indeed feared, on the basis of Roman law and juridical practice, was the death of a minor by the hand of a guardian who came next in the line of inheritance.[6] But this revealed that the exclusion of mothers from patrilinear inheritance turned them into safe guardians of their children: no widow would profit from the death of her offspring, as she never succeeded to their legacy.

6. English law expressed similar preoccupations: see B. Hanawalt, 'La debolezza del lignaggio: vedove, orfani e corporazioni nella Londra tardo medievale', *Quaderni Storici* 86 (1994), p. 467.

Florentine city statutes, as well as those of most Tuscan towns, insisted on the same principle, systematically eliminating all inheritance links between mothers and children. Legal discourse therefore defined mothers as 'above all suspicion' or 'above all hope' of inheriting, and the mother–child bond was repeatedly represented in terms of 'gratuitous charity and affection', effacing the image of purely physical closeness that Renaissance theorists had used to express maternal love.[7]

In their husbands' wills, widows were usually left in the position of the 'donna et madonna' which implied receiving usufruct (life use) over part or the whole of the husband's patrimony, guardianship of offspring, and being allowed to live in the family home. All this was on condition that the widow would not remarry. Should she choose a new husband, she would automatically lose all the prerogatives of her status of 'donna et madonna', as well as guardianship of her children. In this respect a remarried widow, as legal doctrine concisely stated, was like a dead mother to her children.[8]

On the other hand, paternal agnates – uncles and grandfathers – were next in the inheritance line and patrimonies went from male orphans to male kin on their father's side. This relationship of dependence could prove to be extremely dangerous for a male infant or a young boy, whose chances of survival could indeed be weak if entrusted to the guardianship of an uncle with an interest in the child's patrimony. From this viewpoint, girls stood in a safer position as they hardly ever inherited their father's wealth, being only entitled to receive a dowry at the age of marriage.

Between 1648 and 1766, 1503 guardians were appointed in Florence and its territory. They were all named directly by the magistrate as all these cases involved intestate deaths: 72 per cent of all guardians were widowed mothers; 26.1 per cent were relatives on the deceased father's side (uncles); 1.7 per cent were unidentified. We can break down these figures, between urban households, where we find 75.4 per cent of mothers entrusted and 22.6 per cent of uncles, and rural households, where widows acted as guardians in 69.7 per cent of the cases and male kin on the father's side in

7. L.B. Alberti, *The Family in Renaissance Florence*, trans. Renee Watkins (Columbia, SC, 1969), pp. 45–6, 54, or in the Italian original L.B. Alberti, *I Libri della Famiglia* (Turin, 1969), pp. 33–4, 46; Michel de Montaigne, *The Complete Essays* (Harmondsworth, 1991), bk II, ch. 8, pp. 433–4, or *Saggi* (Milan, 1986), pt 2, p. 78.

8. Yan Thomas, 'The division of the sexes in Roman law', in Georges Duby and Michelle Perrot, eds, *A History of Women in the West*, 5 vols (Cambridge, Mass., 1992), I, pp. 83–138.

28.5 per cent.[9] From this data a clear trend emerges: the magistracy operated on the basis of appointing the widow 'without a hope of inheriting' as guardian in preference to uncles or grandfathers with an interest in the inheritance. The widow's guardianship was enhanced by the frequent presence of the widow's brother as guarantor of her administration. Moreover, urban households were more frequently governed by widowed mothers than rural ones, where the administration of land probably required traditional male skills.

Between the sixteenth and the eighteenth centuries the systematic allocation of guardianship to Tuscan widows led them to develop a well-balanced sense of their own status and rights vis-à-vis public institutions and kin. Moreover, widows' guardianship of their children undermined the power of patrilineage. Documentary evidence suggests that women entrusted with legal responsibilities developed a sound knowledge of the law as well as practical skills as negotiators. Thus an institutional policy of protection opened up new space in which women could manipulate rules and exercise initiative.

Let us now turn to our second story, that takes us to another village, Monterchi, a few kilometres away from Anghiari, close to the border with the Papal States. In the first half of the eighteenth century the local population amounted to 435 people, consisting of 98 families and 41 ecclesiastics. Social standing and wealth were connected to agriculture and sheep breeding, as wool production was to be the main source of labour and trade in years to come.[10] Our narrative opens in this milieu, with the sudden death in 1730 of Lando Landucci, a local landowner and cattle breeder, on his way back from the Maremme.[11] Presumably killed by a stroke, Landucci fell off his horse and died, leaving his pregnant wife, Maria Maddalena, and Agata, his six-year-old daughter. The deceased husband left no will and, after the birth of a second daughter, Benedetta, the widow was entrusted with guardianship and custody of her children. Three years went by and the mother, 'having wisely administered her daughters and their patrimony, undergoing the yearly supervision of the magistrate', was involved in a series of disputes with her in-laws, who claimed a right to their deceased brother's property as well as to their young nieces. In need of protection, Maria Maddalena remarried. 'Tenderly loving her children',

9. G. Calvi, *Il Contratto Morale: Madri e Figli nella Toscana Moderna* (Rome/Bari, 1994), pp. 23–4.

10. E. Repetti, *Dizionario geografico-fisico-storico della Toscana*, Vol. 3 (Florence, 1839), *ad vocem*.

11. ASF, MPAP, Memoriali e negozi di Cancelleria, F. 2301, n. 49, 4 May 1739.

so she wrote to the magistrate, she refused to agree to the marriage contract unless a precise condition was spelled out: that she keep custody of both her daughters and their goods.[12]

The new husband, Giuseppe Cerboni, a widower from a nearby village, accepted these conditions and the magistrate judged that the mother could be entrusted as long as eight-year-old Agata entered the local convent of S. Benedetto within a couple of months. The magistrate's decision was the standard line of action in matters of education for the daughters of remarried widows and was probably aimed at avoiding a situation in which an adult male and a young girl verging on adolescence, bound by no blood ties, shared the same household. But the mother refused to separate from her daughter and kept putting off Agata's departure from the family home. Two more years went by and Agata, now eleven, finally entered the convent. Parting was traumatic and the girl fell ill. After a few months her stepfather took her home, where, at the age of twelve, after a painfully long series of discomforts, she died.

On 15 February 1737, ten days before her death, however, a notary and seven witnesses had come to the family home, where Agata dictated her will:

> For the loving and faithful care she received from her mother, she left her the usufruct of her patrimony [i.e. half of her father's patrimony] and should her mother die, she named her universal heir Benedetta Landa her sister. Should her sister die childless before her mother, in that case, she wanted and named her mother only heir to the whole patrimony . . . Should anyone contest the will, she wants it to weigh as a *donatio causa mortis* [a gift made in expectation of death which took effect only if and when the death occurred].[13]

The capacity of a ward to make a will was a highly debatable question, as some jurists claimed that not age but being free from *patria potestas* was the decisive factor in allowing a minor to leave his or her own property *causa mortis.*[14] A child of a madman or of a father who decided to enter the religious profession was in much the same position as a ward and could therefore make a will. In Agata's case, however, the notary had explicitly stated at the end of the document that it was to be considered a simple donation *causa mortis,* and therefore a less compelling deed which could easily be repealed if the girl survived. But, once more, family strategies came

12. Ibid. 13. ASF, Notarile moderno, prot. 21156, n. 16, 15 February 1737.

14. M. Savelli, *Pratica universale* (Florence, 1696); B. Micalori, *Tractatus de fratribus* (Urbino, 1675).

up against public norms, as the local village statutes denied all women and men under 25 the right to make any contract without the formal consent of four relatives on the father's side.[15] Apart from these legal contrasts, what most interests us here is the anomalous construction of a chain of female heirs (the two sisters and the mother) that excluded patrilinear kin such as the two paternal uncles from the Landucci family and their offspring. When no direct male heirs existed, local statutes diverted property into the hands of male cognates and most female wills followed along the same lines, by giving hereditary priority to male kin over daughters and sisters. But here, on the contrary, at the end of the chain stood the slightly disquieting figure of Maddalena, the widow, the ambivalent mother: did she manipulate her dying daughter's will, or simply act out of love?

The question indeed seemed a relevant one for the magistrate, who, in a detailed memo to the Grand Duke, highlighted the widow's ambiguous behaviour: she had never informed the officials about her first child's illness, nor that Agata had left the monastery.[16] Agata had died in her mother's home, where she had also made her will, leaving all her property to Maddalena, should her younger sister Benedetta die childless. The magistrate wrote to the Grand Duke that this scenario – leaving a ward under the custody of a blood relative who is to succeed to his or her legacy – was precisely what the law prohibited, even to the point of contesting a dead father's will should his will allow it to happen. Moreover, the second daughter, then eight, was a weak, sickly child, covered with rashes and suffering from a hernia. In no way would the magistrate allow her to reside in her mother's home, fearing a repetition of what had already happened, and the passing of the whole Landucci patrimony – four farms, plus various fields and woods, hundreds of head of cattle and money – into the widow's hands.[17]

The officials therefore ordered that Maria Maddalena and her daughter be summoned to Florence for investigation: the child could be put in a Florentine monastery and receive medical care in the city.[18] A legal battle began: a health certificate signed by a doctor

15. ASF, Statuti delle comunità soggette, F. 509, Statuti di Monterchi e Mont'Aubello, rubr. 10, ff. 22^{v}–23.

16. ASF, MPAP, F. 2301, n. 49; the Landucci brothers had appealed to the Magistrate for guardianship and custody of their niece: ASF, MPAP, Atti e sentenze, F. 1227, f. 542, 30 December 1738.

17. A complete inventory of Landucci's patrimony is in ASF, MPAP, Filze d'inventari, 2692, n. 16, 21 December 1730.

18. ASF, MPAP, Lettere, F. 2487, 4 March 1739.

appointed by the court supported Maria Maddalena's claim of being the only one capable of treating her daughter's hernia. In spite of a strong disagreement within the officials' board, Benedetta was sent back to her mother's home. But more disquieting news was to reach Florence. Maddalena's second husband, the well-to-do widower Giuseppe Cerboni, had an eighteen-year-old son 'who spends most of the year in his father's home with our ward . . . We deemed it appropriate not to keep the said ward exposed to the frequent allurements of a young man who wishes to make her his bride, thus gaining her rich patrimony.' Planning a ward's marriage without the magistrate's consent was a crime for which the fine was 1000 *scudi*. This was to be Maddalena's last transgression in her relentless conflict with the magistrate's capacity to control what she obviously considered her private sphere of action.

Benedetta was entrusted to the *commissario* (the diplomatic representative of the Florentine government) in Arezzo and, with the assistance of a woman and armed guards should the family oppose the magistrate's decision, put in the monastery of the Trinità in Arezzo.[19] In contrast to general practice, no relatives of either her father or her mother's kin lived in the convent and the eight-year-old child must have experienced a bitter feeling of loss and loneliness. Separated from her daughter, Maddalena renounced custody and officially requested that the patrimony be divided between them.[20] Under the supervision of an appointed arbitrator, mother and daughter were allotted 3000 *scudi* each, half under the administration of a curator appointed by the court, half given in usufruct to the widow. Thus, as the magistrate's decree explicitly stated, the eldest daughter's last will was respected: 'Signora Maria Maddalena Mauri widow of Lando Landucci and now wife of Giuseppe Cerboni shall receive the above mentioned goods as usufructuary heir of Agata Landucci, her now deceased daughter, as mentioned in her will drawn up by Giovanni Franceschi on 15 February 1737.'[21]

In the magistrate's papers this is where the story ends. But looking through the village of Monterchi's notarial archives two more documents give us some final clues. On 15 June 1742 Maddalena signed her will, naming Benedetta her universal heir, on condition that she either married or entered the religious profession. In the mean time the whole legacy would be administered by the rector of

19. ASF, MPAP, Lettere, F. 2489, 11 December 1739; Libro di partiti, F. 135, f. 89, 13 March 1740.
20. ASF, MPAP, Atti e sentenze, F. 1229, f. 1497, 7 August 1739.
21. Ibid. F. 1237, f. 1820, 11 August 1741.

a nearby church, with a yearly salary of three *scudi*. Should Benedetta die childless, her mother's jewellery, clothes and furniture would return to Maddalena's two brothers. A series of bequests to the widow's sisters, husband, mother, and workers as well as bread for the poor and 150 *scudi* for masses and candles would have to be paid from her income. Parting from tradition, she wanted her body to be buried not in her husband's but in her own family's grave.[22]

Five years later, in 1747, Maddalena dictated a second will. The family picture was now completely different. Still in good health and married to her second husband, Maddalena had lost her daughter Benedetta, who had presumably died in the monastery, and so Maddalena named her two brothers universal heirs of her patrimony on an equal standing. The amount of cash she now distributed among a numerous crowd of relatives and poor clients had increased fivefold to over 2000 *scudi*. She doubled the number of masses for herself and left over 400 *scudi* in charity for a number of poor girls. All the rest was passed down to her own family except two comparatively small fields, valued at 150 *scudi*, that she left to her brother-in-law Landucci and his sons.[23] Thus the Landucci had lost the main part of their brother's wealth, owing to the female line of inheritance that Maria Maddalena had skilfully constructed.

Let me now try to draw some final remarks. The first story, Settimia's one, dating back to 1589, was staged around two male protagonists and a seemingly passive widow, whose life was in the hands of her father and brother-in-law. In the late sixteenth century a husband's will could largely determine a widow's future existence, turning her into a legitimate guardian of her children or excluding her altogether from the family household and administration.[24] Gradually, during the 150 years separating Settimia's experience from Maria Maddalena's, widows were systematically entrusted with guardianship even if their husbands had died intestate. Widowhood and guardianship meant accepting institutional control of the private sphere, at a time when public regulation of family conflicts tended to prevail over private arrangements. The responsibility, experience and mutual trust which resulted from widows' guardianship gradually turned what was simply a 'negative right' to be protected against lineages and a pervasive patrilinear culture, into a

22. ASF, Notarile moderno, prot. 2 4870, n. 53, ff. 65^{v}–67^{v}, 15 June 1742.

23. Ibid. n. 79, ff. 104–106^{v}, 22 December 1747.

24. Giulia Calvi, 'Maddalena Nerli and Cosimo Tornabuoni: a couple's narrative of family history in early modern Florence', *Renaissance Quarterly* 45 (1992), pp. 312–39.

positive entitlement to control and negotiate family affairs. The second story shows how widows aimed at discussing the conditions of a remarriage, such as custody of the widow's offspring by the new couple, and then bargained over issues concerning education and health. An impressive capacity to use legal apparatus, rules and regulations led to the final point of this scheme aimed at outlining a formal female hereditary strategy, which linked mother and daughters to one another and in substitution to each other. Doing so placed Maria Maddalena in the suspect position of a male agnate: she indeed had a 'hope of inheriting' the family patrimony after her daughters' death and therefore lost the administration of their goods as well as custody. Thus, as it were, a widow could use the law across gender lines, formally acquiring a juridically male identity.

Between the sixteenth and the eighteenth centuries a significant change in the pattern of family disputes vis-à-vis state intervention seems to have taken place. From the late Middle Ages a viable form of state protection of widows and wards functioned, owing to the imposition of a public system of norms onto the private sphere. Face-to-face violence was suppressed by the systematic intervention of officials in what were perceived as family matters. The widely applied experience of guardianship produced an interiorization of control and a change in the self-perception and social behaviour of widows (in brief, the shift from Settimia's model to Maria Maddalena's). My working hypothesis is that, in the eighteenth century, conflict seems to move back gradually in the direction of a strong private realm under a widow's control. The family attempted to negotiate a wide range of issues and aimed to curb institutional intervention in family affairs. In the second story wills were systematically introduced to redefine the boundaries of the magistrate's intervention along the lines of a well-planned private strategy. From this viewpoint, private and public were not fixed unchanging categories tied by a sort of teleological process such as moving from private to public. Rather public and private were moving points that helped to construct and define the equally mobile and historically changing identity of widows, their families, and the wider social space with which they interacted.

CHAPTER FOURTEEN

Survival strategies and stories: poor widows and widowers in early industrial England[1]

PAMELA SHARPE

In April 1997, a young Bristol widower, Kevin Willis, started a case likely to be heard five years hence, at the European Court of Human Rights in Strasbourg. When his wife, the main income-earner in the family, died of cancer in 1996, Willis found himself ineligible for Widow's Benefit or, indeed, for any other of the social welfare benefits for which widows qualify. Willis's lawyer, employed by the Child Poverty Action Group, argued that Britain lagged behind the rest of Europe and that Willis's exclusion from anything but supplementary benefit was now an anachronism – a hangover from the time when husbands were the main breadwinners in families.[2] The first half of this chapter aims to dig a little deeper on this point by examining the history of the basis of English widows' and widowers' claims to poor relief. However brief, it will offer some suggestions regarding the factors underlying the gendering of social welfare to both single parents and the aged widowed. The second half focuses on survival strategies: how personal narratives of poverty and self-help are used by widows to strengthen their claims to poor relief in the difficult circumstances of early industrialization.

Gender, widowhood and social welfare

The prospect of changed economic circumstances at widowhood lurked within the psyche of both ordinary men and women to a far

1. I am grateful to the University of Bristol Faculty of Arts Research Fund for financial assistance with research at Derbyshire Record Office.

2. BBC Radio 4 'Today' programme, 24 April 1997. In the event, the government pre-empted the European court by extending Widow's Benefit to men in November 1998.

greater degree than is now imaginable. For women of middling status, whose husbands had sunk to poor financial circumstances at the time of their death, widowhood could bring their first real experience of poverty. As one middling-order woman from Suffolk commented on the death of her farmer husband in 1807, 'Death makes strange alterations in families'.[3] She was forced to open a school, and when this failed, become a domestic servant. Many widows had no property to speak of, and no business to go into on the death of their husband. Widows of landless labourers were almost certainly set to struggle without the wage of their husband. On the other hand, the situation of a parsimonious wife might rise on widowhood if she became free of an improvident man. She became able to take full control of the family purse, in terms of children's earnings or management of monies from charity, as a result of becoming entitled to relief in her own right.[4] In a fine article, Isabelle Chabot writes of the strong 'moral' element in widows' poverty. As she argues, the poverty of the widow was so much less questionable than that of the working man.[5] Historically, the poor widow was society's archetypal needy person, the embodiment of the 'deserving poor'.

As noted earlier in this volume, since marital status was not commonly denoted for men, poor widowers are much more difficult to detect in historical documents. But depending on age and ability to work, and bearing in mind the higher earning power of men, the material level of the family of a man whose wife had died would also decline for several reasons. Historical evidence suggests that practical housekeeping abilities and social knowledge were mainly the sphere of women. Testimonies from the poor make evident the vital role of the wife as a manager and this is most apparent in oral history research on a later time period.[6] Widowers lost both their wife's earnings and their domestic capabilities. Although elderly widowers could be beneficiaries of charity disbursements and some

3. Pamela Sharpe, *Adapting to Capitalism: Working Women in the English Economy* (London, 1996), p. 137.

4. Barbara J. Todd, 'Demographic determinism and female agency: the remarrying widow reconsidered . . . again', *Continuity and Change* 9 (1994), p. 422, makes the point that marriage to a poor man cannot necessarily be seen as advantageous to a poor woman.

5. Isabelle Chabot, 'Widowhood and poverty in late medieval Florence', *Continuity and Change* 3 (1988), pp. 291–311.

6. See for example Carl Chinn, *'They Worked all their Lives': Women of the Urban Poor in England 1880–1939* (Manchester, 1988); Ellen Ross, *Love and Toil: Motherhood in Outcast London 1870–1918* (Oxford, 1993); Elizabeth Roberts, *A Woman's Place: An Oral History of Working-Class Women 1890–1940* (Oxford, 1984), pp. 125–68.

lived in almshouses, there was no privileged status for the widower who was of an age to labour.[7] As is evident from case studies of early-nineteenth-century Essex families such as the Halls and the Thurtles, for whom there are substantial collections of poor law evidence, the heart of the family disappeared on the death of a wife. In these two particular cases, after the death of Elizabeth Hall in 1820 and Elizabeth Thurtle in 1832, family budget management went awry and negotiations with poor relief officials became more urgent, less effective and with a greater tendency to be undertaken in an antagonistic way. It is apparent in poor law evidence that labouring men needed a woman to 'do for' them, and although poor relief officials would sometimes provide paid help for domestic duties to widowers, this was often a poor substitute for a wife.

Widowers looking for housekeepers would first resort to daughters, who often became, as a result, 'miniature wives'. This was well described in the legal case of 1821 ensuing from the disputed settlement of Ann Lowe, a 23-year-old single woman from East Derbyshire. Ann, or 'Nanny', became a 'miniature wife' to the extent that she took on her mother's clothes. In 1812, at the age of fourteen, Ann had been hired by her father as a servant to a farmer. When her mother died in 1813, her father asked Ann to go to him to keep house but her employers refused to set her at liberty. However, at the end of the hiring her father said, 'Nanny, I want you to come home and your Sister Hannah to go out.' At this point, Ann took on the management of a cow, and her seven younger siblings. The youngest child had been a week old at their mother's death. She said that 'during that time she was doing all the work in the house and taking care of the pauper children, except a day or two in Harvest, when she was shearing corn with her Father, and during the same period her Father gave her part of her Mother's Cloaths and a pair of New shoes and a new Apron or two'. She needed more clothes but her father gave her sister the remainder of her mother's clothes. She or her sister had to stay at home until the point when their father's banns were published for his second marriage, and the reason for this was made explicit in the case: 'That Witness was so situated that he could not do without a female in his house to do the work and look after the younger Children.'[8]

7. On institutional care of the widower in early modern England, see Margaret Pelling's chapter in this volume.

8. Derbyshire Record Office (hereafter DRO) D1642A/PO275, *Calow* v. *Staveley* 1821.

Reasons such as the relatively privileged status (in terms of societal provision) of the poor widow and the labour market participation and domestic incompetence of many widowers combine with greater female longevity to explain the sex difference in the median interval to remarriage identified by demographic historians. Wrigley and Schofield found, over the period 1600–1799, a median interval to male remarriage of 12.6 months compared to the female interval of 19.4 months for the seventeenth and eighteenth centuries. Men remarried more often and more rapidly.[9] The finding that fewer widows remarried is remarked on in case studies from across north-west Europe.[10] Nevertheless, falling mortality meant that all remarriage was declining over time. In sixteenth-century England some 30 per cent of all those who married were contracting a remarriage, but by the nineteenth century it was only 11 per cent.[11]

In simple human terms, although the departure of a difficult spouse could have been a blessing in disguise, the grief and loneliness of the widowed were pitiable. On the face of it, a mental picture of the early modern widow might bring to mind the black-clad figures of Catholic Southern Europe. However, widow's weeds did not announce the social identity of the poor English widow, for in reality poor women in eighteenth-century England could probably afford little more than a black ribbon or another mourning trimming.[12] However, the act of mourning symbolized transition, and

9. R.S. Schofield and E.A. Wrigley, 'Remarriage intervals and the effect of marriage order on fertility', in J. Dupâquier *et al.*, eds, *Marriage and Remarriage in Past Populations* (London, 1981), pp. 211–27. The interval was shorter in urban areas: for example Vivien Brodsky, 'Widows in late Elizabethan London: remarriage, economic opportunity and family orientations', in L. Bonfield, R.M. Smith and K. Wrightson, eds, *The World We Have Gained* (Oxford, 1986), pp. 122–54, found that in sixteenth-century London there was only a nine-month average interval to remarriage for widows.

10. Susan Wright, '"Holding up half the sky": women and their occupations in eighteenth century Ludlow', *Midland History* 14 (1989), pp. 53–74; Ida Blom, 'The history of widowhood: a bibliographic overview', *Journal of Family History* 16 (1991), pp. 191–210; Gisli Agust Gunnlaugsson and Loftur Guttormsson, 'Transitions into old age: poverty and retirement possibilities in late eighteenth- and nineteenth-century Iceland', in John Henderson and Richard Wall, eds, *Poor Women and Children in the European Past* (London, 1994), pp. 251–68.

11. E.A. Wrigley and R.S. Schofield, *The Population History of England 1541–1871* (Cambridge, 1981), pp. 258–9. On the secular decline in remarriage for widows in a sample of fourteen villages see John Knodel and Katherine A. Lynch, 'The decline of remarriage: evidence from German village population in the eighteenth and nineteenth centuries', *Journal of Family History* 10 (1985), pp. 34–59.

12. Although evidence is accumulating of a consumer revolution extending far down the social scale, there is no evidence of the ownership of mourning clothes among the working class: personal communication with John Styles. See also Phillis Cunnington and Catherine Lucas, *Costume for Births, Marriages and Deaths* (London, 1972).

even if this assumed more significance in peasant communities in terms of the passage of land, it was not without residual value to the landless in the early industrial period. Within local communities, widowhood *per se* conferred a new local identity for the widow, because she became 'Widow Smith', or whoever, in the lists of poor relief or charity recipients.

In early modern England, to be poor, widows were by definition dependants, without substantial kin or connection. But while poverty might construe the widow as a societal subordinate, within the family she was now responsible to and for herself, and therefore had at least some perceived independence. The ambiguities inherent in the independence of widows are apposite to understanding poor relief, because poor relief was not simply economic support. It both underpinned, and was shaped by, social and cultural conditions.

The provision of relief to the settled poor made possible the independent living circumstances of widows. Richard Smith has recently argued that poor relief provision was preferentially given to elderly women in the late seventeenth century.[13] Early modern English widows were often paid twice as much as married couples, and those who had been better-off before the death of their husbands were given higher levels of relief.[14] Historians in fact suggest that the parish poor relief system was at its most generous in the late seventeenth century.[15] Widows were more likely to remain widows, rather than remarry, because they received a measure of community financial support. The work of J.E. Smith has provided a good overview from both a demographic and a welfare point of view. He compared parish listings from Lichfield (1695), Cardington (1782), Ardleigh (1796), and Corfe Castle (1790).[16] In these listings about a fifth of all households were in receipt of parish relief but twice that proportion of widows were 'on the parish'. The proportion of widow-headed households receiving relief varied far less between

13. Richard Smith, 'Charity, self-interest and welfare: reflections from demographic and family history', in Martin Daunton, ed., *Charity, Self-Interest and Welfare in the English Past* (London, 1996), pp. 23–50.

14. Paul Slack, *Poverty and Policy in Tudor and Stuart England* (London, 1988), p. 179.

15. See for example W. Newman Brown, 'The receipt of poor relief and family situation, Aldenham, Hertfordshire 1630–90', pp. 405–20; T. Wales, 'Poverty, poor relief and the life cycle: some evidence from seventeenth-century Norfolk', in R.M. Smith, ed., *Land, Kinship and Life-Cycle* (Cambridge, 1984), pp. 351–404; and Mary Barker-Reed, 'The treatment of the aged poor in five selected West Kent parishes from Settlement to Speenhamland' (Open University PhD thesis, 1988).

16. J.E. Smith, 'Widowhood and ageing in traditional English society', *Ageing and Society* 4 (1984), pp. 429–49.

communities than did the proportions of all households receiving relief. In other words, the condition of widowhood in itself largely qualified these women for relief. A quarter of all recipients of parish relief in the four communities were widows. Todd has described the good provision made for poor widows in almshouses in her study of Abingdon in Oxfordshire.[17] In the town of Colyton in the seventeenth and early eighteenth centuries, widows lived in small independent dwellings. They had access to a double form of relief as the feoffees in Colyton paid poor people's rents on a regular basis and provided quarterly doles. They were relieved by up to 50 per cent more than the actual rental they paid in some cases. Once on the list of 'Widdows Rents' women were paid until death regardless of whether there was any change in their circumstances. Falling prices created a 'welfare state' situation for those with a claim to relief in Colyton such that single households could easily be maintained.[18]

Why were widows so generously supported? Pelling and Smith emphasize the 'nuclear family hardship thesis', stressing that in pre-industrial England, where fertility was lower and mortality higher than in present-day Bangladesh and India, conditions were such that a third of women on reaching 65 would have no surviving children who could look after them, hence the demographic rationale for community support.[19] Much of the research from a 'history of family' point of view has concentrated on residential arrangements. Laslett found that in his sample of a hundred English communities over the time period 1574 to 1821 there were nearly three times as many household heads who were widows as widowers. Widows headed 12.9 per cent of households.[20] Female-headed households seem to have increased in the second half of the seventeenth century.[21] Recently, however, the stress has moved away from the

17. Barbara J. Todd, 'The remarrying widow: a stereotype reconsidered', in Mary Prior, ed., *Women in English Society 1500–1800* (London, 1985), pp. 54–92.

18. Pamela Sharpe, 'Literally spinsters: a new interpretation of local economy and demography in Colyton in the seventeenth and early eighteenth centuries', *Economic History Review* 44 (1991), pp. 46–65. We should note, however, that evidence for this section is disproportionately drawn from the south of England. Steve King has recently argued that relief was less generous in the north in 'Reconstructing lives: the poor, the Poor Law and welfare in Calverley, 1650–1820', *Social History* 22 (1997), pp. 318–38.

19. M. Pelling and R.M. Smith, eds, *Life, Death and the Elderly: Historical Perspectives* (London, 1991), p. 15.

20. P. Laslett, 'Mean household size in England since the sixteenth century', in P. Laslett and R. Wall, *Household and Family in Past Time* (Cambridge, 1972), p. 147.

21. Richard Wall, 'Woman alone in English society', *Annales de Démographie Historique* (1981), pp. 303–20.

independent living arrangements of widows to emphasize more varied and flexible residence in some communities.[22]

If the underlying principle of relief was to support widows' self-reliance, one of the main ways in which this was done was by giving them assistance to find work. In Christian Europe, it was godly that widows should work if work was available. In the Bible, in Kings 17:1, a widow woman serves food and gathers sticks. Parish officials found all kinds of work for poor widows, even if this was the ubiquitous spinning or perhaps lace-making or straw-plaiting.[23] Common rights might be under threat in eighteenth-century communities, but the privileged few who were still given access to exploit them were often widows. Poor widows were less likely to be denied customary rights to pasturage.[24] In 1795 gleaning in Terling in Essex was expressly forbidden to villagers except for widows and children under fourteen.[25] Poor relief officials often arranged for widows to have a role in serving the local community by carrying out jobs such as midwifery, nursing, or waking (watching beside) the dead.[26] Sometimes informal relief for widows was part of work agreements. In Essex, widows who worked as casual farm labourers on the Petre estate in the 1570s were paid higher rates than women with husbands.[27]

If self-reliancy is a cornerstone of social welfare, it reflects both the availability of local resources and the way in which they are distributed, and the cultural inheritance of local communities. Betty Potash's collected essays on widows in contemporary Africa show

22. See D.I. Kertzner and N. Karweit, 'The impact of widowhood in nineteenth-century Italy', in David I. Kertzner and Peter Laslett, eds, *Aging in the Past: Demography, Society and Old Age* (Berkeley, Calif., 1995), p. 238; T. Sokoll, *Household and Family among the Poor: the Case of Two Essex Communities in the Late Eighteenth and Early Nineteenth Centuries* (Bochum, 1993); T. Sokoll, 'The household position of elderly widows in poverty: evidence from two English communities in the late eighteenth and early nineteenth centuries', in Henderson and Wall, *Poor Women and Children*, pp. 207–24.

23. For one example, see Margaret Pelling, 'Old age, poverty and disability in early modern Norwich: work, remarriage and other expedients', in Pelling and Smith, *Life, Death and the Elderly*, pp. 82–4.

24. Jane Humphries, 'Enclosures, common rights, and women: the proletarianization of families in the late eighteenth and early nineteenth centuries', *Journal of Economic History* 50 (1990), pp. 17–42.

25. Essex Record Office (hereafter ERO) D/P 299/8/2, Terling Vestry Meeting Orders.

26. Evidence of this can be found in most parish poor records. See for example Sharpe, 'Literally spinsters' and doctoral research in progress at the Cambridge Group by Samantha Williams, 'Poor relief, welfare and medical provision in Bedfordshire: the social and economic context *c.* 1750–1850'.

27. Sharpe, *Adapting*, p. 79.

that there is generally no communal support there for widows but that many are self-supporting – living alone and heading their own households – and they usually work. They may be helped by gifts from children but these are not vital to support.[28] Support for widows' self-reliancy (which, in unrecorded ways, may have been far more significant than is indicated by the bald payments listed in overseers' account books) reflects the fact that in early modern England, but also in other Christian societies, the treatment of the poor fulfils a godly purpose. Within Christianity poverty is a spiritual asset and the widowed poor are the marginal people who naturally seek refuge in the Lord. Moreover, the welfare of widows, orphans and aliens is the measure by which Yahweh determines the moral fibre of his people. The Bible exhorts the widow's protection and support against oppression, and provides a blueprint of how this should be done. Acts 6:1 outlines a method of organizing a food distribution programme: an official list of widows was to be drawn up with eligibility requirements including age and standards of religious and moral behaviour. Twelve disciples were to appoint a sub-committee of seven men of good reputation to distribute food to widows. 1 Timothy 5 includes a long passage on widows, the tenor of which is 'Be considerate to widows'. Widows should be over 60 and only have had one husband. The passage stresses the duties of relatives to support widows but adds that the church should support those with no relatives. Biblical characters such as Judith (the ideal widow) and the parable of the widow's mite (the giving widow) prescribe the widow's own roles and responsibilities.[29] Notably, biblical widows are wise – there are no fools among their numbers.

Christian theology, then, provides the tenets and organizational structure for the support of widows. But widowers are nowhere in this story. No strictures determine their social welfare and no major male biblical characters tarry long before remarriage. We are offered no models for societal caring for poor widowers. To what extent are these ideas distinctive to Christian culture? There is a lack of historical anthropological research on widows and widowers, which, in itself, suggests that widowhood is a less evident category in other cultures. In Hinduism, widows were considered bad luck, subject to sati and to be kept away from family ritual. In many areas, widows were not allowed to remarry because they belonged to their late husband's household and their behaviour would affect

28. Betty Potash, ed., *Widows in African Societies* (Stanford, Calif., 1986), p. 4.
29. Mark 12:40–4.

the spiritual welfare of the dead husband.[30] Historically, the Chinese also viewed the remarriage of widows as a disgrace. Loyalty to their first husbands was so strong that many widows hanged themselves. Susan Mann argues, by looking at Chinese local histories over the period 1600–1900, that widow chastity was implicit in a hierarchy dependent on loyalty, fidelity and absolute commitment. The Chinese developed honours for chaste widows and even special halls for virtuous widows.[31]

While the economic self-reliance of widows might be upheld in the English case, there are other senses in which widows' independence was a matter of contemporary concern. The unbridled sexuality of widows was seen as dangerous.[32] Their freedom from household restraint meant they were liable to be accused of witchcraft.[33] Poor relief operated as social control and to reinforce patriarchy. Although statutory, the generosity by which it was given obviously varied between individuals, and it could be allocated in a way which upheld moral standards. This is difficult to detect in overseers' records, which tell us only who were the recipients of relief, but further scrutiny of vestry minutes might provide more evidence on this point. In Terling's vestry meeting orders for the late eighteenth century it is evident that the poor were regularly scrutinized to make sure that they were industrious. Middle-order citizens were appointed to monitor the poor and the publican was issued with a list of the official poor so he could check that they did not tipple.[34] In urban areas it was also the case that widows like Sarah Cooke, who was taken to court in Colchester in 1767 for harbouring poor

30. Antony Copley, 'The debate on widow remarriage and polygamy: aspects of moral change in nineteenth-century Bengal and Yorubaland', *Journal of Imperial and Commonwealth History* 7 (1979), pp. 128–48. Anand A. Yang, 'Whose sati? Widow burning in early 19th century India', *Journal of Women's History* 1 (1989), pp. 8–33; D.F.S. Fernando, 'Marriage and remarriage in some Asian civilizations', in Dupâquier *et al.*, *Marriage*, pp. 89–93.

31. Susan Mann, 'Widows in the kinship, class and community structures of Quing Dynasty China', *Journal of Asian Studies* 46 (1987), pp. 37–56; A.P. Wolf, 'Women, widowhood and fertility in pre-modern China', in Dupâquier *et al.*, *Marriage*, pp. 130–47.

32. See for example Lyndal Roper, *The Holy Household: Women and Morals in Reformation Augsburg* (Oxford, 1988), pp. 53–54 and other chapters in this volume.

33. There is now a huge literature on witchcraft. On this point see for example Alan Macfarlane, *Witchcraft in Tudor and Stuart England: A Regional and Comparative Study* (London, 1970); J.A. Sharpe, 'Witchcraft and women in seventeenth-century England: some northern evidence', *Continuity and Change* 6 (1991), pp. 179–99; Lyndal Roper, 'Witchcraft and fantasy in early modern Germany', *History Workshop Journal* 32 (1991), pp. 19–43, reprinted in her *Oedipus and the Devil: Witchcraft, Sexuality and Religion in Early Modern Europe* (London, 1994).

34. ERO D/P 299/8/2.

people (probably migrant lodgers) in her house and bringing a charge on the parish, were likely to be punished.[35]

Widows were viewed very differently from spinsters. Spinsters were also free of direct patriarchal control but the assumption was that they had chosen their state. Widowhood was involuntary. Although there has been little specific research on widows and ideas of honour in this period, we can suggest that the condition of widowhood meant widows were generally held in high esteem, but their unrestrained status meant they were always liable to transgress.[36] The fact that widows had slipped away from patriarchy underlines the gendering of poor relief: social welfare provision can be viewed as a way not only to protect but also to control.

This section has argued that the preferential allocation of relief to widows lies deep in Christian culture, and considerably pre-dates nineteenth-century ideas of the importance of the loss of the breadwinner. Economic support was one reason why widows were a privileged category of the poor, but the need to control masterless women also influenced those who supplied relief. Whereas women are usually invisible in the historical record, poor widowers do not really exist as a historical category. As Kevin Willis has discovered to his cost, there are no historical precedents for widowers' welfare. However, the next section will suggest that during industrialization it did become necessary for widows to strengthen their historic claim to relief.

Constructing stories and strategies

In March 1774 the newly-widowed Dorothy Robinson wrote to the poor law officials at Bakewell in Derbyshire:

> To the overseers of Bakewell aquentin you of my misforten I have lost a Loveing hosband and am beset with another my son Abrahams master Brought him to hies [here?] againe and says he will have nothing to do with him anymore Dere Dere Gentlemen Conseder my Grief and be plesd to help me with what you plese I am Lame and Cannot go about but I can do aleltes [all else]. mester motram is good frend but hes gone jorny.[37]

35. ERO Colchester Borough Draft Minutes of Session 1 July 1767.

36. While not specifically concerned with widows, see the essays on honour and reputation in early modern England in *Transactions of the Royal Historical Society*, 6th ser., 6 (1996).

37. DRO 2057A/PO2/13, 13 March 1774.

Widow Robinson had been disappointed by the men in her life: her departed loving husband, her errant son (or perhaps it was his master who was at fault?), and another, a Mr Motram, who provided support, or even patronage, but had chosen this unfortunate time to go on his travels. Dorothy's immediate need was for sustenance – this was certainly to be financial – she wanted poor relief, but she also expected sympathy. Moreover, writing immediately after the death of her spouse, negotiations perhaps had to be made to organize a pauper funeral.

How did the poor use words as survival strategies? If we are to read these letters from poor people to the poor law officials in the same way that Natalie Zemon Davis reads pardon tales it is evident that they are constructing their stories, emphasizing their poverty to make the strongest case they can for regular relief.[38] But while they offer, to varying degrees, a surface veneer of compliancy, and sometimes a creeping obeisance, it also appears that these testimonies are overt and effective statements of resistance, written from within the 'culture of poverty', inherent in early capitalism. In other words, these petitions, while perhaps appearing in the context of the archives to be little more than miserable fragments of cheap paper, constitute a rhetorical strategy for survival: one of the 'weapons of the weak' of the English poor in early industrialization.[39] These narratives of the experience of poverty change over time in subtle ways which mirror a divergence in the perception of the poor law, between givers and recipients, as we move into the nineteenth century. For by reading the letters as strategic scripts, we gain some appreciation of, at least, contemporary perceptions of rights, obligations and duties.

Anthropologists have given historians a rich endowment in terms of our understanding of adaptive strategies.[40] It has been correctly observed that, when applied to the poor, 'strategy' has inappropriate military associations. But, as David Morgan comments, 'The attractiveness of the use of strategies is that it provides a sense of

38. Natalie Zemon Davis, *Fiction in the Archives: Pardon Tales and their Tellers in Sixteenth-Century France* (Oxford, 1987). On other types of letter from the impoverished see D.T. Andrew, '*Noblesse oblige*: female charity in an age of sentiment', in J. Brewer and S. Staves, eds, *Early Modern Conceptions of Property* (London, 1996).

39. James C. Scott, *'Weapons of the Weak': Everyday Forms of Peasant Resistance* (Yale, 1985).

40. See G. Crow, 'The use of the concept of "strategy" in recent sociological literature', *Sociology* 23 (1989), pp. 1–24; Carol B. Stack, *All Our Kin: Strategies for Survival in a Black Community* (New York, 1970). For perceptive comments on the poor and strategies, see David Vincent, *Poor Citizens: The State and the Poor in Twentieth-Century Britain* (London, 1991), pp. 3–4.

agency while retaining a sense of the significance of power and of structural constraints.'[41] Focusing on widows gives us not only a small sample to work with, to extract from the many surviving pauper letters that are now known to exist for the early industrial period, but a case study to analyse the poor law in terms of the group who were least likely to have to employ strategic behaviour, since widowhood is a human condition and widows were the epitome of the deserving poor.

Turning to pauper letters, important pioneering work on collections of letters has now been carried out by Tom Sokoll and James Stephen Taylor.[42] To put the letters into context we must realize that by the late eighteenth century, due to expanding industrialization and urbanization, migration was becoming more common, and desperate poverty (particularly on a seasonal basis) a more typical experience. Many parishes operated systems of non-resident relief. They would support parish poor living elsewhere, usually in urban and manufacturing areas, through times of slack work, in the hope that they would be able to support themselves when work became available, and perhaps eventually qualify for a settlement in their new parish. Towns like Widow Robinson's native Bakewell would have a large number of non-resident paupers because, while it was a thriving agricultural centre and market town in the late eighteenth century, it had little industry. Yet it was surrounded at several miles remove by a circle of manufacturing areas such as the sprawling hosiery villages of Nottinghamshire, the cutlery capital of Sheffield, and the textile mills of Manchester and points north-west, as well as the Potteries to the south-west. If poor migrants were either sent or returned of their own volition to their place of settlement, they might become permanent poor, and overseers were certainly worried by this prospect. As a result, threats like that issued by widows like Sarah Thornhill were effective. Sarah possibly had a Sheffield overseer writing back to Bakewell on her behalf in October 1773. Whoever wrote it, the letter was blatant: if the overseers did not provide relief, and soon, she and her family would be on their way back to Bakewell with a removal order in the carrier's cart:

41. See reply to Crow by David H.J. Morgan, 'Strategies and sociologists: a comment on Crow', *Sociology* 23 (1989), pp. 25–9.

42. J.S. Taylor, 'A different kind of Speenhamland: nonresident relief in the Industrial Revolution', *Journal of British Studies* 30 (1991), pp. 183–208; J.S. Taylor, *Poverty, Migration and Settlement in the Industrial Revolution* (Palo Alto, 1989). Also essays by Sokoll, Sharpe and Taylor in Tim Hitchcock, Peter King and Pamela Sharpe, eds, *Chronicling Poverty: The Voices and Strategies of the English Poor 1640–1840* (London, 1997).

> Sirs James Thornhills widow sends this To Inform you of her severe want and Distress. And as the Overseers of Sheffield inform her that she belongs to bakewell parish She hopes you woud Immediately send her some relief and if you Dont think Proper to send it the Sheffield overseers will send her and her two Children with an Order so Quickly let her know whether you will send her relief or not – Sarah Thornhill
>
> PS the Overseers of Sheff[d] have for some time Relieved her till they Discover'd to where she belongd.[43]

We have only very recently become aware that collections of these letters can be wrested from the miscellany of poor law papers. A town like Bakewell, where local administration was overseen by the major property holder in the parish, the Duke of Rutland, ran a tight ship and, as a result, most of the parish poor law material survives. Even after the passing of the New Poor Law, Sarah Brown, a 64-year-old widow resident in Manchester, used perhaps every rhetorical strategy available to her when writing in 1835. After stressing that her parents were Bakewell natives, she persuaded the officials of her age and ill health: 'delicacy prevented me from making Application to you sooner . . . for the decays of nature has laid hold on me together with old age'. She then issued a threat similar to that made by Sarah Thornhill: 'if it is not in your power to allow me something weekly without removing me I shall be under the necessity of removing to my Parish which will be more disadvantageous to you'. Such a phrase was almost formulaic, or at least was found in the majority of pauper letters. It emphasizes the need for regular relief and the determination to return to the parish if it is not provided. She then asserted her own perception of a customary right, although imputing it to the Bakewell overseers 'Sir considering the matter throughout I think you have a Just right to attend attentively to me.' Finally, she evoked pity and empathy: 'I am Completely in want of [clothing] and now the Winter fast Approaching Consider Old age you are the son of a mother whether she is living or dead prudence forbids me to say any farther.'[44]

43. DRO 2057A/PO2/5, 5 October 1773.

44. DRO D2057A/PO2/219, 15 November 1835. Some paupers used model letters: see J.S. Taylor, 'Voices in the crowd: the Kirkby Lonsdale township letters', in Hitchcock, King and Sharpe, *Chronicling Poverty*, p. 115. A comparable, later case of a widow negotiating charity is that of Delia Kennedy in Michael B. Katz, 'The history of an impudent poor woman in New York City from 1918 to 1923', in P. Mandler, ed., *The Uses of Charity: The Poor on Relief in the Nineteenth-Century Metropolis* (Philadelphia, 1990), pp. 227–46.

It is clear that the poor's knowledge of their legal rights and disabilities was both full and functional.[45] For widows, this is most apparent when we consider the Settlement Law. Whereas we can show the generosity of parishes to their settled poor, outsiders could be harshly expelled. Women took their husband's legal settlement on marriage and every parish for which overseers' records survive shows the removal of widows to their husband's place of settlement. From 1662 to 1795 removal of new widows took place if they were likely to fall on the poor rates, after 1795 if they became actually chargeable. In a mobile society this might mean removal to another part of the country, possibly one that the woman had never previously visited. We can unearth gruesome deathbed interrogations of poor men regarding the settlement of their widows-to-be. An example of this is the case sent to the Inns of Court in 1801 regarding the settlement of Martha Shipman and the oddly named four-year-old John Le Child (perhaps he was an adopted foundling) from Selston in Nottinghamshire to Barlow, Derbyshire. In his final illness and on his deathbed, Martha had had to cross-question her husband, John, about his settlement parish. She tried to piece together the history of his hirings and labour agreements. John Shipman knew the law but could not readily comprehend the possibility of her forced eviction. When she said she was afraid of removal he said, 'remove you, where should they remove you to, you belong where you are'.[46]

While this more punitive side of the poor law was readily apparent, it is nevertheless reasonable to argue that the poor saw their settlement and their claim to funds as a customary right in the eighteenth century. Two cases from the large collection of pauper letters which exist for Essex parishes exemplify this for the mid-eighteenth century. About 1750 Mary Barrett wrote to the overseers of Great Chesterford from Saffron Walden parish about her justifiable case for relief: 'My time I hope will not be long if Please God as I am Eighty next September you may suppose I cannot gett my Bread.' Relief was her due: 'It is but returning ye Money my Husband has Paid if [in] ye Parish & his Family before him for above A centrey I have a friend still a Walden than Acquaint a Gentlemean how ill I am used.' And she threatened to go home: 'if ye Feoffees dont think proper to send next week by Mr Pilgrim I must come Down I have been a Widdow 23 years & have a ginnea & a half'.[47] Mary

45. Hitchcock, King and Sharpe, *Chronicling Poverty*, pp. 10–13.

46. DRO D975A/P0383, 17 November 1801.

47. ERO D/P 10/25/7, *c.* 1750.

Parret's equally colloquial letter to her brother-in-law, sent in March 1748, was probably designed to be a strategic transcript in itself:

> I must be first to com to [Rain] ham parish and with whot things I have got I can Mak Shift Just to Live aand if [Rain] ham parish Will is to be at the Charge Desier them to send a note from thare hands but I shall be glad if you Will Com Down for ther is som things that will be of servis to you in your Way of Business he came hom of the Saturday Night and Died Amonday Noon he Not got a Coffin Nor I have got No Money Soe pray Send me Word by th Barer from you[r] Loving Sister Mary Parret.[48]

Although writing to her husband's brother, Mary always intended, or at least expected, the overseers to see this letter. Not only did they need to take responsibility for the funeral but Mary was now moving to her husband's place of settlement. He seems likely to have been a tramper or a migrant worker and his tools, or perhaps clothes, were to be passed on to his brother-in-law.

Although E.P. Thompson gave poor relief short shrift, by the late eighteenth century we can see the defence of these customary rights to relief within the context of the moral economy.[49] Under conditions of escalating poverty, rapid population rise and more anonymous and cost-conscious vestries who applied the logic of political economy, the migrant poor, in particular, were put into situations where they needed to defend their rights with increasing vigour or sagacity. While the Christian notion of honouring and supporting widows was still adhered to in principle, in practice it was less in evidence. Individuals were overlooked as standard packages for labouring families were applied. In comparison with single women, widows could still expect to be supported, especially if they were military widows. (This is an area still under-researched by historians, but it was a problem brought into sharp relief by the French Wars.) Overall, for women, relief seems to have changed from an inclusive to an exclusive system. Rather than the continuance of the high level of support suggested by Snell and Millar, the evidence is tending towards Jane Humphries's view that female-headed households were poor, and getting poorer, into the early nineteenth century.[50] Young widows were not as well supported as they had been a century earlier. In general poor relief moved away from

48. ERO D/P 202/18/13, 2 March 1748.

49. E.P. Thompson, *Customs in Common* (London, 1991).

50. K.D.M. Snell and J. Millar, 'Lone families and the Welfare State: past and present', *Continuity and Change* 2 (1987), pp. 387–422; Jane Humphries, 'Female-headed households in early industrial Britain: the vanguard of the proletariat?', *Labour History Review* 63 (1998), pp. 31–65.

young women, except in maternity – whether legitimate or illegitimate. This shift was exacerbated by the lack of access to work in rural areas, especially in the south-east of England. Young, poor widows gravitated to urban areas, which offered more employment, especially for children, but then struggled to afford the rent.[51] The greater co-residence of widows with kin in the late eighteenth century, which Tom Sokoll argues for, and the consequent diminishing 'independence' in terms of household arrangements, are perhaps signs that widows' sustenance was becoming more insecure.[52]

While widows could assert a strong *a priori* claim to relief, validated by the Bible and enhanced by traditional social welfare methods in small village communities, towards the late eighteenth century they needed to employ proactive strategies to secure relief, particularly if they had moved to the more precarious world of urban living. Individual paupers might still assert their customary claims but the propertied were more likely to question them.[53] If relief were secured, it was less likely to be forthcoming on a continuous basis, and this is one reason why often not one but a series of pleading letters were sent by paupers to overseers. By reviewing several hundreds of these letters it is possible to suggest strategies by which widows made convincing cases. First, they increasingly adopted the methods of their paymasters and wrote down their claims in ways which left no doubt about their position in the social hierarchy. If unable to write themselves they persuaded or perhaps paid someone to write for them. Secondly, they stressed their moral claim to relief and, perhaps most significantly, they moved from simply 'being' a widow, to 'doing', solidifying their claim by asserting not just need, and traditional right, but also respectability and self-help, for example. By the 1820s, all of these elements seem to have been necessary to construct a plausible narrative.

First, in their self-definition, widows were adopting and appropriating the language of the parish officials: they were invariably

51. See, for example, the cases of widows Elizabeth Ann Manning and Sarah Withnell in Sharpe, *Adapting*, pp. 42, 146.

52. Sokoll, *Household and Family*; Sokoll, 'The household position of elderly widows in poverty'. Michael Anderson, *Family Structure in Nineteenth-Century Lancashire* (Cambridge, 1971), pp. 46–50, found that many more widows than widowers headed their own households and fewer lived in lodgings than took in lodgers in Preston in 1851. See also Marguerite W. Dupree, *Family Structure in the Staffordshire Potteries 1840–1880* (Oxford, 1995), p. 120, who found it was not clear cut from their living arrangements whether the widowed were providing or receiving mutual assistance.

53. Hitchcock, King and Sharpe, *Chronicling Poverty*, pp. 10–13. A sophisticated overview of the interaction between givers and receivers is Marco H.D. van Leeuwen, 'Logic of charity: poor relief in pre-industrial Europe', *Journal of Interdisciplinary History* 24 (1994), pp. 589–613.

'humble', but in describing themselves could also be an 'object of parochial aid', 'an object deserving of relief' and, if aged, 'the ould creature'. Adam Fox sees writing as a source of power, as 'both a symbol and an agent of authority'.[54] By writing about their circumstances rather than visiting parish officials or waiting for someone to report on their state of poverty, paupers saved time but also adopted the methods of an elite culture. Typically their tone struck a balance – submissive and deferential yet firm. Sarah Burley wrote to the Baslow overseers from London in 1830 with such an opening: 'y humbly ask pardon for the liberty y now take in trobling you but y should be obliged to you if you would have the goodness to take my case into your serious consideration'.[55] An expectation of justice was often intermingled with the need to prove a claim to respectability. Biblical phrases were used and inferences made.

Secondly, overall, it was no longer sufficient merely to be poor – widows had to assert their moral value and spell out what they were doing to overseers or the vestry. They increasingly tended to stress self-help, respectability and reputation. Of Ann Mills, a pauper in Durham, the overseer wrote to Bakewell in 1824: 'she is a very infirm old woman of a good moral character, and I believe truly grateful for the bounty which she receives'.[56] Widow Bown from Lichfield was 'a hardworking, respectable woman . . . she has a lodger and goes out washing etc.' in 1837.[57] Apart from remarrying, young widows could put their children out as apprentices (and often it was the first resort of parish officials to help them to do this) or they could appeal to kin for help. George Rose of Stockport, writing to the Bakewell overseers on behalf of his relative Rebekah Rose in 1825, asked for their help to place her illegitimate grandson to shoemaking. Rebekah had had to bring him up herself and needed their help to bind him. He wanted decent clothing to go to a place and, as Rose wrote, 'you verry well know that this would be much more than what a widdow can do who hath nothing to subsist upon herself'. She was supported by what some of her sons could spare out of their scanty earnings as cotton weavers.[58]

54. Adam Fox, 'Custom, memory and the authority of writing', in Paul Griffiths, Adam Fox and Steve Hindle, eds, *The Experience of Authority in Early Modern England* (London, 1996), pp. 89–90.

55. DRO D2380A/P015/12, 10 November 1830.

56. DRO 2057A/PO2/64, 18 July 1824.

57. DRO 2057A/PO280, 31 March 1837. These cases show widows establishing their credentials through a propertied local.

58. DRO 2057A/PO2/79, 3 February 1825. On apprenticing of widows' children see Pamela Sharpe, 'Poor children as apprentices in Colyton, 1598–1830', *Continuity and Change* 6 (1991), pp. 262–64.

Other widows stressed their efforts to work, usually with insufficient earnings to make ends meet. Women's work was declining in some regions, particularly for women who were not young, childless and energetic.[59] Participation in the informal economy was very insecure. In 1824 fourteen well-to-do neighbours of an Essex widow resident in London got together to write a petition on her behalf:

> This Humble Petition of Mrs Ann Marsh of Sugarloaf Court, Long Alley, Moorfields
>
> Sheweth . . .
>
> That your poor Petitioner is a Parishoner of Chelmsfd and is left a widow with 7 Children 6 of whom are dependent on the poor pittance which the kindnes of a few neighbours supply her with by sending her a few Cloathes to Mangle for them which at present is so trifling that they are now literally half-starving and in winter time she knows from past experience her supply will be near wholly cut of as her few employers do not mangle in the Winter season as in Summer. So that she now has a long dreary Winter to look forward to with numerous infants whom she fears will be crying to her for Bread; which it will not be in her power to provide. She therefore is impelled herself to humbly beg your pity & humanity to assist her utmost endeavour this Winter, to provide for her numerous infant charge (without which She never can keep them from starving) 4 of them being under 9 years of age which she hopes will claim your kindest Sympathy which She will ever acknowledge with grateful thanks to her kind benefactors.
>
> Your very Humble Supplicant
>
> Ann Marsh[60]

This petition reveals the seasonality and general precariousness of the laundry work which was so common for widows – indeed, we might see the mangle as a symbol of widowhood. On the death of their husbands, it was extremely common for widows to beg, borrow or be bought a mangle. We know something of the later history of Ann Marsh. The neighbours later appealed to her siblings in Chelmsford. Seven years later, she was still mangling and existing on the minimum of parish support, although by this time she only had the four youngest children as dependants. To the Chelmsford overseers she appeared 'a very industrious woman . . . her principal

59. Sara Horrell and Jane Humphries, 'Women's labour force participation and the transition to the male-breadwinner family, 1790–1865', *Economic History Review* 48 (1995), pp. 89–117.

60. ERO D/P 94/18/42.

means of support is a mangle, her children have a comfortable appearance, the boy (12) goes errands for a surgeon and is in hopes that he will soon be able to earn something but at present has only a little victuals for what he does do'.[61] The Widow Marsh petition stressed both what she was being and doing: deserving, self-helping and respectable. The historian James Winter estimates for early Victorian Britain that a third of widows' income must have come from informal relief – for widowed mothers it would have been more than this, and he gives instances of landlords condoning rent payments. He also cites the case of six fishermen's widows who, given neighbourly help, were able to run a North Uist farm on a collective basis.[62] It does seem necessary to stress, however, that this degree of mutual and informal support would have been much more forthcoming for the widow established in a community, either by birth or long residence. For recent migrants to urban areas, support was likely to have been much less available. Widows might also demonstrate that they had made appeals to charity or that their friendly society had failed.[63] An example is Widow Stone of Stoke-on-Trent, who reported to the Bakewell overseers in 1816 that she was '10s 6d bad in her club'.[64]

Letters which came from afar could mislead overseers. How did they know that paupers told a true story? Adam Fox emphasizes that writing was prized as a standard of proof – but could also be seen as a means of deception.[65] Poor law officials were certainly alive to the possibilities of being double-crossed – people's slight illnesses might be described as critical: deathbed cases who made a swift recovery when a pound note appeared on the carrier's cart.[66] Larger parishes did send out overseers or prominent citizens to check on their poor from time to time, to ensure that they were not overpaid. They also received reports like the following anonymous letter written in 1830 and signed 'FM', about a widow whose character, respectability and visible appearance were questionable, and

61. ERO D/P94/8/5, 19 April 1831.

62. James Winter, 'Widowed mothers and mutual aid in early Victorian Britain', *Journal of Social History* 17 (1983), pp. 115–26.

63. On women and friendly societies see Shani D'Cruze and Jean Turnbull, 'Fellowship and family: oddfellows lodges in Preston and Lancaster *c.* 1830–1890', *Urban History* 22 (1995), pp. 25–47; Dot Jones, 'Self-help in nineteenth century Wales: the rise and fall of the female friendly society', *Llafur* 4 (1984), pp. 14–26.

64. DRO XM1/321, 16 May 1816.

65. Fox, 'Custom, memory', p. 90.

66. For an example see Pamela Sharpe, '"The bowels of compation": a labouring family and the law *c.* 1790–1834', in Hitchcock, King and Sharpe, *Chronicling Poverty*, pp. 87–108.

whose family did not try to help themselves. Widow Fenton was imposing on Bakewell:

> While you continue to pay her Rent she will not work, She has a Son at home who works as a glazier & she has a daughter which she Keeps at home 18 or 19 Years of Age & will not let her go out to Service, what would you think of a pauper's daughter dress in the stile with no less than 6 flounces on the bottom of her gown which is the case with her. It is not 12 months since Mr Owen was Obliged to seize upon her goods in order to get her out of the house but she paid no rent, he let her go, I think while you continue relieving her as you have done, you certainly are doing wrong for [the] practice of applying to the Parish for her rent is well known thro Dronfield, Only tell her when she applies againe to come into the house at Bakewell I will answer for it . . . I am oblige to write in disguise.[67]

If conditions were worsening for women as a whole, amid the upheavals of industrializing England, widows did their best to exploit whatever opportunities did exist for poor relief. Underlying their claims was the long-standing tendency for charity and alms to be extended to widows more readily than to widowers. Although officials could sometimes cut funding, letters were generally effective, because overseers often sent back a pound note and, where the correspondence continued, went on to relieve people over several years. In James Scott's terms of the 'weapons of the weak' these are partial transcripts and, on a superficial level, they show everyday acts of compliance, not resistance. Only written testimonies survive for us to see, and it is apparent that some paupers employed verbal strategies – making a trip home and giving an expectant knock on the door of the vestry, perhaps, or, as some of the letters suggest, with a thought to opportune timing or with persuasive flourishes, which appealed to a sense of place or a need for flattery. Whatever the strategy, there was a belief that petitioning in a time-honoured way would be effective. The poor retained the sense of the parish as an extended community and maintained an investment in the continuance of the fruits of paternalism.[68] Their stories show the power of the poor to influence, if not control, the circumstances of their own lives.

67. DRO 2057A/PO2/230, 4 February 1830.

68. See Gregory C. Smith, '"The poor in blindness": letters from Mildenhall, Wiltshire 1835–6', in Hitchcock, King and Sharpe, *Chronicling Poverty*, pp. 211–38.

Suggestions for reading on widowhood

Medieval and early modern sources on widowhood
Conduct books, autobiographical writing and law codes

EUROPE

Amt, Emilie, ed. *Women's Lives in Medieval Europe: A Sourcebook* (London, 1993), an anthology with some sources on widowhood such as patristic literature, conduct books and extracts from legal codes across Europe.

Augustine, St. 'The excellence of widowhood', in Roy Deferrari, ed., *Treatises on Various Subjects,* Vol. 16 (New York, 1952).

Erasmus, Desiderius. *De vidua christiana* (1529), trans. J.T. Roberts, *Collected Works of Erasmus,* Vol. 66 (Toronto, 1988).

O'Faolain, Julia and Martines, Lauro, eds. *Not in God's Image: Women in History from the Greeks to the Victorians* (New York, 1973) contains documents from manorial courts, guilds, statutes and law codes about the widow's portion, guardianship, remarriage, and poor law petitions.

Vives, Juan Luis. *De institutione feminæ Christianæ* (1523), available in the original Latin with parallel English translation (Leiden, 1996), translated into English (1529?) as *The Instruction of a Christian Woman,* French (1542) German (1544), Spanish (1528), Italian (1546) with numerous reprints and editions in each language.

ENGLAND

Aughterson, Kate, ed. *Renaissance Woman: Constructions of Femininity in England* (London, 1995), excerpts from Jane Owen's advice to Catholic widows, *An Antidote against Purgatory* (1634); extracts from J.L. Vives (1523) on second marriages; from Thomas Becon's *Cathechism* (1564) on the 'office and duty of old and ancient women'; from *Advice to the Women and Maidens of London* (1678) on preparation for widowhood.

Chaucer, Geoffrey [*c.* 1343–1400]. *The Wife of Bath's Prologue and Tale,* in *The Riverside Chancer,* Larry D. Benson, ed., 3rd edn (Oxford, 1988). The 'wife' is a many-times-remarried widow.

[Dunton, John] [1659–1733]. *An Essay Proving We Shall Know Our Friends in Heaven Writ by a Disconsolate Widower on the Death of his Wife and Dedicated to her Dear Memory* (London, 1698), available in the Early English Books 1641–1700 microform series.

Goldberg, P.J.P., trans. and ed. *Women in England c. 1275–1525* (Manchester, 1995) includes sources translated from Latin on 'Widowhood, poverty and old age' with examples of wills and an example of a vow of chastity taken by widows known as vowesses.

Hervey, Sir Thomas [1625–94]. 'Verses written by Sir Thomas Hervey on each of the seven anniversaries of the death of Isabella, his wife', in *The Letter-Books of John Hervey First Earl of Bristol. With Sir Thomas Hervey's Letters During Courtship and Poems During Widowhood 1651–1750,* 3 vols (Wells, Gloucs., 1894), I, pp. 32–9.

Keeble, N.H. *The Cultural Identity of Seventeenth-Century Woman: A Reader* (London, 1994). Chapter 15 on widowhood, celibacy and female friendship has short extracts from Thomas Overbury, *A Wife* (1614), on the virtuous widow.

Klein, Joan Larsen, ed. *Daughters, Wives and Widows: Writings by Men about Women and Marriage in England, 1500–1640* (Urbana, Ill., 1992) includes extracts from Juan Luis Vives on mourning, remembrance and second marriages as well as extracts from *The Lawes Resolutions of Women's Rights* (1632) on dower and widows' legal status.

Moulsworth, Martha. 'The memorandum of Martha Moulsworth/ Widdowe [1632]', in R.C. Evans and Barbara Wiedemann, eds, *'My Name was Martha': A Renaissance Woman's Autobiographical Poem* (West Cornwall, Conn., 1993).

Wycherley, William. *The Plain-Dealer,* in Arthur Friedman, ed., *The Plays of William Wycherley* (Oxford, 1979), comic portrayal of the litigious Widow Blackacre.

FRANCE

Arbaleste, Charlotte. *A Huguenot Family in the Sixteenth Century,* trans. Lucy Crump (London, 1926), a widow's account of the death of her husband, decisions about their child and her eventual remarriage, pp. 114–21 and 140–5.

Benton, John, ed. *Self and Society in Medieval France: The Memoirs of Abbot Guibert of Nogent* (1064–*c.* 1125), 2nd edn (Toronto, 1984), an account of a noble widow's life from her child's perspective. See bk I, ch. 4, and especially chs 12–14 and 18; bk II, ch. 4.

Corneille, Pierre [1606–84]. *La Vefve ou Le Traistre Trahy, Comédie* (1634), M. Rogues and M. Lièvre, eds (Geneva, 1954).

La Fontaine, Jean de [1621–95]. 'La Jeune Veuve/The Young Widow', in Norman B. Spector, ed. and trans., *The Complete Fables of Jean de la Fontaine* (Evanston, Ill., 1988), bk 6, XXI, pp. 281–3.

Le Long [Le Leu], Gautier. 'La Veuve (*c.* 1267)', in A. de Montaiglon and G. Raynaud, eds, *Recueil Général des Fabliaux des XIIIe et XIVe siècles*, 2nd edn, 6 vols (Paris, 1964), II, pp. 197–214.

Molière, Jean-Baptiste Poquelin [1622–73]. *L'Avare [The Miser]* (1668), in John Wood, ed. and trans., *Five Plays* (Harmondsworth, 1953). The 'miser' is a widower, an old man foolishly in love with a young girl.

Molière, Jean-Baptiste Poquelin [1622–73]. *The Misanthrope and Other Plays* (Harmondsworth, 1959). The misanthrope Alceste is in love with Célimène, a young, rich, independent widow.

Pizan, Christine de [1365–1430?]. *Treasure of the City of Ladies* (Harmondsworth, 1985), moral and practical advice written by a widow: pt I, chs 21 and 22, 'Of the behaviour of the wise princess who is widowed' and 'Of the same: advice to young widowed princesses'; pt III, ch. 4, 'Of young and elderly widows'.

Sales, St Francis de [1577–1622]. *Introduction to the Devout Life* (London and New York, 1961), bk III, ch. 40, 'Advice to widows' gives a commentary on St Augustine's and St Paul's views on widowhood.

GERMANY

Davis, N.Z. 'Glückel of Hameln, Jewish merchant woman', in N.Z. Davis and Arlette Farge, eds, *History of Women: Renaissance and Enlightenment Paradoxes* (Cambridge, Mass, 1993), a widow's account of her decision to remarry. See also below in section 'Widowhood, the Church and Religion'.

Glückel, of Hameln [1646–1724]. *The Memoirs of Glückel of Hameln*, trans. Marvin Lowenthal, 2nd edn (New York, 1977). See also below in section 'Widowhood, the Church and Religion'.

[Hoyers, Anna Owena]. Brigitte Edith Archibald, 'Anna Owena Hoyers: a view of practical living', in Katharina Wilson, ed., *Women Writers of the Renaissance and Reformation* (Athens, Ga. and London,

1987), a biography of a widow and translations of her 'Advice, which she has given to all old widows to live thereafter' and 'Brief reflections on the marriage of old women . . .', pp. 304–26.

ITALY

Androzzi, Fulvio. 'Stato lodevole della vedova [The laudable widow's state]', in *Opere Spirituali . . . Divise in Tre Parti* (Milan, 1579), in English translation as *The Widdowes Glasse: abridged out of . . . Fulvius Androtius . . . and others*, in Lennardus Lessius, *The Treasure of Vowed Chastity in Secular Persons* (St Omer, 1621).

Boccaccio, Giovanni [1313–75]. *Il Corbaccio [The Old Crow]*, in English translation as A.K. Cassell, ed., *The Corbaccio* (Urbana, Ill., 1975), a satire about an old widow and her sexuality.

Cabei, Giulio Cesare. *Ornamenti della Gentil Donna Vedova* (Venice, 1574).

[Colonna, Vittoria]. Joseph Gibaldi, 'Vittoria Colonna: child, woman and poet', in Katharina Wilson, ed., *Women Writers of the Renaissance and Reformation* (Athens, Ga. and London, 1987), a biography of Colonna, who was widowed at 35 and entered a convent but did not take the veil, with translations of her love poems and spiritual poems written during her long widowhood, pp. 22–46.

Dolce, Ludovico. *Dialogo . . . della Institutione delle Donne Secondo li Tre Stati che Cadono nella Vita Humana* (Venice, 1545).

Drew, K.F., trans. *The Lombard Laws* (Philadelphia, 1973), a translation of the medieval law codes of Lombardy.

Fusco, Horatio. *La Vedova* (Rome, 1570).

Goldoni, Carlo [1707–93]. *La Vedova Scaltra [The Artful Widow]* (1748), in English translation in *Four Comedies* (Harmondsworth, 1968).

Piazza, Carlo Bartolomeo. *Cherosilogio Overo Discorso Dello Stato Vedovile* (Rome, 1708).

Savonarola, Girolamo. *Libro della Vita Viduale* (Florence, 1491).

Trissino, Giovanni Giorgio. *Epistola del Trissino de la Vita, che dee Tenere una Donna Vedova* (Rome, 1524).

Trotto, Bernardo. *Dialoghi del Matrimonio e Vita Vedovile* (Turin, 1578).

Valerio, Agostino, Cardinal. *De viduitate, ad Hadrianani Contarenam juniorem, viduam* (Patavia, 1719).

LOW COUNTRIES

[Tesselschade, Maria]. Ria Vanderauwera, 'Maria Tesselschade: a woman of more than letters', in Katharina Wilson and Frank J.

Warnke, eds, *Women Writers of the Seventeenth Century* (Athens, Ga. and London, 1989), includes a biography, translations of a poem on suitors and letters to a widower.

SPAIN

Ignatius of Loyola, St [1491–1556]. *Letters to Women*, Hugo Rahner, ed. (New York, 1960), a letter to the Widow Boquet in Barcelona, 1554, pp. 246–7.

Ignatius of Loyola, St. *Lettres*, trans. Gervais Dumeige (Paris, 1958), letters of condolence to a widower on the deaths of his wife and son, letters 55 and 57, pp. 214–16 and 218–20.

Vega, Lope de [1562–1635]. *La Viuda Valenciana* (Madrid, 1967), play dating from 1620.

General studies of widowhood

EUROPE

Bremmer, Jan and van den Bosch, Lourens, eds. *Between Poverty and the Pyre: Moments in the History of Widowhood* (London, 1995), essays on widowhood ranging from Anglo-Saxon England to the practice of sati in India.

Hufton, Olwen. 'Women without men: widows and spinsters in Britain and France in the eighteenth century', *Journal of Family History* 9 (1984), a seminal article on women alone, reprinted in Bremmer and van den Bosch, eds, *Between Poverty and the Pyre.*

Hufton, Olwen. *The Prospect Before Her: A History of Women in Western Europe 1500–1800* (London, 1995), ch. 6 on widowhood provides an excellent pan-European summary.

Mirrer, Louise. *Upon My Husband's Death: Widows in the Literature and Histories of Medieval Europe* (Ann Arbor, Mich., 1992), a very good and wide-ranging collection of articles also listed individually in this bibliography.

Parisse, Michel, ed. *Veuves et Veuvage dans le Haut Moyen Age: Table Ronde* (Paris, 1993), articles in French and German.

ENGLAND

Barron, Caroline and Sutton, A.F., eds. *Medieval London Widows, 1300–1500* (London, 1994), a series of biographies of individual widows.

Hanawalt, Barbara. *The Ties that Bound: Peasant Families in Medieval England* (Oxford, 1986), ch. 14 on widowhood and ch. 15 on old age and death.

Rosenthal, Joel T. 'Other victims: peeresses as war widows, 1450–1500', *History* 72 (1987), pp. 213–30 considers the effects of war on the experience of widowhood.

Walker, Sue Sheridan, ed. *Wife and Widow in Medieval England* (Ann Arbor, Mich., 1993), an excellent collection of essays.

Wall, Richard. 'Women alone in English society', *Annales de Démographie Historique* (1981).

FRANCE

Gibson, Wendy. *Women in Seventeenth-Century France* (New York, 1989), ch. 6 on the dissolution of marriage describes the legal position of and moral attitudes to widows.

Hardwick, Julia. 'Widowhood and patriarchy in seventeenth-century France', *Journal of Social History* 26 (1992), pp. 133–48 compares cultural attitudes to widows and widowers, and the difficulties widows encountered running the household, managing property and retaining custody of the children.

IRELAND

Clarkson, L.A. and Crawford, E.M. 'Life after death: widows in Carrick-on-Suir, 1799', in Margaret MacCurtain and Mary O'Dowd, eds, *Women in Early Modern Ireland* (Edinburgh, 1991), pp. 236–54, examines the demography of widowhood and how widows made their livings.

ITALY

D'Amelia, Marina. 'Scatole cinesi: vedove e donne sole in una società d'antico regime', *Memoria* 3 (1986), pp. 58–79, a fine study of widows' living arrangements, their economic activities and family networks based on parish listings in Rome.

LOW COUNTRIES

Hempernias-van Dijk, Dierneke. 'Widows and the law: the legal position of widows in the Dutch Republic during the seventeenth and eighteenth centuries', in Jan Bremmer and Lourens van den Bosch, eds, *Between Poverty and the Pyre: Moments in the History of Widowhood* (London, 1995), pp. 89–102.

Marshall, Sherrin. *The Dutch Gentry, 1500–1650: Family, Faith and Fortune* (Westport, Conn., 1987), ch. 4, 'Survivors and status: widows and widowers in gentry families', is one of the few studies to compare attitudes to and the legal status of widows and widowers.

SPAIN

Vassberg, David E. 'The status of widows in sixteenth-century rural Castile', in John Henderson and Richard Wall, eds, *Poor Women and Children in the European Past* (London, 1994), pp. 180–95, a valuable assessment of the legal status and economic fortunes of widows in Castile.

Historiographical and methodological works

Aubry, Y. 'Pour une étude du veuvage feminin à l'époque moderne', *Histoire, Économie et Société* 8 (1989), pp. 223–36.

Blom, Ida, 'The history of widowhood: a bibliographic overview', *Journal of Family History* 16 (1991), pp. 191–219.

Cabibbo, Sara. 'La capra, il sale, il sacco. Per uno studio della vedovanza feminile tra Cinque e Seicento', *Archivio Storico per la Sicilia Orientale* 85 (1989), pp. 117–67.

Widowhood in drama and literature

EUROPE

Dulac, Liliane. 'Mystical inspiration and political knowledge: advice to widows from Francesco da Barberino and Christine de Pizan', in Louise Mirrer, ed., *Upon My Husband's Death: Widows in the Literature and Histories of Medieval Europe* (Ann Arbor, Mich., 1992), pp. 223–58.

Kelso, Ruth. *Doctrine for the Lady of the Renaissance* (Urbana, Ill., 1956) provides a very good overview of European literature on advice to the widow, especially good on Italian sources, pp. 121–35.

ENGLAND

Bacon, J.L. 'Wives, widows and writings in Restoration comedy', *Studies in English Literature 1500–1900* 31 (1991), pp. 427–43.

Carlton, Charles. 'The widow's tale: male myths and female reality in 16th and 17th century England', *Albion* 10 (1978), pp. 118–29.

Mikesell, Margaret. 'Catholic and Protestant widows in the "Duchess of Malfi" (John Webster)', *Renaissance and Reformation* 7 (1983), pp. 265–79.

Sisson, Charles. 'Keep the widow waking: a lost play by Dekker', *The Library: Transactions of the Bibliographical Society* 8 (1927–28), pp. 39–57 and pp. 233–59, based on Star Chamber court records from the prosecution of the playwrights whose dramatization of a widow's forced marriage provided the plot of a lost seventeenth-century play.

FRANCE

Arden, Heather A. 'Grief, widowhood and women's sexuality in medieval French literature', in Louise Mirrer, ed., *Upon My Husband's Death: Widows in the Literature and Histories of Medieval Europe* (Ann Arbor, Mich., 1992), pp. 305–19.

Biet, Christian. 'De la veuve joyeuse à l'individu autonome', *XVIIe Siècle* 187 (1995), pp. 307–30.

Lafouge, J.P. 'Sincerité et veuvage: Corneille, Racine, La Fontaine, Mme de Villedieu, Mme de Lafayette', *Cahiers du Dix-Septième: An Interdisciplinary Journal* 4 (1990), pp. 151–66.

Spielmann, Guy. 'Viduité et pouvoir dans le discours comique, 1683–1715', *XVIIe Siècle* 187 (1995), pp. 331–43.

Thomas, R.P. 'Twice victims: virtuous widows in the eighteenth-century French novel', *Studies on Voltaire and the Eighteenth Century* 266 (1989), pp. 433–49.

GERMANY

Taylor, Irmgard C. *Das Bild der Witwe in der deutschen Literatur* (Darmstadt, 1980), on the image of the widow in German literature.

ITALY

Cabibbo, Sara. 'Marcella Romana, vedova nell'età della Controriforma', in Giulia Barone, Marina Caffiero and Francesco Scorza

Barcellona, eds, *Modelli di Santità e Modelli di Comportamento* (Turin, 1994), pp. 283–93, examines seventeenth-century hagiographical and moralistic literature and new models for the widow devised by the post-Tridentine church.

Jordan, Constance. *Renaissance Feminism: Literary Texts and Political Models* (Ithaca, NY, 1990), discusses the works of the Italian humanists Barbaro, Trissino and Trotto on widows.

De Maio, Romeo. *Donna e Rinascimento* (Naples, 1995), a short section on the widow with other material interspersed throughout the book.

SPAIN

Estow, Clara. 'Widows in the chronicles of late medieval Castile', in Louise Mirrer, ed., *Upon My Husband's Death: Widows in the Literature and Histories of Medieval Europe* (Ann Arbor, Mich., 1992), pp. 153–67.

Gericke, Philip O. 'The widow in Hispanic balladry: *Fonte Frida*', in Louise Mirrer, ed., *Upon My Husband's Death: Widows in the Literature and Histories of Medieval Europe* (Ann Arbor, Mich., 1992), pp. 289–303.

Montserrat, Piera and Rogers, Donna M. 'The widow as a heroine: the fifteenth century Catalan chivalresque novel *Curial and Guelfa*', in Louise Mirrer, ed., *Upon My Husband's Death: Widows in the Literature and Histories of Medieval Europe* (Ann Arbor, Mich., 1992), pp. 321–42.

Vasvari, Louise O. 'Why is Doña Endrina a widow? Traditional culture and textuality in the *Libro de Buen Amor*', in Louise Mirrer, ed., *Upon My Husband's Death: Widows in the Literature and Histories of Medieval Europe* (Ann Arbor, Mich., 1992), pp. 259–87.

Bereavement and mourning

Aston, M. 'Death', in Rosemary Horrox, ed., *Fifteenth-Century Attitudes: Perceptions of Society in Late Medieval England* (Cambridge, 1994).

Chabot, Isabelle. '"La sposa in nero". La ritualizazione del lutto delle vedove fiorentine (secoli XIV–XV)', *Quaderni Storici* 86 (1994), pp. 421–62.

Gittings, Clare. 'Venetia's death and Kenelm's mourning', in Ann Sumner, ed., *Death, Passion and Politics: Van Dyck's Portraits of Venetia Stanley and George Digby* (London, 1995), pp. 54–67.

Gittings, Clare. 'Expressions of loss in early seventeenth-century England', in P.C. Jupp and Glennys Howarth, eds, *The Changing Face of Death: Historical Accounts of Death and Disposal* (London, 1997), pp. 19–33, on widows' commemoration of their deceased husbands.

Houlbrooke, Ralph. *The English Family 1450–1700* (London, 1984), ch. 8, 'Death and the broken family', examines bereavement and the experiences of families at the death of father or mother.

Houlbrooke, Ralph, ed. *Death, Ritual, and Bereavement* (London and New York, 1989) focuses on Britain.

Strocchia, Sharon. 'Funerals and the politics of gender in early Renaissance Florence', in Marilyn Migiel and Juliana Schiesari, eds, *Refiguring Woman: Perspectives on Gender and the Italian Renaissance* (Ithaca, NY and London, 1991), pp. 155–68.

Strocchia, Sharon. *Death and Ritual in Renaissance Florence* (Baltimore, 1992).

Remarriage

(See also under widowhood and children)

Brundage, James. 'Widows and remarriage: moral conflicts and their resolution in classical canon law', in S.S. Walker, ed., *Wife and Widow in Medieval England* (Ann Arbor, Mich., 1993), pp. 17–32.

Brundage, James. 'The merry widow's serious sister: remarriage in classical canon law', in Robert Edwards and Vickie Ziegler, eds, *Matrons and Marginal Women in Medieval Society* (Rochester, NY, 1995), pp. 33–48.

Dupâquier, Jacques, *et al.*, eds. *Marriage and Remarriage in Populations of the Past* (London, 1981), the standard reference on remarriage which covers Western Europe as well as the Nordic countries, Eastern Europe, Africa, Latin America and Asia.

ENGLAND

Boulton, Jeremy. 'London widowhood revisited: the decline of female remarriage in the seventeenth and eighteenth centuries', *Continuity and Change* 5 (1990), pp. 323–55, should be read in conjunction with Barbara Todd's articles on remarriage.

Brodsky, Vivien. 'Widows in late Elizabethan London: remarriage, economic opportunity and family orientations', in L. Bonfield, R.M. Smith and K. Wrightson, eds, *The World We Have Gained* (Oxford, 1986).

Collins, Stephen. '"A kind of lawful adultery": English attitudes to the remarriage of widows, 1550–1800', in P.C. Jupp and Glennys Howarth, eds, *The Changing Face of Death: Historical Accounts of Death and Disposal* (London, 1997), pp. 34–47, an analysis of the constant disparagement of remarrying widows in didactic literature on marriage.

Franklin, P. 'Peasant widows' liberation and remarriage before the Black Death', *Economic History Review* 39 (1986), pp. 186–204.

Griffith, J.D. 'Economy, family, and remarriage: theory of remarriage and application to preindustrial England', *Journal of Family Issues* 1 (1980), pp. 479–96, on the frequency of remarriage among men and women and the effect of property and children on the choice to remarry.

Hanawalt, Barbara. 'Remarriage as an option for urban and rural widows in late medieval England', in S.S. Walker, ed., *Wife and Widow in Medieval England* (Ann Arbor, Mich., 1993).

Rosenthal, Joel T. 'Aristocratic widows in fifteenth century England', in B. Harris and J. McNamara, eds, *Women and the Structure of Society* (1984), pp. 36–47, on the length of widowhood and the frequency of remarriage among widows of peers.

Todd, Barbara, 'The re-marrying widow: a stereotype reconsidered', in Mary Prior, ed., *Women in English Society 1500–1800* (London, 1985), pp. 54–92, a seminal article on remarriage.

Todd, Barbara, 'Demographic determinism and female agency: the remarrying widow reconsidered . . . again', *Continuity and Change* 9 (1994), pp. 421–50, takes up the debate with Jeremy Boulton's interpretation of remarriage in early modern England.

Wright, S.J. 'The elderly and the bereaved in eighteenth-century Ludlow', in Margaret Pelling and Richard Smith, eds, *Life, Death and the Elderly: Historical Perspectives* (London, 1991), pp. 102–33, examines household structure and its effects on the rates of remarriage by widows and widowers.

FRANCE

Bideau, Alain. 'A demographic and social analysis of widowhood and remarriage: the example of the Castellany of Thoissey-en-Dombes (1670–1840)', *Journal of Family History* 5 (1980), pp. 28–43.

Burguière, André. 'The charivari and religious repression in France during the Ancien Regime', in R. Wheaton and T. Hareven, eds, *Family and Sexuality in French History* (Philadelphia, 1980), pp. 84–110, includes information on charivari and its relation to remarriage.

Diefendorf, Barbara. 'Widowhood and remarriage in sixteenth-century Paris', *Journal of Family History* 7 (1982), pp. 379–95, an excellent article on the legal position of the Parisian widow with a study of marriage contracts of remarrying widows.

GERMANY

Knodel, John and Lynch, Katherine. 'The decline of remarriage: evidence from German village populations in the eighteenth and nineteenth centuries', *Journal of Family History* 10 (1985), pp. 34–59.

NETHERLANDS

Vanpoppel, F. 'Widows, widowers, and remarriage in nineteenth-century Netherlands', *Population Studies: A Journal of Demography* 49 (1995), pp. 421–41.

Poverty and provisions for the widowed

EUROPE

Bothelho, Lynn. '"The old woman's wish": widows by the family fire? Widows' old age provision in rural England', forthcoming in *Journal of Family History*.

Henderson, John and Wall, Richard, eds. *Poor Women and Children in the European Past* (London, 1994); see especially the essays by D. Vassberg on Castile and T. Sokoll, 'The household position of elderly widows in poverty: evidence from two English communities in the late eighteenth and early nineteenth centuries'.

Riley, J.C. 'That your widows may be rich: providing for widowhood in Old Regime Europe', *Economisch- en Sociaal-Historisch Jaarboek* 45 (1982), pp. 58–76, on the genesis of life insurance, with special emphasis on Germany, England and the Netherlands.

BRITAIN

Cullum, Patricia. '"And her name was charitie": charitable giving by and for women in late medieval Yorkshire', in P.J.P. Goldberg, ed., *Women is a Worthy Wight: Women in English Society c. 1200–1500* (Stroud, Gloucs., 1992), pp. 182–211.

McIntosh, Marjorie K. 'Networks of care in Elizabethan English towns: the example of Hadleigh, Suffolk', in P. Horden and R. Smith, eds, *The Locus of Care: Families, Communities, Institutions, and the Provision of Care Since Antiquity* (London, 1998), examines the frequency with which widows and widowers figure among recipients of poor relief and in institutional care.

Pelling, Margaret. 'Old age, poverty and disability in early modern Norwich: work, remarriage and other expedients', in Pelling and Richard Smith, eds, *Life, Death and the Elderly: Historical Perspectives* (London, 1991), pp. 74–101.

Smith, J.E. 'Widowhood and ageing in traditional English society', *Ageing and Society* 4 (1984), pp. 429–49, examines the age structure of widowhood in seventeenth- and eighteenth-century England, the living arrangements of widows and their reliance on parish relief.

Smith, Richard M. 'Charity, self-interest and welfare: reflections from demographic and family history', in M. Daunton, ed., *Charity, Self-Interest and Welfare in the English Past* (London, 1996), pp. 23–50.

Wales, Tim. 'Poverty, poor relief and life-cycle: some evidence from seventeenth-century Norfolk', in M. Pelling and R.M. Smith, eds, *Land, Kinship and Life-Cycle* (Cambridge, 1984), pp. 351–404.

Whyte, I.D. and Whyte, K.A. 'Debt and credit, poverty and prosperity in a seventeenth-century Scottish rural community', in Rosalind Mitchison, ed., *Economy and Society in Scotland and Ireland 1500–1939* (Edinburgh, 1988), pp. 70–9, examines social groups, landholdings, assets and debts of people on the Pamure estates in Forfarshire, with information on 'single women and widows' as one group, and 'elderly and single men' as another group.

GERMANY

Wunder, Berndt. 'Pfarrwitwenkassen und Beamtenwitwen. Anstalten vom 16–19. Jahrhundert. Die Entstehung der staatlichen Hinterbliebenen – versorgung in Deutschland', *Zeitschrift für Historische Forschung* 12 (1985), pp. 429–98, on the church widows' fund and the rise of state-sponsored survivors' care in Germany from the 16th to the 19th centuries.

ITALY

Chabot, Isabelle. 'Widowhood and poverty in late medieval Florence', *Continuity and Change* 3 (1988), pp. 291–311.

Skinner, Patricia. 'Gender and poverty in the medieval community', in Diane Watt, ed., *Medieval Women in Their Communities* (Toronto, 1997), pp. 204–21.

Trexler, R.C. 'A widow's asylum of the Renaissance: the Orbatello of Florence', in R.C. Trexler, *Dependence in Context in Renaissance Florence* (Binghamton, NY, 1994).

Economic and public roles of widows

Bennett, Judith M. 'Widows in the medieval English countryside', in Louise Mirrer, ed., *Upon My Husband's Death: Widows in the Literature and Histories of Medieval Europe* (Ann Arbor, Mich., 1992), pp. 69–114.

Collins, James. 'The economic role of women in seventeenth-century France', *French Historical Studies* 16 (1989), pp. 436–70, an excellent survey of the economic roles of women as daughters, wives and widows.

Crabb Morton, Ann. 'How typical was Alessandra Macinghi Strozzi of fifteenth-century Florentine widows?', in Louise Mirrer, ed., *Upon My Husband's Death: Widows in the Literature and Histories of Medieval Europe* (Ann Arbor, Mich., 1992), pp. 47–68, based on the correspondence between a widowed mother of four and her sons, this article offers a detailed insight into the economic and political roles of patrician women after the death of their husbands.

Hanawalt, Barbara, ed. *Women and Work in Preindustrial Europe* (Bloomington, Ind., 1986), an important collection on women's economic roles outside the family. See especially the articles by J. Bennett, N.Z. Davis, M. Howell, M. Kowaleski and K. Reyerson.

Holderness, B.A. 'Widows in pre-industrial society: an essay upon their economic functions', in M. Pelling and R.M. Smith, eds, *Land, Kinship and Life-Cycle* (Cambridge, 1984), pp. 423–42.

Kalas, R.J. 'The noble widow's place in the patriarchal household: the life and career of Jeanne de Gontault', *Sixteenth Century Journal* 24 (1993), pp. 519–39, based on a widow's management of family property and her relationship with her son.

King, C. 'Women as patrons: nuns, widows and rulers', in D. Norman, ed., *Siena, Florence and Padua: Art, Society and Religion,* 2 vols (London 1994), II, pp. 243–66, a study of funerary images and other works of art and architecture paid for by women, this article considers whether these commissioned works conformed to conventional representations of gender roles.

Palazzi, Maura. 'Work and residence of "women alone" in the context of a patrilineal system (eighteenth- and nineteenth-century northern Italy)', in M.J. Maynes *et al.*, eds, *Gender, Kinship, Power: A Comparative and Interdisciplinary History* (New York, 1996), pp. 215–30.

Tallan, Cheryl. 'Medieval Jewish widows: their control of resources', *Jewish History* 5 (1991), pp. 63–74, on property rights and business activities of widows, especially moneylending.

Tallan, Cheryl. 'Opportunities for medieval Northern European Jewish widows in the public and domestic spheres', in Louise Mirrer, ed., *Upon My Husband's Death: Widows in the Literature and Histories of Medieval Europe* (Ann Arbor, Mich., 1992), pp. 115–26.

Wiesner, Merry. *Working Women in Renaissance Germany* (New Brunswick, 1986), a helpful section on widows and guilds, pp. 157–63.

Property, inheritance and legal status

MEDIEVAL

Archer, Rowena. 'Rich old ladies: the problem of late medieval dowagers', in T. Pollard, ed., *Property and Politics: Essays in Later Medieval English History* (Gloucester, 1984), pp. 15–35.

Archer, Rowena. '"How ladies . . . who live on their manors ought to manage their households and estates": women as landlords and administrators in the later Middle Ages', in P.J.P. Goldberg, ed., *Women is a Worthy Wight: Women in English Society c. 1200–1500* (Stroud, Gloucs., 1992), pp. 149–81.

Broida, E. 'La viudez, triste o feliz estado? (Las últimas voluntades de los barceloneses en torno al 1400)', in C. Segura Graiño, ed., *Las Mujeres en las Ciudades Medievales* (Madrid, 1984), pp. 27–41, a study of the testamentary practices of widows in Barcelona.

García-Herrero, M.D.C. 'Viudedad foral y viudas Aragonesas a finales de la edad media', *Hispania: Revista Espanola de Historia* 184 (1993), pp. 431–50, on the application of laws concerning the widow's control over family property, based on notarial acts.

Hanawalt, Barbara. 'The widow's mite: provisions for medieval London widows', in Louise Mirrer, ed., *Upon My Husband's Death: Widows in the Literature and Histories of Medieval Europe* (Ann Arbor, Mich., 1992), pp. 21–45, on husbands' provisions for their widows and contested dowers.

Howell, Martha. *The Marriage Exchange: Property, Social Place and Gender in the Cities of the Low Countries 1300–1550* (Chicago, 1998).

Klapisch-Zuber, Christiane. 'The "cruel mother": maternity, widowhood, and dowry in Florence in the fourteenth and fifteenth centuries', in Christiane Klapisch-Zuber, *Women, Family and Ritual in Renaissance Italy* (Chicago, 1985), pp. 117–31.

Loengard Senderowitz, J. '"Of the gift of her husband": English dower and its consequences in the year 1200', in Julius Kirshner and Suzanne Wemple, eds, *Women of the Medieval World* (Oxford, 1985), pp. 215–55, a detailed reconstruction of the English 'dower' and of its problems in practice.

Lorcin, Marie-Thérèse. 'Veuve noble et veuve paysanne en lyonnais d'après les testaments des XIVe et XVe siècles', *Annales de Démographie Historique* (1981), pp. 273–88, a study of husbands' provisions for their widows and of widows' standards of living.

Miskimin, Harry A.'Widows not so merry: women and the courts in late medieval France', in Louise Mirrer, ed., *Upon My Husband's Death: Widows in the Literature and Histories of Medieval Europe* (Ann Arbor, Mich., 1992), pp. 207–21, examines the lawsuits involving widows brought before the Parlement de Paris.

Mitchell, L.E. 'The lady is a lord: noble widows and land in thirteenth-century Britain', *Historical Reflections* 18 (1992), pp. 71–87.

Nelson, Janet L. 'The wary widow', in Wendy Davies and Paul Fouracre, eds, *Property and Power in the Early Middle Ages* (Cambridge, 1995), pp. 82–113, on the widow's endowment and her actual control over it in the Carolingian period.

Rivers, Theodore John. 'Widows' rights in Anglo-Saxon law', *American Journal of Legal History* 19 (1975), pp. 208–15.

Skinner, Patricia. 'Women, wills and wealth in medieval Southern Italy', *Early Medieval Europe* 2 (1993), pp. 133–52.

EARLY MODERN

Calvi, Giulia and Chabot, Isabelle, eds. *Le Richezze Delle Donne. Diritti Patrimoniali e Poteri Familiari (XIII–XIX sec.)* (Turin, 1998), essays stressing the *longue durée* of laws concerning women's property and inheritance rights, and the tensions between norms and testamentary practices in various Italian regions.

Diefendorf, Barbara. 'Women and property in *ancien régime* France: theory and practice in Dauphiné and Paris', in John Brewer and Susan Staves, eds, *Early Modern Conceptions of Property* (New York, 1995), pp. 170–93.

Erickson, Amy Louise. *Women and Property in Early Modern England* (London, 1993).

Gates, L.A. 'Widows, property and remarriage: lessons from Glastonbury Deverill Manors', *Albion* 28 (1996), pp. 19–35.

Hardwick, Julia. 'Widowhood and patriarchy in seventeenth-century France', *Journal of Social History* 26 (1992), pp. 133–48, on widows as female heads of household, control of property and child custody arrangements.

Hempernias-van Dijk, Dierneke. 'Widows and the law: the legal position of widows in the Dutch Republic during the seventeenth and eighteenth centuries', in Jan Bremmer and Lourens van den Bosch, eds, *Between Poverty and the Pyre: Moments in the History of Widowhood* (London, 1995), pp. 89–102.

Kuehn, Thomas. *Law, Family and Women: Towards a Legal Anthropology of Renaissance Italy* (Chicago, 1991).

Marshall Wyntjes, Sherrin. 'Survivors and status: widowhood and family in the early modern Netherlands', *Journal of Family History* (1982), pp. 396–405.

Palazzi, Maura. 'Female solitude and patrilineage: unmarried women and widows during the eighteenth and nineteenth centuries', *Journal of Family History* 15 (1990), pp. 443–59.

La Richesse des Femmes, Actes du Colloque de Paris, 6.12.1996, special issue of *Clio: Femmes, Histoire, Sociétés* 7 (1998), includes essays on Italy and France stretching from the early Middle Ages to the 19th century. Includes a comprehensive bibliography of works on women's property.

Stretton, Tim. *Women Waging Law in Elizabethan England* (Cambridge, 1998).

Swett, K.W. 'Widowhood, custom and property in early modern North Wales', *Welsh History Review* 18 (1996), pp. 189–227.

Todd, Barbara. 'Freebench and free enterprise: widows and their property in two Berkshire villages', in John Chartres and David Hey, eds, *English Rural Society, 1500–1800: Essays in Honour of Joan Thirsk* (Cambridge, 1990), pp. 175–200, compares how widows from two villages (with different landholding customs and property rights) fared in their management of property.

See also Schereschensky, Ben-Zion. 'Widows', in Menachem Elion, ed., *The Principles of Jewish Law* (Jerusalem, 1985).

Widowhood, the church and religion

Baernstein, P. Renée. 'In widow's habit: women between convent and family in sixteenth-century Milan', *Sixteenth Century Journal* 24 (1994), pp. 787–807.

Benvenuti Papi, Anna. 'Mendicant friars and female Pinzochere in Tuscany: from social marginality to models of sanctity', in Daniel Bornstein and Roberto Rusconi, eds, *Women and Religion in Medieval and Renaissance Italy* (Chicago, 1996), pp. 84–103, discusses the place of widows in medieval religious life, especially as holy women and saints.

Bowman Thurston, Bonnie. *The Widows: A Women's Ministry in the Early Church* (Minneapolis, 1989) examines widows in Christian doctrine.

Davis, N.Z. *Women on the Margins: Three Seventeenth-Century Lives* (Cambridge, Mass., 1995) discusses the lives of 'Glückel of Hameln', a Jewish merchant widow (see also above, in section 'Medieval and Early Modern Sources on Widowhood: Germany'), and Mère Marie de l'Incarnation, a French widow who entered the convent.

Dunn, Marilyn R. 'Spiritual philanthropists: women as convent patrons in seicento Rome', in Cynthia Lawrence, ed., *Women and Art in Early Modern Europe: Patrons, Collectors, and Connoisseurs* (University Park, Pa., 1997), pp. 154–88.

Jussen, Bernhard. 'On church organization and the definition of an estate: the idea of widowhood in late antique and early medieval Christianity', *Tel Aviver Jahrbuch für deutsche Geschichte* 22 (1993), pp. 25–42.

Ramis, G. 'La benedicion de las viudas en las liturgias occidentales', *Ephemerides Liturgicae* 104 (1990).

Scaraffia, Lucetta and Zarri, Gabriella, eds. *Donne e Fede* (Rome, 1994); the articles by G. Zarri and M. Caffiero deal with the presence of widows in convents, cloistered religious communities of women and the exaltation of female widowed saints.

Valone, Carolyn. 'Roman matrons as patrons: various views of the cloister wall', in Craig A. Monson, ed., *The Crannied Wall: Women, Religion, and the Arts in Early Modern Europe* (Ann Arbor, Mich., 1992), pp. 49–72, examines the early Christian matrons who patronized St Jerome and their influence as models for wealthy widows in 16th-century Rome.

Valone, Carolyn. 'Piety and patronage: women and the early Jesuits', in E. Ann Matter and John Coakley, eds, *Creative Women in Medieval and Early Modern Italy: A Religious and Artistic Renaissance* (Philadelphia, 1994), pp. 157–84.

Willen, Diane. 'Godly women in early modern England: Puritanism and gender', *Journal of Ecclesiastical History* 43 (1992), pp. 561–80, information on the clerical contacts of Protestant widowed women.

Widowhood and children

(See also under remarriage)

Baulant, Micheline. 'The scattered family: another aspect of seventeenth-century demography', in Robert Forster and Orest Ranum, eds, *Family and Society: Selections from the Annales ESC* (Baltimore and London, 1976), pp. 104–116, on remarriage, family structures, guardianship and custody arrangements for children and stepchildren.

Calvi, Giulia. *Il Contratto Morale: Madri e Figli nella Toscana Moderna* (Rome, 1994).

Carlton, Charles. *The Court of Orphans* (Leicester, 1974).

Clark, Elaine. 'City orphans and custody laws in medieval England', *American Journal of Legal History* 3 (1990), pp. 168–87.

Collins, Stephen. 'British stepfamily relationships, 1500–1800', *Journal of Family History* 16 (1991), pp. 331–44.

Collins, Stephen. '"Against reason, nature and order": step-parents in the English Renaissance', in R. Phillips, ed., *The History of Marriage and the Family in Western Society* (Toronto, 1995).

Coster, W. '"To bring them up in the fear of God": guardianship in the diocese of York, 1550–1668', *Continuity and Change* 10 (1995), pp. 9–32.

Hanawalt, Barbara A. 'Patriarchal provisions for widows and orphans in medieval London', in M.J. Maynes *et al.*, eds, *Gender, Kinship, Power: A Comparative and Interdisciplinary History* (New York, 1996), pp. 201–13.

Hardwick, Julia. 'Widowhood and patriarchy in seventeenth-century France', *Journal of Social History* 26 (1992), pp. 133–48 shows how widows' rights of guardianship and their roles as heads of household were disputed by the family and required constant negotiation.

Hempernias-van Dijk, Dierneke. 'Widows and the law: the legal position of widows in the Dutch Republic during the seventeenth and eighteenth centuries', in Jan Bremmer and Lourens van den Bosch, eds, *Between Poverty and the Pyre: Moments in the History of Widowhood* (London, 1995), pp. 89–102, examines guardianship and child custody arrangements.

Houlbrooke, Ralph. *The English Family 1450–1700* (London, 1984), ch. 8, 'Death and the broken family', examines bereavement and the experiences of families at the death of father or mother.

Klapisch-Zuber, Christiane. 'The "cruel mother": maternity, widowhood, and dowry in Florence in the fourteenth and fifteenth centuries', in Christiane Klapisch-Zuber, *Women, Family and Ritual in Renaissance Italy* (Chicago, 1985), pp. 117–31.

Images of widowhood

Franits, Wayne. *Paragons of Virtue: Women and Domesticity in Seventeenth-Century Dutch Art* (Cambridge, 1993); see the chapter on 'Weduwe' for representations of widows, widowers, ageing men and women.

Llewellyn, Nigel. *The Art of Death* (London, 1991).

Matthews Grieco, Sara. 'Persuasive pictures: didactic prints and the construction of female identity in sixteenth-century Italy', in L. Panizza, ed., *Culture, Society and Women in Renaissance Italy* (Manchester, in press).

Murphy, Caroline. 'Lavinia Fontana and depictions of female life-cycle experiences', in Geraldine Johnson and Sara Matthews Grieco, eds, *Picturing Women in Renaissance and Baroque Italy* (Cambridge, 1997), pp. 111–38.

Placing widowhood in context

EUROPE

Gottlieb, Beatrice. *The Family in the Western World from the Black Death to the Industrial Age* (Oxford, 1993), especially helpful on inheritance practices.

King, Margaret. *Women of the Renaissance* (Chicago, 1991) includes a short section on widowhood, pp. 56–62.

Wiesner, Merry. *Women and Gender in Early Modern Europe* (Cambridge, 1993).

ENGLAND

Barron, Caroline M. 'The "Golden Age" of women in medieval London', *Reading Medieval Studies* 15 (1989), pp. 38–42.

Bennett, Judith. *Women in the Medieval English Countryside* (Oxford, 1987).

Cressy, David. *Birth, Marriage and Death: Ritual, Religion and the Life Cycle in Tudor and Stuart England* (Oxford, 1997), ch. 17, 'Death comes for all', investigates the social and religious understanding of death in the 16th and 17th century from theology, liturgy to secular social activity, the separation of body and soul, burial, Protestant funerals, interment and memory.

Laurence, Anne. *Women in England 1500–1760: A Social History* (London, 1994).

Tadmor, Naomi. 'The concept of household-family in eighteenth-century England', *Past and Present* 151 (1996), pp. 111–140, reconsiders the concept of the nuclear family as defined by demographers. Focuses on alternative sources such as the diaries of the widower Thomas Turner.

Thompson, Janet. *Wives, Widows, Witches and Bitches: Women in Seventeenth Century Devon* (New York, 1993), information on issues of inheritance and property as well as on widows in trade.

FRANCE

Troyansky, David. *Old Age in the Old Regime: Image and Experience in Eighteenth-Century France* (Ithaca, NY, 1989).

GERMANY/LOW COUNTRIES

Nicholas, David. *The Domestic Life of a Medieval City: Women, Children and Family in Fourteenth Century Ghent* (Lincoln, 1985).

Roper, Lyndal. *The Holy Household: Women and Morals in Reformation Augsburg* (Oxford, 1989) pp. 49–54, focus specifically on widowhood.

Wiesner, Merry. *Working Women in Renaissance Germany* (New Brunswick, 1986), see especially ch. 1 on political, economic and legal structures.

Wiesner, Merry. 'Spinning out capital: women's work in the early modern economy', in *Gender, Church, and State in Early Modern Germany* (London, 1998), reprinted from Susan Stuard *et al.*, eds, *Becoming Visible: Women in European History* (Boston, 1987), on widows and work, legal and guild restrictions.

Wunder, Heide. *He is the Sun, She is the Moon: Women in Early Modern Germany* (Cambridge, Mass., 1998), a chapter examines widowhood.

SPAIN

Perry, Mary Elizabeth. *Gender and Disorder in Early Modern Seville* (Princeton, 1990).

Vassberg, David. *The Village and the Outside World in Golden Age Castile: Mobility and Migration in Everyday Rural Life* (Cambridge, 1996), many examples of widows, widowers and their children can be found in this study of rural life.

Index